CW00763128

RELIGIONS OF THE ANCIENT NEAR EAST

This book is a history of religious life in the Ancient Near East, from the beginnings of agriculture to Alexander the Great's invasion in the 300s BCE. Daniel C. Snell traces key developments in the history, daily life, and religious beliefs of the people of Ancient Mesopotamia, Egypt, Israel, and Iran. His research investigates the influence of those ideas on the West, with particular emphasis on how religious ideas from this historical and cultural milieu continue to influence the way modern cultures and religions view the world.

Designed to be accessible to students and readers with no prior knowledge of the period, this book uses fictional vignettes to add interest to its material, which is based on careful study of archaeological remains and preserved texts. This book provides a thoughtful summary of the Ancient Near East and includes a comprehensive bibliography to guide readers in further studies of related topics.

Daniel C. Snell is L. J. Semrod Presidential Professor of History at the University of Oklahoma, Norman. He has also taught at the University of Washington, Connecticut College, Barnard College, Gustavus Adolphus College, and Otterbein College. He is the author of eight books, the most recent of which is *A Companion to the Ancient Near East* (2005).

RELIGIONS OF THE ANCIENT NEAR EAST

DANIEL C. SNELL

University of Oklahoma, Norman

CAMBRIDGE
UNIVERSITY PRESS

CAMBRIDGE UNIVERSITY PRESS
Cambridge, New York, Melbourne, Madrid, Cape Town,
Singapore, São Paulo, Delhi, Tokyo, Mexico City

Cambridge University Press
32 Avenue of the Americas, New York, NY 10013-2473, USA

www.cambridge.org
Information on this title: www.cambridge.org/9780521683364

First published 2011
Reprinted 2011

A catalog record for this publication is available from the British Library.

Library of Congress Cataloging in Publication Data
Snell, Daniel C.
Religions of the ancient near East / by Daniel C. Snell.
   p. cm.
Includes bibliographical references and index.
ISBN 978-0-521-86475-6 (hardback)
1. Middle East – Religion.   2. Middle East – Religious life and customs.   I. Title.
BL1060.S64 2010
200.939′4 – dc22   2010026015

ISBN 978-0-521-86475-6 Hardback
ISBN 978-0-521-68336-4 Paperback

CONTENTS

FIGURES AND MAPS

FIGURES

MAPS

PREFACE

Let us start without preconceptions. Of course, we all have some preconceptions about what religion is or should be, and how it got to be the way it is now. Here we delve into the distant past to see whether we can recognize what appears to have happened. We freely admit that in our self-conscious age, this is nearly impossible.

I do not write to prove or disprove any particular theory about religion. I have ideas about them, which I talk about toward the end of this book. However, I also have a, doubtless, Romantic conviction that one of the things historians should be doing is recounting what is known, usually in chronological order, to see whether we can sniff and feel the force of events, of ceremonies, and of words. My epigraphs are drawn especially from modern studies of religious life; I do not mean to endorse the views expressed by others, but I bring them in to show the continuities and discontinuities in human experience.

We will not be able to experience the same things that others have lived through and heard, but if we do not try to get close to their experiences, we consign our studies to the irrelevance of catalogs and the vapidity of technical detail. There was life back then – human life – and we cannot hope to catch it all. But we can try to feel. And we should.

ACKNOWLEDGMENTS

My formulation of the issues and problems of the history of religions owes a great deal to my forebears, both in the disciplines I have studied and in my own family. Everyone in the generation that preceded mine was either an ordained minister of some confession or other or married to such a minister. I particularly recall my late aunt, the Rev. Marjorie Hawkins Call, longtime minister of the Free Methodist Church, who came to Oklahoma to grow old with my then small children, so that each of them would clearly remember what a determined woman of religion can now do in this world.

With regard to disciplines, I remember the noble effort of Thorkild Jacobsen, always kind to all, who wrote a challenging if idiosyncratic history of Mesopotamian religion. In what follows, all will see how I rebel against his views, but I cherish the clarity of their expression and the obvious depth of thought that he devoted to Sumerian developments. I have profited too from the intuition of Bill Hallo, from whom I learned to hold open the possibility of the continuity of traditions, even over millennia. Further, I owe much to scholars I have never met but have studied, including, especially, Henri Frankfort, who dared to think broadly and wrote more clearly than most on Egyptian religion.

I have also profited from discussions with a number of colleagues in various institutions on the nature and practice of religion. In the spring of 2008, the University of Oklahoma's president David L. Boren sponsored my "dream" course on Ancient Near Eastern religions. In that course, my students and I heard lectures and had extended discussions with Professor Gary Beckman of the University of Michigan, Professor Benjamin Foster of Yale University, Professor Ann Macy Roth of New York University, Professor Tonia Sharlach of Oklahoma State University, and Professor David Sperling of the Hebrew Union College and Jewish Institute of Religion in New York City; they cannot be held responsible for my interpretations, but they are to be praised for their openness and willingness to discuss religion. Professor Sharlach also kindly read and made useful comments on a late version of this work.

I thank my wife, Dr. Katie Barwick-Snell, for reading and commenting on the manuscript of this book, as well as working on its maps. My dear friend, artist Adrienne Day, created three wonderfully clear line drawings for it.

My brother, David Snell of Atlanta, Georgia, gave drafts of this book his sensitive readings. In thanks for his support over the years and that of his wife, Mary Lou Snell, I dedicate this book to them.

1

DEFINING TIME AND SPACE

The student who tries to penetrate the essence of Assyro-Babylonian literature will have to put aside all conventional methods of examination.
— Edward Chierra, *They Wrote on Clay*, 1965, 44

It was a dry place back from the river, pockmarked by the recent rains and with weeds luxuriating in the basins. When there was a wind, it could be positively pleasant, even in the very hot afternoons of summer. It was not at all the blowing sand of other deserts that he had expected. It was not the American Southwest but more like the fruitful plains of the Midwest, which could in a bad year turn inhospitable, especially if the wind kicked up the dirt.

Later he would stand in such a dirt storm, and his mouth would fill with grit – and laughter, too, because he and his crew could accomplish nothing while the wind howled and the grit blew beneath the perfectly blue skies. Treated properly, watered properly, this place could be a paradise, he thought. Then he remembered that in the very early stories, including some from the Bible, it actually had been depicted that way:

> A river issues from Eden to water the garden, and it then divides and becomes four branches. The name of the first is Pishon, meaning Frisky, the one that winds through the whole land of Havilah, meaning Sandy, where the gold is. The gold of that land is good; bdellium, a gum for incense, is there, and lapis lazuli, the prized stone of deep blue. The name of the second river is Gihon, meaning Bubbly, the one that winds through the whole land of Cush in Africa. The name of the third river is Tigris, the one that flows east of Assur. And the fourth river is the Euphrates. (Genesis 2:10–14, after the Jewish Publication Society)

* * *

This was my own first impression of the part of Syria on the Euphrates, where I first encountered what was long ago called Mesopotamia. I was working as a dirt archaeologist, with emphasis on dirt, and I was hoping the team would discover some cuneiform tablets that I could read. That eventually happened. But meanwhile, I got very dirty and very tired. The parts of the Middle East where most people live and have lived for millennia are not really deserts, or at least not always deserts. They can flourish and frequently have.

Here we study the areas usually understood as the Ancient Near East, starting with Mesopotamia, including the modern countries of Iraq, Syria, Turkey, Lebanon, Israel, Palestine, and Iran. We also strive to place Ancient Egypt in this same context, through its writings and monuments. The time treated spans from prehistory to the arrival of the Greek conquest led by Alexander the Great around 330 BCE, although in some matters, we drift further down in time; in others, we stop earlier.

This area is the same as that referred to nowadays as the Middle East, although the Middle East can sometimes include areas to the east, including Afghanistan, Pakistan, and Central Asia, and to the West along the Arabic- and Berber-speaking coast of North Africa. The term "Middle East," although more widely understood and used in the modern languages of the area, is not really descriptive. It derives from the American naval historian Alfred Mahan's perception that the East – the Orient – had a culturally different swath that ran west to east along what we would now term the northern tier of the Middle East, which he thought should be seen as different from India and China (Lewis 1994; Mahan 1902).

The term "Near East" is newer, probably deriving from Russians referring to the area in which they were concerned, including Afghanistan and Persia, as *blizhny vostok*, the "near east," near to them. Both this term and the term Middle East are European coinages that show how Europeans viewed these areas. A geographically more descriptive term would be "Western Asia," but we would need to add "Northeast Africa" to include Egypt and Sudan. Thus, there may be no really satisfying modern term for what we are talking about, but this is just one of our terminological problems.

Some other definitions are needed. "Sumerian" refers to the language earliest attested in the south of Mesopotamia, a language unrelated to any other. It was apparently the language for which the cuneiform, or nail-shaped, writing system on clay was devised. The earliest materials we have that bear on religion appear in that language, but it must have been overshadowed very early by Akkadian, the language spoken by neighbors to the north. At some point, Sumerian died out as a spoken language, but we are unsure exactly when. It remained a scholarly language until the end of the tradition of cuneiform writing in the first century of our era.

Sumer was the south of Iraq, and Akkad was more to the north – central Iraq now, Baghdad and its environs. Religiously, however, there was

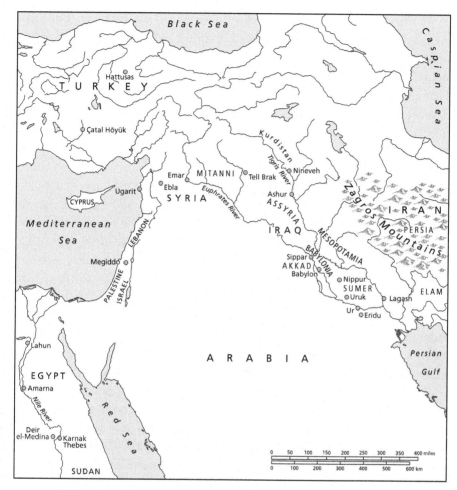

MAP 1.1. The Ancient Near East.

continuity with the south, although there was also a complex process in which gods known to one society were equated with those known in another. This identification could be exact or inexact. Mother goddesses might translate easily, but goddesses of love and war might not. Looking back, we cannot say whose gods' characteristics actually dominated.

Many aspects of religious life were first seen among people who wrote Sumerian. However, some speakers of Akkadian were working and living alongside people with Sumerian names at the earliest periods, and thus combinations of practices from different origins may have happened in times before writing. We find it difficult to sort out what might have been exclusively Sumerian and what might have been originally Akkadian.

The first city-states appear to have been Sumerian-speaking, but some Akkadian-speaking states also showed up in the early king list, which probably did not come into being until a thousand years after the formative periods (Jacobsen 1939). The older idea that something nomadic might have been preserved among the Akkadian speakers seems unlikely; Akkadian was a Semitic language, meaning it is related to the still-living languages of Arabic and Hebrew, both of which may have had their nomadic periods. There is no indication, however, that Akkadians lived in a simpler society than the Sumerians.

Another term we need to know is "Assyrian." This refers first to a dialect of Akkadian that was spoken in the far north of Iraq and in the late second millennium and into the first millennium BCE. It was the name given to the expansive state that dominated Iraq and most of the rest of the Near East. Assyrians saw themselves as culturally distinct, but they consciously collected texts from the south of Iraq and appropriated southern texts for their own chief god, Assur. There were some different cultural emphases that may not have been appreciated in the south, which was mostly politically alienated from the Assyrians, fearful of their organization and might and distrustful of their motives. Assyria did constitute a different culture, and yet its language and attitude were conscious of the debt to the earlier traditions of the south.

The analogy might be that Assyria was to southern Mesopotamia as the United States once was to Great Britain before anyone bothered to read an American book. Before Emerson, all culture seemed to flow from the mother country, even though there were many immigrants in the United States from elsewhere, and the political bonds with Britain had definitively been cut.

"Babylonian" is another geographic term used in some periods. It refers to the city of Babylon and its area, which was roughly the same as the area of Akkad. Babylon, however, only became important as a city after 2000 BCE, and the kingdom of Babylon became the most successful of the little states that emerged from the collapse of a more unified state. The language of Babylon was probably Akkadian, but there was an admixture in the ruling classes of people who spoke Amorite. Amorite was never written as a separate language, and we know it only from the personal names people had. The term "Babylonian" continued to be used after that Old Babylonian kingdom ceased to be important, and the whole of Iraq, or at least southern Iraq, tended to be referred to as Babylonia.

It is a difficult question whether one may speak of a separate religious tradition as being Babylonian. The contemporary opposite would be Assyrian, but the connections in religious traditions were close, even if politics alienated the bearers of those traditions.

A final term to define is "Mesopotamia" itself. This was what the Greeks called the area of Syria and Iraq, and they were translating with "between rivers" what the Aramaic speakers they met called "across the two rivers." To the Aramaic speakers, this meant the great bend in the Euphrates that swings through Syria and Turkey today, and it probably included a great deal of the area to the east of that bend, including modern Iraq. Mesopotamia was never a political term until the twentieth century, and its cultures have always been diverse (Finkelstein 1962).

There were nonetheless continuities among the religious traditions referred to by all the terms discussed here. Polytheisms do not tend to be interested in orthodoxy, and they are frequently open to new customs and gods. Still, some of the places with very early religious sites, such as the city of Uruk in the south of Iraq, continued through more than three millennia to be religious centers. Some of the gods worshiped persisted as well. There was development over time, and yet the traditions seem to have had a certain coherence of concept that appears early and late, and we have tended to view them as a single tradition. Nonetheless, within those traditions, in different places and times, there were differing emphases and interests.

Polytheism is difficult for modern Westerners to take seriously because our own traditions have moved in different directions. Hinduism is a modern polytheistic system that seems to show the flexibility and adaptability that you find in the Ancient Near East, but with Hinduism, too, you must reckon with the long interaction in dialogue and dispute with Islam, which may have forced Hindu thinkers to solidify their teachings and regularize the way they talked about religious phenomena. Hinduism cannot be taken as a mirror for the Ancient Near East, and yet there are some intriguing aspects that seem similar. The association of gods with their animals seems comparable, although it would be rash to argue that at some point, animals were the gods in every case or that anthropomorphic tendencies have always intervened. The emphasis on sight, on seeing the gods and thus partaking of the holiness of the gods, does seem to echo the Ancient Near East (Babb 1975). Yet much space and time separates Hinduism from the Ancient Near East.

As Ernest Renan, the leading Semitist of the nineteenth century, once said, monotheism dulls the taste for all other forms of religion (Renan 1974: 208). This means that we who have been brought up in monotheistic ways cannot see the attraction in polytheisms (Augé 1982). Obviously, however, our own traditions have a history that stretches back to the Ancient Near East, and even if we only understand where we stand, it is important to try to see how the ancients thought about the central concerns of humanity.

Time Line

	Mesopotamia	Turkey	Syria-Palestine	Egypt
10,000–5500 BCE	Neolithic villages	Çatal Höyük	–	o
5500–3100 BCE	Ubaid Cultures	o	–	4000–3000 Naqada Cultures
3100–2000 BCE	3100–2300 Early Dynastic	o	Ebla	3000–2600 Early Dynastic
	2300–2100 Old Akkadian, Gutian	o		2600–2160 Old Kingdom
	2100–2000 Ur III			2160–2055 1st Intermediate
2000–1600 BCE	Old Babylonian	1800–1700 Old Assyrian	–	2055–1650 Middle Kingdom
		1700–1600 Old Hittite		1650–1550 2nd Intermediate
1600–1200 BCE	Middle Babylonian	Hittite New Kingdom	1400–1200 Ugarit	1550–1069 New Kingdom
	Late Babylonian			1069–664 3rd Intermediate
1200–539 BCE	883–625 Neo-Assyrian	–	1000–925 Israel United Kingdom	664–332 Late Period
	625–539 Neo-Babylonian	–	925–722 Israel Divided Kingdom	
			722–586 Judah alone	
			586–539 Babylonian Exile	
539–330 BCE	Persian Empire	–	–	–
330 BCE	Macedonian States: Seleucids	–	–	Ptolemies

o means there are few or no similar phenomena in the period.
– means there are similar phenomena in the period.

6

2

EARLY INKLINGS

The marvelous was not for him exceptional; it was the normal state.

– Ernest Renan, *Vie de Jesus*, 1863, 137

The foreigners were coming. They did not even speak the language, but they brought very good shards of shiny obsidian, perfect for working into blades. The blades would be sharp enough to cut flesh and even bone.

So those who lived in the village gladly accepted the shards and made sure the foreigners were included when the meal of goat meat and milk was served on the roof in the evening.

The foreigners stayed, however. Perhaps they wanted a glimpse of the Lady as she passed. She might bring a blessing to them as she did to the villagers. You could not tell with foreigners. Clearly, they were fascinated by how many people came and went, impressed with the large number of sheep crowded into town at evening.

They were on edge, especially as the leopard dancers spread out into the dusk. The dancers carried the plastered heads of their venerable ancestors, some dripping red with fresh paint to keep the ancestors full of blood and alive. The men wore loincloths of leopard skin and made sounds of moaning and keening, although leopards attack secretly and silently. The women and men turned and walked backward around the perimeter of the village, each chanting his or her family's secret song, holding the plastered head before them in the thickening dark. They carried no torches and returned suddenly, like big cats, to deposit the ancestors again in their houses.

There was a fire burning by the main entrance of the village, and the foreigners gathered there with the other men and children. A shaman, an old man steeped in cattle lore, arose from the circle and began the song. It was in old language, and even people who had heard it many times did not fully understand it. It was about the hunt and its success; it praised particular ancestors for their skills at baiting bulls and killing boars.

The old man was also trying to gauge the purity of intent of the foreigners, men and women and a baby or two huddling all together. This was most unusual, that foreigners should be present, and not everyone bringing offerings knew the secrets of the village.

Their presence, though, might ruin the effect of the prayer that was about to begin. Or their gifts might instead please the Lady and lead to a most propitious prayer and subsequent season. They seemed receptive enough, a little nonplused by the shaman's headdress and wild language, which, of course, they could not understand.

It grew late, and some of the foreigners had fallen asleep. The shaman stopped chanting, and an expectant silence fell upon the assembly. In the distance, outside the circle of light, a leopard man moaned.

Then She was in their midst, large, tall, wearing a red mask and flailing about and yelling Her will: the foreigners should be fed, for three days. They should be given skins to wear, flint to use, invited to come at the equinox, bearing more of their stone. They were most welcome, She yelled, most welcome.

The men and children rose and cheered and hugged the foreigners. The Lady stalked off into the night. The men laid skins out for the foreigners and drifted off to their own roofs. It would be warm still tonight, and they would sleep on the roofs. The women already lay within.

At dawn, however, the village was aroused and the foreigners were, too. There, on the horizon, stalked a real leopard. It was a lean and hungry cat looking for leftovers from the meats of the night before, but too afraid of humans to come very near the village. This was a most auspicious sign.

* * *

Çatal Höyük ("Fork[-shaped] Ruin") is a large mound in southern Turkey now, but around 8000 BCE, it was a center of trade that happened perhaps as imagined in the preceding paragraphs. It was a large town before plants were domesticated, and the animal domesticates were also few. The obsession with leopards is clear in the preserved art. Perhaps the leopards were the sacred animals of the site, and you did not normally kill them.

The site of Çatal Höyük is odd among the Neolithic villages of which we know. It lasted from the time before people made pots into a time when ceramics were common. It had the domesticated wheat and goats other sites had, but it also had buried treasures of obsidian, the glass from volcanoes that makes especially sharp knife points. Flourishing around 7000 BCE, the place was noteworthy for being a rather big village, but its many houses had no doors. You entered them through holes in the roofs.

The dead were buried in the floors of the houses, but some had their heads removed and covered with plaster. The plaster was frequently renewed, sometimes covered with red paint. Revered ancestors but also children were commemorated in sites in this way (Bonogofsky 2004). The custom presumably meant that the dead person's life was being renewed with blood. House walls sometimes were decorated with scenes of hunts, and some are still preserved in lively colors. Prominent among the animals that appeared were leopards. But they were not necessarily hunted. Some merely lounged catlike on walls, and there were leopard skins that people depicted on the walls were wearing. Oddly, thus far only a single leopard bone has been recovered in the site, found in a burial of a high-status woman who may have been wearing it as a pendant because it had a hole in it. Was there some reason people did not hunt leopards even as they were obviously important in their art? Clearly there were still leopards living nearby.

The site was apparently an important trade depot for obsidian, but we do not understand why people buried hordes of it under their floors. There were also depictions of cattle in the art, and residents did not have scruples against eating cattle, as the bones show.

Perhaps the site was of religious importance to people in the region. It certainly seems as though the people at the site could draw on resources beyond those that they might themselves have raised or hunted. The concerns that seem to us religious at Çatal Höyük were fertility of flocks and crops and also the question of life after death. Some, but apparently not all, of the dead seemed to live on in the sense of being involved in the life of the community to the extent of having their heads preserved and plastered and replastered. We cannot tell how it was decided which people would be celebrated in this particular way or if such treatment was considered an honor (Hodder 2006).

As the Ancient Near East was being revealed through archaeology to the world of the Victorians in the 1800s, Western society was in a process of apparent secularization. This meant that religious authorities were losing power and becoming marginalized when it came to making decisions about what governments did and how money was spent. However, many of the scholars who were participating in the secular miracle of the revival of knowledge of the Ancient Near East had trained for the priesthood, ministry, or rabbinate if they were not actually ordained. Their views of earlier ages may have been more sympathetic to religion than others of their contemporaries. Furthermore, the data they were discovering teamed with the names of hitherto unknown or only slightly known gods. This world seemed to have been animated by religious sentiment that reverberated with their experiences.

Victorian-era excavators found temples to be the biggest and most interesting buildings uncovered in their excavations. They guessed that the temples must have been the motivating and organizing factor in the creation of the early civilizations. Their publications were rich in titles with temple documents and religious texts. They came to feel that these early societies had been pious and had seen religion as a major organizing feature. The ancient kings boasted that they built temples to please the gods; modern scholars, although recognizing the bombast and political motivation, tended to take the piety at face value.

It is ironic that the culmination of this approach may have come from a very secular anthropologist, Robert McC. Adams in his book *The Evolution of Urban Society* (Adams 1966). There he argued that both Mesopotamia and Mesoamerica were formed under the guidance of priest kings, men who used their close connections with the supernatural to frighten and cajole their fellows into cooperating in the creation of large religious projects. There is extensive evidence to support this contention for late periods for which archives revealed large amounts of land and large numbers of people under the control of the House of the Lady, a temple complex run by the wife of the city governor of Lagash, a large city in southern Iraq. This was in 2400 BCE, however, long after the establishment of Mesopotamian civilization in the Iraqi plain around 5500 BCE.

In Adams's book, he paints a plausible picture of early developments in Mesopotamia and in Mesoamerica, and yet this is inevitably a sketchy and theoretical picture. It is also based on a mildly Marxist idea of how to motivate people, by offering them spiritual solace in exchange for physical work. Its corollary is that these ancient peoples were somehow more religious than we are. Some have argued that they believed religious leaders had extraordinary powers that could afflict them with pain if they did not obey. There is little direct evidence of such an attitude, however, and the great physical mobility in Mesopotamian society shows people voting with their feet. Overbearing city leaders found themselves with fewer followers and, in worst cases, saw their cities abandoned.

Scholars now may wish to see the distant past as determinedly religious, but we do not want to see ourselves and our societies as determined or attracted by religious mandates. Yet our society, too, has advocates of greater religiosity in politics. To the nonreligious, this looks self-serving, and perhaps that perceived selfishness is all Adams really meant to address. Certainly from this distance, it is hard to assess sincerity in religion, especially when the religious expression seems too alien to modern observers.

What happened next? After the Near East was scattered with farming communities that were probably linked to each other only by occasional exchanges of goods and innovations, there may have sometimes been problems with rainfall agriculture. We think that from at least 3000 BCE, the area was as dry as it is now, meaning fairly dry. Thus, in bad years, villages might be abandoned or partly abandoned, and some people would go further into the hills where the rains were better or leave agriculture completely to follow their domesticated animals, sheep, and goats in their quest for food. Such moves leave little trace in archaeological sites, but they may have made people much more sensitive to the vicissitudes of the rain. This may have led people to try to placate gods of rain.

The nomads went into the hills sometimes but also into the deserts, but they did not really like the desert, and as far as we know later nomads' religious concerns were concentrated on the god of the moon. This may have had something to do with navigating in relatively trackless wastes.

The important step for the history of religion was the move from the foothills, in Iraqi Kurdistan today, into the Iraqi plain. The foothills continued to be farmed productively, but the plain is fed by the two big rivers and by innumerable natural canals. It was easy to tap these watercourses to water stream-side fields, and it turned out that irrigated crops produced up to ten times the yield as rain-fed crops. The plain was otherwise dry and barren, and it became very hot in the summers, but the productivity seems to have been worth it to lure the village farmers out onto the plain.

We can see what the settlers did for religion at the far southern site of Eridu, modern Abu Shahrain, where an Iraqi team carried out a modern scientific excavation that they then published in an exemplary way (Safar et al. 1981). According to the much later Sumerian King List, kingship first came down from heaven at Eridu, meaning that social complexity was felt to have arisen there, and although it may not be the earliest site occupied on the plain, it was settled very early, perhaps around 5500 BCE (Jacobsen 1939: 70–1).

At Eridu the Iraqis found an old mud brick building, the floor of which was strewn with fish bones, another benefit of living in a river zone. This structure was rebuilt many times down to historical periods, where it could be identified as the temple of the god Enki. He apparently liked to receive fish as an offering, and he was eager to share his bounty with his human devotees.

Later, we see he was a god of freshwater, and his name in Sumerian means "lord earth," but he was not really an earth god. Rather he was a god of what made the earth good, the water that created the surpluses bursting out of the storehouses. It is unknown whether he corresponded in some way with earlier ideas about rain gods. You could expect only winter rains on the plain.

Probably this temple was an organizational center for its community, and it was the biggest building and represented a significant pooling of people's resources. There were daily meals of fish, and perhaps everyone got to participate. Or maybe it was a set of ceremonies restricted to people who made the key community decisions, perhaps not even including the fishermen themselves.

Our idea about how elites formed is a fuzzy one, based on the sense that there probably was a hierarchy of good fields you might farm. That kind of resource may have been distributed unevenly, and even if it were not, some people had skills and talents that others did not; over time they had more influence on community decisions. Among them may have emerged not only community leaders in practical matters but also priests. The basic Sumerian word for priest, E N, was translated into Akkadian as "priest" but also as "lord," and this implies that early on, there may not have been much distinction between practical and ideological leadership in communities. If we see these developments as only self-serving and pernicious, we may be evaluating them from our present standpoint. Later we can see that these same people were the ones responsible for supporting the poor, and so there was at least some altruism in their approach.

Other early settlements may have worshiped other gods besides the god of freshwater, although they, too, must have been dependent on the waters. What their qualities may have been is speculative, but in later times, cities had chief gods who were worshiped in the biggest buildings. Those gods had families of gods who might share some of the main temple, or they might have smaller shrines of their own. The construction of groups of gods into families seems ancient, although our evidence for it definitely comes only from times when people could write about it (Sallaberger 2004).

Another way to relate gods to each other was through syncretism, the identification of one god with another of a different name but somewhat similar characteristics. This seems to be a basic feature of polytheism made necessary by the multitude of gods and the needs of humans to categorize them. There may have been a political need to cooperate with other towns that had different gods but were viewed as friendly, and the interaction of the gods was assumed to have been benign. Polytheisms seem especially good at avoiding religious conflict, partly because they are open-ended and can admit any number of new names of gods. Syncretism allows them to simplify a burgeoning system and yet retain the names and panoply preferred in each locality. We may draw the analogy to the various forms of the Virgin Mary, some of which may have gone back to various pre-Christian deities, who have been brought together under the mantle of Christianity. What you do in front of them may be slightly different, and the feelings that are developed may be different, even though no one now would doubt that references were to the same Virgin Mary.

The mechanism was available to create a pantheon that included the gods of various towns, but no one may have bothered when the early farming villages, dependent on irrigation, did not amalgamate into larger political entities. When they began to combine, the issue arose, however, and gods became identified with other gods, their qualities becoming homogenized. This is the earliest polytheism we know much about. Religious feelings may have been different in different towns as the objects of religion varied, but religion itself did not appear to be divisive.

3

GODS, GODS, GODS

The religious world is but the reflex of the real world.
— Karl Marx, *Capital*, 1906, 91

WHAT GODS WERE FOR

The young priest had been told exactly what to do, and he had been up all night, keeping watch on the sacred things, the first dates anyone had harvested from anywhere throughout the city. They were green and mushy and not particularly appetizing. He preferred them dried, but the goddess wanted the very first and as soon as possible. He was drowsy but attentive as the first light of dawn appeared over the horizon, and gradually he could make out the web of the basket and the sleeping city, with only one or two plumes of smoke rising from the homes of early risers.

The old priest had told him exactly how to do it, and the priest could no longer mount the stairs to the terrace, so he had better get it right. He had thought he would be a little cold in the night because he had been supposed to sit there, in front of the mud brick temple, with absolutely nothing on. But in fact, it was still high summer, although the harvesting of the rest of the dates would stretch into autumn. The night had been almost pleasant after the scorching day. The nakedness was to show his purity to the goddess; it might have been embarrassing except that no one else was around at all. Even the day-shift priests had not yet arrived to clean up the temple terrace and to prepare the rest of the goddess's breakfast. For his was a special offering that had to be made on the dawn after the first pickings were available. So here he was, naked.

There, the sun had finally peaked onto the plain. He arose and walked slowly into the temple. The goddess sat in effigy facing him, the light beginning to illuminate her gold-plated hair. The image was of wood with gold attached. It was taller than a human, and the garments in which she was depicted, too, were studded with that expensive blue stone that came from the east. Her coal-black eyes seemed to look at him intently as he came in holding the basket up before him.

He began the prayer he had memorized, "Lady of all the divine qualities, light outspreading, upright woman, surrounded by overwhelming splendor, loved by both heaven and earth . . . "

She really was, he realized, as he plunked the basket before her, then averted his eyes and backed out, if perhaps she would wish to begin eating the dates immediately. He finished the recitation outside the temple, and the sun was already stoking up the day.

⋆ ⋆ ⋆

This may have been something like the experience of a priest presenting the goddess Inanna with the first fruits. The poem we know is from much later (Hallo and van Dijk 1968: 14–15), and in the earliest times, the young priest would probably have had Sumerian as his first language and so could understand it all. Eventually Sumerian ceased to be a spoken language, and it would have been an academic effort to have memorized it and presented it correctly. To do it incorrectly would displease the goddess.

Religion is for us, the human beings now making our way on earth. This is brought forth eloquently by an art-historical fact. Although in some cultures there are depictions of a series of gods all off in their own world, this is not true in Ancient Mesopotamia. Perhaps the most well known of the depictions of an all-divine world is from Turkey in the second millennium BCE, at Yazilikaya, apparently a center for worship of the Hittite pantheon, where there is a marching parade of gods carved on a mountainside in relief. In southern Iraq, however, there is apparently no such thing in any period. There are, instead, always human beings present, either as worshipers or as givers of gifts. The Uruk vase, from the Uruk period in the fourth millennium BCE, does have a snazzy picture of a goddess receiving goods, but a naked worshiper, the political leader of the city, is seen giving her a big pot, probably full of dates, a staple crop in the south. Human beings were always there, perhaps on the periphery of myths and stories, an afterthought sometimes, but still the real reason for the story being told. We have gods because we wish to understand how the world works, but most importantly, we have gods to see how we fit into the world (Boemer 1957–71).

WHAT WAS A GOD?

The words for "god" in general are well understood in the languages of the Ancient Near East, and yet what exactly is meant by them is harder to say.

FIGURE 3.1. Uruk vase: This view of the top portion of the alabaster vase from the Uruk Period around 3100 BCE shows a naked, and therefore presumably pure, representative of the community bringing a basket of dates to the goddess, who graciously accepts them, perhaps to tuck away in her storehouse. The flaglike symbols behind her show she is to be understood as Inanna, the goddess of heaven, associated with the morning and evening star and with storehouses, a key to community success. Sketch by A. Day.

Certainly there is linguistic continuity from *ilum* in Akkadian through *el* in texts from the second millennium in Syria and Hebrew *el* and *elohim*, a plural that probably is meant to emphasize the majesty not the plurality of the object, to *Allah*, the Arabic name for the one God. The root of this word has to do with power, and certainly a god is seen as a focus of power, meaning the skill to make things happen in the world.

The Sumerian word from the first written language in Mesopotamia is DINGIR, written with the sign for star and sometimes itself read as AN, the name for the sky god, ⁂. It is unclear what DINGIR is related to, and that is true of the Egyptian word we translate as god, *neṭer*, ⌐. It is possible that *neṭer* is related to *neṭery*, meaning "natron," a salt for drying and cleaning, and consequently meaning "clean, pure." Or perhaps the idea of god was primary and was assumed to be clean and pure.

Because the contrast with our own views is frequently extreme and surprising, we may find ourselves generalizing about the ancients' experiences, but this is not actually such a good idea because the ancients were mostly not interested in generalizing. They were concerned about the particular god and her or his particular power. The qualities of some gods include the following.

Some gods were not immortal. Their dying was a central fact of their stories and apparently also of the worship of them – that is to say, the acts that their communities did to commemorate them. In particular, the cycle of the Mesopotamian goddess Ishtar and of her husband Tammuz was important. In these stories, the goddess conceived a desire simply to visit the underworld, usually a place of no return where the dead barely survived as individuals. Her sister reigned there, and she had never gotten along with her sister. When she arrived, she was struck dead, and her death led to the cessation of fertility back on earth. The other gods became concerned and sent emissaries to revive the goddess, by now a mere slab of dead meat. The sister objected, but a deal was struck through which Ishtar might return topside, but half of the year she had to be replaced by her insouciant spouse, the boy-god of fertility, Tammuz, or Dumuzi ("Righteous Youth" in Sumerian). He presumably represented all easy fecundity, and when he was gone, it was the heart of the rainless Iraqi summer, with unmerciful heat and dryness in which nothing would grow (Pisi 2001).

Gods also were not omniscient. An incident was in the story of the flood, in which most of the great gods agreed to destroy humans because they were so noisy, but one secretly dissented and alerted the flood hero to build a boat and save life from extinction. When this transpired and the other great gods perceived that they had been tricked, they were angry, but the dissenter managed to convince them that it was unjust to destroy everybody. The great gods did not know everything that was happening, even in connection with important decisions they had made (Foster 2005: 252).

Gods also were not all powerful. They were seen as specialized, some dealing with some phenomena, and others with different ones. Enlil, "lord wind" in Sumerian, had charge of the weather and was a god almost universally honored on the Iraqi plain. He was the main mover in bringing the flood. But there was also lord earth, Enki, who was the god of freshwater, who made everything bloom and made it possible for humans to live. Yet when assembled the gods could wield great power, and certainly when they agreed on something, it was likely to happen, like the flood. Yet their power was not absolute, and applying it in any particular direction was not an easy thing to do.

Famous heroes after death could become gods, as with Gilgamesh. Those people tended in life to be people of high status and wide renown, and what it meant to have become a god was not always clear. In Egypt from a very early period, kings were gods, a specific kind of god, the *neter nefer*, "the good god," who might therefore affect what actually happened now. This term, however, could also refer to a recently deceased king, whose power in this life was diminished with death. Clearly such gods died and were not always available as personalities for intervention in the lives of others. There were also people who were cultural heroes, such as the putative pyramid builder Im-hotep, who became gods after their deaths. In his case, this meant that there were temples built to him and that at least architects and builders paid some attention to him in later times. Perhaps they imagined him intervening to perfect their buildings and works, much as a medieval Christian saint would have done (Wilkinson 2003: 111–13).

The situation in Ancient Iraq was more complex. There rulers were happy to have themselves seen as the chosen ones of gods and even as the children of gods, but around 2200 BCE, the king of Akkad, Naram-Sin, claimed to be a god.

In practice, this meant that kings had their names written with the DINGIR sign before it. We do not know whether this meant it was actually pronounced; perhaps it was merely a note for scribes. However, kings took up the custom, perhaps unconsciously, for another three hundred years, over the falls of dynasties and changing of traditions. Some of them had temples built to themselves and sacrifices given, and yet they governed as flawed human beings, did not always make successful decisions, and certainly eventually died.

It is unclear how other Mesopotamians felt about these developments, but there is a certain irony that later Mesopotamian tradition held that Naram-Sin, who was actually not the last king of his line, was blamed for the fall of his dynasty through impiety toward the great gods. There is no evidence contemporary to him that this was so, and it is not particularly likely. However, Mesopotamians had the view that someone must have been to blame when there was a great upheaval, and, because he was famous, Naram-Sin was blamed. Perhaps part of his impiety perceived by later ages included his claim of divinity, but the tradition did not say so.

Later kings were happy to take on this particular aspect of his mantle. Modern students see this as a crass attempt to pull rank, to assert the specialness of kingly office somewhat analogous to the European idea of the divine right of kings. Ordinary people may not have taken this claim too seriously, however. There is one indication that some of them may have tried to flatter the reigning king when giving their children names including his, but this continued even after the deification of kings stopped. One of these names was a compliment to the king who ended the custom, Hammurabi: a boy grew to adulthood with the name *Hammurabi-nuḥdi-matim* – "Hammurabi is the plenty of the land" – around 1750 BCE. Presumably he had a shorter nickname.

One aspect of the deification included the idea that only the king who controlled the religious center of Nippur near modern Baghdad could have royal hymns composed in his honor. Kings after Akkad seem to have respected the idea that although there could be several kings vying for power in later periods, the one who held Nippur was the paramount king. Maybe others could deify themselves, but the ruler of Nippur certainly did (Hallo 1963). Some have seen in Hammurabi's renunciation of royal deification a self-conscious assertion of the foreignness of kings of Amorite, or Western descent, arguing that somehow Amorites were offended by deification. However, most of the kings for the two hundred years before Hammurabi who had happily deified themselves were also of Amorite extraction. Ethnicity does not seem to be an adequate explanation for the end of deification. Later kings, although they had no other trappings of deification, did sometimes have their names written with the divine determinative.

So if kings and heroes could be gods, what might a god have been? A god was someone with extraordinary power and success and someone who might exert that power over distance and perhaps over time. Having kings and heroes as gods meant that the gods were not so far away or so totally "other," as has been thought in later times. An old poem begins, "When gods were men...," and in a sense that phrase might hark back to what was happening in people's attitudes to Mesopotamian gods; they were not so far away or so different, but of course they were powerful and sometimes dangerous (Foster 2005: 227).

KINDS OF GODS

Mesopotamians thought their gods belonged to different types. Our sources for understanding their views range from scholarly lists to the personal names of actual people. Archaeology sometimes allows us to see what exactly was done for a particular god, but not usually to penetrate the thinking even of elites about their feelings on religious occasions. We also hear tales about gods from literary texts that were part of the way scribes learned to write; these presumably corresponded in some periods with the views of others in society, but they did not in any sense constitute an orthodoxy to which you had to adhere. Thus, if we happened to be plopped down in an antique Iraqi city and were up to speed in our Sumerian or Akkadian so that we could understand and be understood, it is doubtful whether everyone we talked to would have heard of all of these gods or know their stories. Some would, we think, because the scholarly medium of writing conveys information to us, but the connection to the rest of society is not known. Perhaps we need to think about these portraits of gods the way we would about portraits of medieval Christian saints; peasants would see pictures if they were lucky enough to visit a nice up-to-date church or shrine, and they might hear some priest preaching in a language they could understand about the saint – or they might not (Gurevich 1992: 95).

Among the gods were the primordial gods, those who existed at the first. They were present in scholarly genealogies of the gods, and they continued to show up in mythological thinking, but they were not likely to have shrines in historical periods nor to loom large in normal people's ideas about how the world worked. They had names such as ANŠAR and KIŠAR, meaning "all-sky" and "all-earth." They had sex and produced other gods who again did not make too much impression on later thinkers. Yet there must have been gods at the beginning, and there must have been an idea of generations of gods progressing down to later times.

One of these descendants continued to be noteworthy, ABZU, who was the freshwater abyss, and from whose name our word "abyss" may be distantly descended, although Greek *a-bussos,* "without depth," seems plausible, too. This primordial place was in some sense still with us because freshwater did bubble up in springs from the depths and came along most conveniently in rivers. In English we do tend to say *the* ABZU, meaning that we think of it as an impersonal force, but in neither of the Mesopotamian languages was there a definite article, and so this is our idea and not theirs. There was something unreliable and chaotic about the ABZU as well, and so when there is a story about rebellions against the order imposed by the gods, you find the ABZU on the wrong side of things. Furthermore, the ABZU appeared as a primordial place, the lowermost place imaginable, filled with freshwater. It was also the seat of later gods who were more active, especially lord earth, Enki, the god of freshwater (Sjöberg 1994: A 2, 184–202).

This earlier generation of gods had faded by the time writing was invented around 3100 BCE; they had been supplanted, at least in some people's views, by other gods, who seemed to be active gods who might be involved in the lives of people. They had temples kept up for their use, and they had prayers written to them. People hoped they would do something for them.

Lord wind, Enlil, was the chief executive of the gods. He could be arbitrary and unfair, but he convened the assembly of the gods and could get them to intervene on behalf of rulers and other humans. Princes who hoped to be paramount in southern Iraq built temples to him and made him offerings. Apparently, he was worshiped all over the south, but he had a city that was special to him, Nippur – in many ways the religious capital of all of Mesopotamia. As far as we can see, it was never a political capital. The late Thorkild Jacobsen guessed that its preeminence, and Enlil's, may have been due to a custom of convening a council of the city-states there to deal with threats to the river valley. Jacobsen saw Nippur as a neutral place where peace could be maintained and calm, multilateral discussions could take place. However, his evidence for this Sumerian League, as he called it, is in fact only the later mythical texts that showed the council of the gods functioning (Jacobsen 1957; Steinkeller 2002).

The case of Nippur calls into question the generalization that religious capitals are always, or were once, connected to politics. Jerusalem was important because it became a royal city, and Rome and Istanbul as well. Mecca was economically important before the Prophet of Islam and after his rise was never the political capital, but its religious function was reasserted by the revelation to Muhammad.

In cuneiform, the name of the city of Nippur was written simply "Enlil place," and we owe the reading of Nibru and Nippur to glosses to that writing. The name persists in its modern place-name, Nuffer. However, the god as a character seems like the kings who prayed to him, distant and elegant, powerful and inscrutable, able to wield vast power but potentially unreliable. He owed his power to his descent from the primordial gods, and Nippur was the showcase of it.

In contrast, lord earth, Enki, was a trickster and Wile E. Coyote of a god who always had his own idiosyncratic approach to things. As god of freshwater, his abode was the ABZU, and from there he contrived to help human beings.

Enki was not just the god of agricultural success but also the god of wisdom, endowing his favored humans with "a wide ear," as they said in Sumerian – that is, a wide understanding of how things worked. This wisdom also made

FIGURE 3.2. Enki seal: This is a sketch from a modern impression of an ancient seal showing the god of fish and freshwater and wisdom mounting the mountains, good things spewing off his shoulders. Next to him stands his sidekick, Ishum, a useful appendage given that his many faces allow him insight in different directions and contribute to Enki's wisdom and magic skill. The seal's owner's name appears at left; he is "Adda, the scribe." Sketch by A. Day.

him uniquely qualified to instruct people in the spells that would allow them access to magic. Many spells were attributed to him and to his son, the god of Babylon, Marduk.

Enki's city was Eridu, far to the south on the river plain. By 2000, if not earlier, Eridu had been abandoned by most of its inhabitants, and only a rear guard of priests who were keeping up the Enki shrine dwelt there. Thus, here, too, as with Enlil, there is an odd connection to a city lacking political importance; Enki's town was basically a ghost town through the historical period. It was not maintained by governments for economic reasons, probably because its river meandered away and its canals had run dry. It was maintained, however, for the honor of Enki and because the kings remembered, correctly, that this was the foremost of the early cities (Safar et al. 1981).

Moderns have speculated that there was an Eridu theology in contrast to a later Nippur theology, strands of written tradition that emphasized different aspects of the relations of the gods in earlier times. The Eridu stories stressed the primordial elements of water and earth and included appeals to underworld gods because Eridu stood at the entrance to the primordial abyss. The Nippur stories, however, stressed the celestial bodies that might affect humans. In the long run, the Nippur theology dominated, but scribes continued to copy the Eridu material long after Eridu had ceased to exist (Hallo 1996).

The most notable thing about Mesopotamian religion, however, was the presence of powerful goddesses, many of whom seem to have been of two types. One type was goddesses of birth and motherhood, much prized in a world where children died in droves from childhood diseases; simply to replace themselves, women and men needed to have perhaps three times as many children as they hoped would live. Another type of goddesses was that of love and war.

The mother goddesses had many names, but all shared the quality of being nurturing and supportive. In early times, they were depicted with exaggerated breasts and vulvas to stress the success they could impart in childbearing. In historical times, they seem narrowly focused and yet obviously popular, especially among women who faced the nitty-gritty tasks of reproduction.

Ishtar was the name in Akkadian for the most famous of the goddesses of love and war. In Sumerian, she was known as Inanna, which appears to mean "queen of heaven." Another set of goddesses was involved in healing the sick.

Wherever cultures met, they compared gods and suggested that gods with different names and from different milieus were at base the same. The Egyptologist Jan Assmann has argued that such equations of gods were in fact conceptual breakthroughs of a high order (Assmann 1997: 46). People were abstracting from their particular god and seeing the similar qualities in someone else's. This identification took place in a polytheistic context, meaning that both of the gods compared were parts of systems that were theoretically open, able to accept new gods with different duties and characteristics. Sometimes one system did accept a god that did not seem to have analogues within its system. With gods who were considered great, there was considerable activity of identification and translation.

In these equations, however, some characteristics of one god could rub off on another. It is possible that Sumerian Inanna was a star goddess representing the planet Venus and perhaps aspects of sexual love. Ishtar seems to have been oriented toward protecting her favored Akkadian kings in battle. Yet the two goddesses came to share all these qualities. It is not likely that this sharing was a self-conscious effort of the Akkad dynasty to equate its goddess with a firmly ensconced southern one. It is much more likely that this kind of equation had been going on among scribes and probably in others as well for as long as speakers of Akkadian and Sumerian had been together, meaning as early as we have any writing at all from southern Iraq (Wilcke 1976–80).

Jacobsen saw Inanna not just as a part of the date palm but also as a personified storehouse. Her name does not mean that, but her symbol did show up adorning storehouses, which probably were important community centers for keeping surpluses and for distributing them when famine threatened. They may well have been the foci and the most obvious successes of the early community, not just in southern Mesopotamia (Jacobsen 1976).

The symbol of the goddess was a spire draped by a shawl that was partly bound at the top and then allowed to hang free. It may have been a part of a tiara worn by high-class ladies (Beaulieu 1998; Steinkeller 1998). Flying over buildings, especially storehouses, these spires must have conveyed the message that the Lady had again created a surplus, and there would be plenty for all.

The figure of Ishtar was feminine in southern Iraq, but in second millennium Syria, there was a god Ashtar, which seems to be the same word as Ishtar, who was masculine. This god, perhaps to be identified with Venus as a morning star, was also honored by the pre-Islamic Arabs (Pope and Röllig 1965: 249–50). Although not a major god, he raises the question about the consistency of identification of gods and the continuity of their names.

Inanna-Ishtar was especially honored in Uruk, where apparently writing first developed and where we have a set of stories about Early Dynastic kings. The goddess in literature was seen as eager to fulfill her wifely duty and to spread the blessing of fertility among all her people. A mechanism to achieve fertility was the so-called sacred marriage where the king would personify Inanna-Ishtar's spouse, and a priestess would play the goddess; their union would guarantee fertility. The hymns connected to this custom mentioned only Iddin-Dagan, king of the city of Isin, from the 1900s BCE. We do not know whether this custom was practiced elsewhere or at other times (Renger 1972–5).

Another aspect of interest regarding Inanna was her husband, who personified the dry season of southern Iraq and yet who also functioned as a symbol of fertility. He was early identified with another once-independent god, Amaušumgalana, a dragon or reptile, and his role as a shepherd meant that he spent a lot of his time outside of the cities, in the uncultivated areas between their green fields. This area we call the "steppe," although the image of the Russian steppe the word conjures in English is wrong; the EDIN in Sumerian, the ṣēru in Akkadian, was the area that was not irrigated by the rivers and canals. Only scrub would grow there, but scrub was enough for

FIGURE 3.3. Uruk seal: This is a rendering of a modern impression of an Uruk Period seal from around 3100 BCE that seems to boast of the owner's bounty, represented by storehouses, with their flaglike symbols waving, stuffed with small animals and probably milk products. Beyond, cattle gambol, showing that there is plenty more on the way. Sketch by A. Day.

the sheep and goats that Dumuzi herded. The steppe, however, was for most Mesopotamians a forbidding place where there were also wild animals and where one could get lost and hurt. Not for them the Romantic connection with nature. In contrast to Israel and Greece, sacred places were not likely to be found in the steppe. Dumuzi was from there, however, and to woo Inanna, he had to come into the city, where all the good things were, to help disburse the benefits of fertility. Dumuzi was not among the great gods, but he does seem to have been important early on, and it is interesting that his origins were not in the cities. His characteristics underline how important the cities were seen to be. They were where the great arts of civilization were found most thickly and where real human life could be most fully lived.

There was another great god of importance who appeared early and late but who did not have interesting stories written about him. The god of the sun was sobriety and justice incarnate, perhaps for the obvious reasons that in a land mostly without rain, the sun shines every day and looks into every nook and cranny. Kings wished to have his assent to their ruling and to their rule making. In Sumerian, he was UTU, and in Akkadian Šamaš, and for him, too, we have a similar deity in Syria who rather clearly was female. Her name, related to his, was Šapaš, and she seems also to have been connected to impartiality and justice (Pope and Röllig 1965: 308–9). Šamaš's town was Sippar, north of Babylon, but he was worshiped elsewhere as well, and especially in legal disputes, people tended to invoke him above other gods.

The great gods were revered in many places under several names. Although their greatness derived perhaps from their initial associations with powers of nature important to the survival and success of humans, they did not each have a set personality or even gender in every place. They were powerful but not all powerful, long-lived but not necessarily immortal, knowledgeable but not omniscient.

It is tempting to speculate on the models for these gods, to guess what experiences human beings in Mesopotamia were responding to that they thought of their gods in these ways. Jacobsen was interested in seeing especially Inanna and Dumuzi as manifestations of the success of date-palm agriculture, but there is no way to validate his suggestions. The later epithets used for those gods do seem to accord with such an origin (Ringgren 1973: 5). Yet the later fates of these gods may have nothing to do with their origins. Perhaps the great gods were somehow modeled on the experience of human leadership. Such leadership, we guess, arose from people in agricultural villages who were able to produce a slightly bigger surplus and organize irrigation projects among their fellows. At best, from the point of view of the governed, such men (probably almost always and not women) could be approachable consensus builders, but they could be offended by slights and concerned about losses, especially to themselves and the community. At worst they could be arrogant and domineering. Nonetheless, we know from historical periods that Mesopotamians were always able to get away from bad situations and people and to move up- or downriver and find other places to farm. Some ran to the hills and tried rainfall agriculture; others disappeared into the desert with some sheep and were not bothered again by sedentary leadership. Hence, perhaps, we see the limitations of the leaders' power and also of the perceived powers of the gods.

We should not reduce the great gods to reflections of human rulers, however, even historically more firmly attested ones than the "big men" of early Mesopotamia. These possible human images do not explain the longevity of interest in these gods, but they may contribute a bit to some of their continuing qualities. It seems not unlikely that people's views of the divine qualities did change over time, and the great gods became in some sense greater, more powerful, and wiser in the long run.

GODS OF CITIES

The great gods sometimes had different names in different cities, indicating that, for example, a mother-sex-war goddess of one place had been equated with Inanna of another. Yet the similarities were enough to allow a shared name. Ishtar of Nineveh in the north attracted different people from Inanna of Uruk, and yet there was something in common between them.

There were also many lesser gods who found special devotion in particular cities. They may have been thought of sometimes as heads of their local pantheon and so have been equated with other more famous gods. In the southeastern city of Lagash, for example, the head god Ningirsu (the name means "lord of Girsu," a section of the city) faded eventually from memory but became associated with Ninurta ("lord of the earth"), a god of Nippur; they shared warlike qualities and powers over fertility, and of course their names began with Nin-, meaning either "lord" or "lady." The city gods reigned locally, but they also sometimes made visits to other cities and their gods in waterborne processions that must have impressed everyone along the way (Sjöberg 1957–71). Systematic thinkers incorporated local gods as the children of more widely revered gods.

We can see the importance of local gods, especially in the names given to persons. Some only showed up within their own cities, and their popularity in names waned with the importance of their towns. Over the course of Mesopotamian history there may have been a certain homogenization of names, because the great gods appeared to take over from the local gods. Yet even among the great gods, there were tendencies in particular towns to favor some over others.

In personal names, we feel as though one can gauge the sentiments of parents or relatives who gave the names. Those sentiments may be not only religious; style and fashion may play a role as well, although perhaps in a more subdued and slower role than in our day. I am thinking of the 1988 *New Yorker* cartoon of the mothers calling kids home to supper in "The All-Christopher Neighborhood." But that was some time ago, and those Christophers have gone on to name their children other things.

PERSONAL GODS

An aspect of Mesopotamian religion that must remain elusive to us is the existence of the personal god. This was a god who was concerned with the individual person and sometimes apparently had no other functions than to look after that person. Great gods could sometimes be personal gods. Rulers like the Akkadian kings had Ishtar, a really important goddess, as their personal god, and Gudea, prince of Lagash, was personally connected with Ningirsu.

There are references to "his or her god" from many periods, and sometimes that might refer to one of the major gods who was especially worshiped, but other times the reference was to a minor deity concerned with the individual. These gods were not mere angels or emanations of other deities, however; we see them in the ubiquitous presentation scenes on cylinder seals.

Sometimes the person was led in before a great god, who was seated in regal splendor. The seal owner did not presume to come forward because of his own virtue but was conducted in by the personal god, who was depicted as a god and not a person, as may be seen from the horned headdress. The personal god approached with the same humble attitude as the human toward the great god. Still, the little god walked on the same topographic plane as the other god, and the lesser god had some acquaintance with the great one that would be of benefit to the lowly human.

In a way, the existence of the personal god is a simplifying element in what must have been for the ancients a confusing mess of gods. You might know which god could help you in a given situation – say, one of sickness – but to approach such an august being directly would be scary. If you had an advocate who knew your problems, in the realm of the gods as in the realm of the city, your way might be eased.

The concept of the personal god was not a late one. It was already attested in the personal names from the third millennium (di Vito 1993: 272–5).

DEMONS

There were other spirits abroad, however. Some were ghosts, spirits of the dead people who prowled, unhappy with their fates. Ghosts were a problem to be placated. There were other spirits, some of evil intent and others benevolent. In fact, it is not unlikely that the protective personal god, in Akkadian the *šēdu*, was seen as another minor spirit, but a sensible one to whom one might turn for sympathy and help. The bad spirits were unlikely to help you. On the contrary, they could maliciously afflict you for no reason at all. From medical texts, we see that the way to rid oneself of such afflictions was to invoke sympathetic magic, to commit an act directed at something that was deemed to be the equivalent of the ill-intentioned demon. You did not have to be especially nice to such a spirit. Really, such spirits were felt to be stupid, and they did not understand much in any human language, so they had to be addressed most effectively with insults and yells (Scurlock 2005).

Mesopotamian pantheons are hard to understand – and were for the ancients, too – but we can comprehend the sort of world the sets of gods reflected. It was a world in which there was a hierarchy, but it was unclear where effective power lay in any particular instance. The great gods might not pay any attention to a person, but their occasional malevolence had to be reckoned with. There were many ways to offend them, and yet misfortune might not come from them at all. There were quite enough smaller spirits that could bother you, and dealing with them might require an experienced practitioner in magic as well as the intervention of your own personal god. This world was uncertain and unstable, but the personal god would help you, and sometimes even the great gods would deign to smile on you.

At the bottom of the divine food chain but also of concern to humans was the existence of magic. From late stories, it is known that even the greatest gods used spells, key sets of words that brought into effect powers that accomplished particular things. In the thick of the battle described in the Akkadian poem called the creation epic, the poem that began "When on high," the god of Babylon used spells that were better than the spells invoked by the goddess of chaos whom he was overcoming (Foster 2005: 459–60). It is as if behind and above the gods there was an awesome power that was amoral and undirected but that could be accessed through the use of the proper words. This power could be used by wise humans, and the keeping and passing down of successful spells was a major task of the tradition of writing. Ritual, in Sumerian literally "the things done," might tap into the particular power of a god or the amorphous power of the sphere of magic behind and above the gods.

In the modern world, the debate about the connection between religion and magic is a long one, and they seem to have been closely connected in Mesopotamia (Cunningham 1999). However, if one thinks that religion is just about the gods, one will miss the pervasive sense that the universe was also affected by forces that might not be personal and divine at all and that might be accessed through the proper words, an "Open Sesame" unconnected to justice or fairness or anything else but competence in the spell. For us this raises the question of the relation between nature and religion, because some of the workings of magic seem to be the sudden invocation of a law of nature unleashed by the right words. Magic was impersonal and arbitrary for the Mesopotamian. It could be used by anyone, but it would be senseless to worship it because, unlike the great gods, it could not respond personally.

4

CITIES, STATES, AND GODS

For Germany the criticism of religion is in the main complete, and criticism of religion is the premise of all criticism.... The basis of irreligious criticism is Man makes religion, religion does not make man.

> – Karl Marx (quoted in Niebuhr 1964: 41)

She looked beautiful in death, her hair done up elegantly, as it had not been in the few weeks of her last illness, and she wore her favorite jewelry, a necklace of gold and the rich blue stone, lapis lazuli. Laid on her bier, she looked most regal, almost peaceful, and certainly not in distress as in her last days. The servants were gratified that it was finally over, but they were aware of their duty now, and they met that future with mixed emotions. Most were quite young themselves and not ready to die. The lady had requested it, however, and those around her were ostensibly ready to comply.

It was true that their futures were in fact uncertain. The ruler might take another wife or promote another from among his concubines, and she would inevitably have her own attachments to her favorites. Her family would benefit from favor and offices, and the entourage of the dead lady would be demoted, just how far there was no telling. The dead lady's family would be concerned about erasing her memory completely, but it might be wise for the courtiers to end their lives, too. It would simplify matters for the ruler, and the lady had asked it of them because she did not want to go alone into the underworld, which she imagined was an unpleasant place where rank was mostly ignored, and food and drink were scarce. Even the hero Gilgamesh, the king of the underworld, was a shadow of his earthly self and could not be expected to care for a new arrival, even if she had been consort of the ruler of Ur. Better to bring your own help, she had reasoned, to the extent she had been able to reason toward the end.

So the harpists came into the pit that had been dug where the lady lay, set up their instruments, and began to play their sad songs. The chief butler brought in the maidservants and arranged them around the lady, then the guards, then, struggling down the ramp, a cart full of good things and the oxen pulling the cart.

They all stood solemnly for a moment, not including the oxen, who continued to chew the cud and complain slightly. A priest, who was not of the entourage, offered a final prayer, invoking the lady's forebears to accept her and her servants and the gods of the underworld to deal kindly with them all.

The maidservants wept, remembering all the happy times with the lady and of course in mourning for their own lives soon to be ended. The soldiers stood stolidly, and the harpists played on, trying to make their last song the best they could possibly play, full of complex fingerings and pleasing combinations of tones.

Then the ruler came, flanked by his soldiers and servants, and the lady's family, including the small boys who had survived birth. In each hand, the ruler held a helmet of the costliest gold, and each inscribed in the cuneiform script with the name of each ruler to whom she had been married. He advanced solemnly and placed them near her feet, paused to look at her and then quickly withdrew along with the family.

The pharmacist moved among them and gave them the small poison doses, and slowly they dropped dead in their places. The oxen were dispatched with quick knife thrusts, and the harpists drank last of all. The workmen standing around the top of the pit set to work filling it up and making a little mound above the grave, though there would be no other monument.

* * *

That was how the burials were found in the 1930s by excavators working for Sir Leonard Woolley of Great Britain in the ruins of Ur, from which the river had moved away, and so it now stood in a desert. Excavators also found the lady's seal, giving her name as Pu-Abi, meaning "the mouth of my father," signifying probably that she was the favored and hoped for child. She had fulfilled her promise. The names of the rulers with whose helmets she was buried are still not otherwise known; they do not occur in inscriptions or in the Sumerian King List. They are remembered only for their association with Pu-Abi.

The suicide of an entourage was unique in Ancient southern Iraq. Although such practices are known from Central Asia in later times, and perhaps once from Early Dynastic Egypt (David 2002: 75), it never recurred. We can see the general idea that the great personage would have need of her entourage in another existence, but this was an unusual practice. It has some parallels from other cultures, but because it would discourage service to any worthy who planned to put it into effect, it could not have been widespread. The objects buried with these dead show a wealth of materials not available in Mesopotamia itself, including stone from the Iranian mountains, lapis lazuli from what is now Afghanistan, and gold, which may have come either from the far north or perhaps from Egypt and other parts of Africa.

The period from about 3500 BCE to 3100 BCE named after the sprawling site of Uruk, in the south of Iraq, was marked by large monumental buildings and the creation of a sacred precinct with several large temples within it. The residents of those temples may have been seen as a divine family. From later times we see that the god of the sky, AN, was the father of the family, and his coy and lovely daughter, Inanna, "queen of heaven," was the main female deity. Her mother was later seen as Antum, a feminine grammatical form for the word for "sky" in Akkadian, and her personality does not seem to have been as marked as the daughter's.

Inanna was a goddess of fertility and also of love and childbirth, but there may have been other mother-goddesses who were locally celebrated. Sometimes we can see that Inanna was combined with them, and she took on more maternal qualities over time.

Something was happening to the size of settlements that affected religious buildings. Both were growing more rapidly than natural population increase. Uruk itself became enormous, housing perhaps forty thousand people within a 3-kilometer, or 2-mile radius. With the growth came the abandonment of smaller settlements near the bigger cities. People were still working the same riverside fields as before, but they tended not to live out among them. Instead, they would walk out daily to tend the fields, and so the limit of the areas centered in cities tended to be about 15 kilometers, about 9 miles (Adams 1981).

The religious traditions of abandoned villages must have come into the cities that grew, or perhaps they were overwhelmed by the successful concentration of resources and splendor in the city temples. The zones of domination of cities were not usually circular but elliptical, flowing along rivers and canals.

Late in the Uruk Period, around 3100 BCE, bureaucrats systematized their record-keeping efforts and began to write pictures of the things they were trying to keep track of on clay tablets, little pillows of clay they had carefully prepared without any added straw to make them hold together, unlike pottery. This device, at first apparently used for economic records only, allows us to see the religious life of at least elites with considerably more detail than ever before. Animals were allocated, as were scarce resources such as silver, among various agencies, including the houses of the gods. It was some time before writing was used for what we would see as purely religious purposes, but it was a tool to extend the memory of individuals, and it allowed the preservation of detail about larger and larger quantities of material that elites could bring together and give away.

In the Early Dynastic Period, 3000 BCE to 2300 BCE, cities actually built walls around themselves, and that bespeaks hostility among them but might also make more obvious the advantages that peasants may have felt in clustering together. They could be more easily defended, although their fields might be pillaged.

The cities of the Early Dynastic Period used the new device to record dedications by kings to gods and to make sure people remembered the exertions of individuals in rebuilding temples and making other sorts of donations. There were also documented conflicts among city-states, and in one famous and extended case, the fight between Umma and Lagash over the field of Ningirsu was depicted as a struggle between the main gods of the two cities, Shara of Umma and Ningirsu of Lagash (Cooper 1983a). This may be the earliest clear example of a holy war, in which the struggle for some agriculturally productive land was depicted as a fight among gods. The people of Lagash had better preserved their views of the conflict, but it was Umma who won in the end. Yet that victory, although probably seen as a triumph of the god Shara over Ningirsu, did not lead to a curtailment of the cult of the beaten god or any realignment of the pantheon of either city. The religious ideologies remained polytheistic and open still, although one god had been bested.

The world of these Early Dynastic city-states was a wide one, because they used some of their surpluses to draw in fancy goods from far away. Death for them can be seen as an extension of the luxurious life some people were living. Most people were not living that life, although their hopes for an afterlife not unlike their present lives may have been similar.

AMALGAMATION AND EMPIRE

The victory of the city of Umma over Lagash foreshadowed a union of the south, and that may have begun to happen under the last independent ruler of Umma. That is not what happened, however, politically or religiously. Instead, from the north, the area around Baghdad and north of there today, a new power emerged unexpectedly in the form of a king who practically admitted he had no real claim to rule when he took the name Sargon, meaning "The king is legitimate." Because he came from the north, we understand his social context much less than if he had emerged from the southern city-states. He probably spoke Akkadian, the Semitic language of Mesopotamia, as his first language, but he certainly paid a lot of attention to the gods of the Sumerian-speaking southern cities. Maybe he had associations with Akkadian speakers in the north who practiced nomadism in preference to sedentary farming. Clearly, though, he was interested in taking advantage of the surpluses generated by the farmers and in making sure their religious ideas were taken into account (Westenholz 1997).

One way to understand the impact of Sargon and his successors on Mesopotamian religion is to look at the gods honored before and after them. Douglas Frayne's Pre-Sargonic volume (2008) has a helpful index that shows many gods mentioned in royal inscriptions. The local gods played an important role. Baba and Gatumdu and Nanshe of Lagash-Girsu were there, but the gods that seem to have larger than local importance were revered too, especially An, Enki, Enlil, Inanna, as well as Ningirsu, also locally important in Lagash, and Ninhursag, "the lady of the mountain," a mother goddess. Oddly, in light of later developments, Suen, the moon-god, appeared only three times, and Shamash, the sun-god, only once, in an inscription by a king whose name included Shamash. Utu, a sun god later assimilated to Shamash, also seems slighted because there were only six mentions of him. Other gods that seem later to shrink in importance were there, including Shul-MUSHxPA from Lagash (Frayne 2008). (This writing in all capitals means we do not know now how to read the god's name, let alone his characteristics or roles.)

By Ur III times, another two hundred years later, some of these gods had dropped from view, but Enki, Enlil, and Inanna were still important, and Nanna, especially, the Sumerian moon-god, appeared in a number of inscriptions, although he had only been mentioned once in the Pre-Sargonic material. Local gods were still important to the later rulers, and Ningirsu and Shara of Umma were still revered (Frayne 1997).

Texts from and about Sargon continued to be copied long after his dynasty faded in importance. The reason for this was that he was remembered as founding the first effort to unite all of the river valley in one political unit. He also built a new city, which was called Akkad. This became the name for the northern region of central Iraq and also gave its name to the Semitic language spoken there. So the later importance is clear, but it is dicey to try to find in this material a reflection of the religious policy, if any, of Sargon and his people.

Foremost among these later bits of writing are the poems attributed to his daughter, Enheduana. She was appointed a priestess in the south, had a Sumerian name, and presumably wrote in Sumerian, if she really was directly involved in the production of these texts. Her compositions seem to show that the dynasty of which she was a part sought to praise many of the earlier religious centers and their gods. Her temple hymn lauded the various southern temples and made them all seem equal. An interesting aspect of the hymn is that although it was attributed to her, it was attested much earlier as well, in Early Dynastic copies long before the princess was born (Sjöberg and Bergmann 1969). This must mean that she or her scribes used a traditional text known to at least the more erudite of the southerners to assert her dynasty's concern.

Another of her poems has been called "The Exaltation of Inanna." It seems to make the goddess of war and love more important among her peers (Hallo and van Dijk 1968). It may also be taking qualities enjoyed by the presumably northern Mesopotamian goddess Ishtar and massaging them into the figure of Inanna, who may earlier have been more of a mother goddess. Clearly the resulting figure was a scary deity who was quick to intervene in battle on the side of her favorites, among whom the Sargonic kings certainly thought they were. She was also a god of fleshly love, of young women and their concerns, and young men and their hopes. This identification of one god with another may not have originated with Enheduana or her circle but may have been part of a much older process in which different female deities were brought together. The result was a formidable and attractive mixture that remained important through to the end of cuneiform-using civilization in the beginning of the Common Era.

From an institutional point of view Sargon was the first to try to combine the priesthoods of Inanna at Uruk and of Nanna, the moon-god, at Ur in the person of his daughter. The economic results of this combination are not clear to us; the cities were 45 miles, or about 72 kilometers, apart, so she might have functioned at each place. This may have made the daughter the most important single person in the religious hierarchy in all of Iraq. Down to the middle of the Old Babylonian Period, the right to appoint this priestess lay with the most important and successful dynast ruling when the last priestess died. In later times, too, the first priestess, Enheduana, may have been treated as a god herself after her death, for her name is sometimes written with a divine determinative (Hallo and van Dijk 1968: 5).

Another aspect of the dynasty's religious policy was the innovation of claiming that rulers were divine during their lifetimes. The first king to claim this was the fourth in the dynasty, called Naram-Sin, "beloved of the moon-god," and grandson of the founder. He had himself depicted with a horned helmet that was later reserved for actual gods. It is not clear that he had himself worshiped as if he were a god, but later kings sometimes did do that, and he may have been the first to do so.

Is this the height of hubris, of overweening pride so typical of people in power and so deplored by all nonpoliticians? Possibly. It may also be that Naram-Sin was up against formidable opponents, including, in principle, the ancient gods of the cities of the south. The blessings of his own northern gods may not have seemed enough, although the force of arms served him and his forebears rather well. The claim of the city rulers was that ancient gods had actually appointed them, and so to remove the rulers was doubtless seen as impiety. Sargon had tried to retain those rulers as subordinates after his takeover, but after another generation or two, that situation may have offered difficulties for the king of Akkad. The city rulers might have had a more ancient lineage than the ruler of the whole valley, or at least they thought they had. But they did not rule as gods themselves. Thus, Naram-Sin's claim, backed by brute force, may have assuaged the consciences not of the southern supporters of the old city-state hierarchies but perhaps of his own northerners.

It is hard to say to what extent he or his supporters believed he was a god, and yet he had campaigned with his armies widely and subdued many groups previously on the edge of Mesopotamian consciousness. He had achieved a great deal. If this assertion eased the way to control the old city-states, elites might not object. Nonetheless, we can see that later there was objection.

The interesting thing about the religious legacy of the Old Akkadian Dynasty is that it lived on. The memory of it did not always reflect the historical record even as we can imperfectly reconstruct it, but later dwellers in the river valley remembered these kings and their achievements and brooded on their meanings for many centuries. Later stories told of Sargon's lowly birth, of which there is no trace in records contemporary to him or his dynasty. The idea seems to have been that as an orphan child of a discredited woman, he showed exemplary good luck in being found at all when set adrift in a river, like the later story of Moses, and then being blessed by the goddess Ishtar, who brought about his later kingly honors and success (Westenholz 1997: 36–49). This is perhaps the first but not the last of stories told of great men born with few advantages who nonetheless persevered to greatness.

Another longer poem tells of Sargon's concern for Mesopotamian merchants in distant Anatolia, now Turkey. He was said to have organized an army and came to their rescue despite the long distance involved – 790 miles, or about 1270 kilometers – and the hardships. Again, there is no contemporary evidence of such an expedition, but there is archaeological trace of the conqueror in northern Syria, not so very far from western Anatolia. The point of the poem seems to be to show later rulers that a great Mesopotamian king was sensitive to the fates of his subjects wherever they traveled and traded.

As noted earlier, the Mesopotamian view of history was colored by the idea that the dynasty fell because of the impiety of its last significant king, Naram-Sin. There is no hint of such impiety in contemporaneous records, but this idea was current as early as the Ur III period, within a hundred years or so of the actual fall, and it encapsulated the idea of the bad ruler who could bring down the wrath of the gods because of his overweening pride and abuse of power, especially in the religious arena. The historical Naram-Sin would not have desecrated Enlil's temple at Nippur, but the later stories show that only gross impiety could explain the gods' wrath and the subsequent downfall. This idea, that political power and success were gifts of the gods and came only to those who were deserving of them, was a persistent one in Mesopotamian thought. The converse was also felt to be true; political disaster, especially overwhelming disaster of the sort that led to the fall of dynasties, was a result of the impiety of kings. This idea does not seem to have been generalized into a sense of decadence of an entire society or its ruling elite but from perhaps its earlier formulation in the Sumerian composition called "The Curse of Agade," this individual's impiety was painted as having led to economic and social misfortune for the entire society. The trade goods were simply not arriving because of the civil unrest around the capital city, the poem complains; people were starving and dying. The fault was laid, not as we politically minded observers might do, at the feet of a series of late and perhaps incompetent rulers or in the lap of a period of less rain, caused by climate change that made agricultural productivity less dependable. The fault was blamed on one supercilious and irreligious man, Naram-Sin, who had been dead half a century before the dynasty actually fell (Cooper 1983b).

The lesson for later rulers, and for later Mesopotamians, was that overvaluing one's own role in affecting matters could lead to sins that, for a ruler, might have far-reaching implications for his society. For anyone, however, the implication was that failure to pay due attention to the gods would have negative results – perhaps not immediately, but eventually. A king had the freedom to get away with a lot, and rich people could, too; but the poor had to watch their behavior, for their disaster could be closer at hand.

This web of ideas reveals a society in which religious values were in fact being threatened, sometimes even from the top of the society, and yet the thinkers who gave us the texts acknowledged that the recompense would not necessarily be immediate for violating norms. It would come, however, unless diverted by other acts of piety and, especially, concern for the poor. It is not clear that one should derive from these concerns that Mesopotamians necessarily lived in a highly structured and regulated society in which authority figures were obsessed with dictating morality. It may be that these ideas imply the opposite: that there were lots of people ignoring traditional morality, and they needed to be reminded that there were results that derived from their actions, even if the immediate consequences were not automatically visited on wrongdoers.

The centralized state probably had tried to impose some kinds of regulations at least on the elites of the cities, and its detailed lists of forced labor affected many less privileged individuals who were unlucky enough to live near government building projects. However, the fact that village sites were frequently abandoned throughout Mesopotamian history seems to argue that if things became too oppressive, people just moved away, as noted earlier. The cities may always have been in competition for population, and so measures that placated even the lowly were always a consideration of leaders, even if they did not always write about it (Stone 2005).

The disaster that intervened to break apart the areas controlled by the Akkad dynasty was blamed on kings from the Iranian mountains known as Gutians. They were seen in later texts as the embodiment of impiety, and they left few contemporary inscriptions. They probably did not control the whole area that the Sargonic kings had, and their religious ideas are unclear to us (Glassner 1986).

They were the dominating power in the days of Gudea, a ruler of the southern city of Lagash who has left an astounding mass of evidence and the longest religious poem preserved in Sumerian. The main activities of this city-governor, as he styled himself, seem to have been rebuilding temples. This would have been a constant need in southern Iraq because temples, like most structures, were built of mud brick, and the slightest rain, which does sometimes fall, would necessitate repairs. The unusual aspect of Gudea's work was the extent to which he went to publicize the rebuilding. There are many statues of him that boast of this work and lots of clay cones and other inscriptions in addition to the long hymn. We have the hymn in an odd form; it is on two clay barrels that might have been drafts of texts that were to be transferred to stone. We have several stone fragments that seem to be related, but we have not found a monumental form of the poem.

Gudea wanted to present himself in his inscriptions and poem as a pious man who heeded the omens that the gods sent him, but the omens were ambivalent. He needed to test their correctness by trying to induce confirming dreams from the gods. He was careful to note that the people who did the actual building were not compelled to do so. "No one was lashed by the whip," he claimed in connection with the Ningirsu's temple (Statue B, iv, 10–12, Edzard 1997a 32). Part of his task was certainly to try to have some debts remitted and to make slaves briefly feel equal to their owners (ibid., vii, 29–33, p. 36). He saw himself as a "reverent slave" whose goal was to build as the gods wanted (Statue E, ii, 1–4, Edzard, 43 and F, ii, 6–11, 47).

Gudea wished to be seen as meticulous in carrying out the god's command for a new temple, careful in all things, checking twice about the messages he thought he was getting from the god, and punctual in carrying out tasks. Because these inscriptions came to light in the late 1800s of our era before archaeological method had become as rigorous as later, it is not possible to reconstruct exactly where his building may have taken place or how.

But its rhetoric is still clear in his writings. This indicates that human beings, even special ones like the ruler himself, felt they needed direction from the god through dreams and omens, and even when they got that direction, they needed to check it out with other omens and dreams. Not all omens were really reliable; to attain certainty took a string of omens with the same message. Gudea noted that he "refused (to listen to) chance utterances (as omens), (and) he had 'spittle' (of sorcery) removed from the roads" (A, viii, 4–5, p. 74). This seems to mean that there were illegitimate means of affecting the gods' commands, and they should be avoided.

Gudea succeeded, he said, but he lived in an uncertain world, where wrong omens could be had and where the wills of the gods needed to be systematically probed to get at their real wills. To be unsure was in itself not a bad thing but actually a good thing, and the gods would not mind it. The god appeared to Gudea in a dream, saying,

When to my house, the house honored in all lands,
the right arm of Lagash, the thunderbird roaring on the horizon,
the House of Fifty, my royal house, O able shepherd Gudea,
you effectively put forth your hand for me,
I shall call up a wet wind that will bring abundance for you from on high,
and the people will spread out their hands on the plenty.
May abundance come with the laying of the foundations of my house! . . .
Gudea rose; it was a sleep; he shuddered; it was a dream.
To Ningirsu's command he assented.
Into the white omen kid he reached his hand, got the omen,
and it was favorable: Ningirsu's wish was clear to Gudea as daylight.
Great of knowing he was, and great too at carrying out. . . .
(Cylinder A xi.1–21, after Jacobsen 1987: 401–3.)

Although the ruler received a dream omen from the god, he immediately carried out a sacrifice of a sheep so that he could be sure that he understood the omen and that he really was directed to build the house.

UR III PIETY AND SUPPLY

Gudea never acknowledged in all his writings his relations, if there were any, with the Gutian rulers who had come in after the fall of Akkad, but the next rulers of Mesopotamia prided themselves on their relatives' having expelled the Gutians. These kings ruled from Ur, the southernmost of the great cities and an important seaport. They, too, saw themselves as chosen by the great gods to rule, but they continued the late Akkadian custom of referring to themselves as divine even when they were still alive. They looked forward to being able to name the priestesses, especially the one who served at Ur and Uruk, from among their own daughters. The kings of Ur looked backward, though, and envied the Old Akkadian kings; they were proud to claim to be related to Gilgamesh of Uruk, the legendary figure of the Early Dynastic Period. The Ur III kings probably had his stories and those of his relatives collected and placed into the curriculum for educating scribes as models for human and especially royal behavior.

The kings had themselves depicted in their building inscriptions in a very traditional way. They were happy to be seen, like Gudea, as pious rebuilders. They were also gods, however, at least after the first king's death. Being a god could bring perquisites, including having your own temple with offerings and a priesthood to serve your statue. This custom is known only in a provincial city of the Diyala region, and when the influence of the dynasty waned, the temple reverted to the worship of the head of the local pantheon (D. Frayne 1997, Shu-Sin 12, pp. 322f., is the dedication to "his god" of the city governor; Number 13 records such a temple in Girsu, 14 and 15, in Ur by different officials, p. 435). Perhaps this means that the worshipers, if any, saw the Ur king as an embodiment of the power of their local god. It must have been flattering to the ruler to be celebrated, but the reversion to the local god may show that there was some resentment of the practice among the population.

Here is how one dedication read:

Shu-Sin, the one called by name by the god An,
beloved of the god Enlil, the king whom Enlil
in his pure heart chose for the tending of the land
and of the four quarters, a mighty king, the king

of Ur, king of the four quarters, his beloved god [sic!],
Ituria, governor of Eshnunna, his servant,
built his temple for him.

The Ur state was the most fully organized of any period of Mesopotamian history, as we can see from the thousands of preserved tablets that record economic transactions mainly within the state apparatus. A major focus of the transactions was supplying the temples. A cattle pen was even built near the religious capital of Nippur, in central Mesopotamia, to receive the contributions and to redistribute the animals to the temples and to royal favorites. In the flurry of activity that is documented, it is hard to catch a glimpse of the piety and sacrifice that the donations and distributions reflected, although we do see that sometimes some quite minor gods were favored by the king's scribal minions. We do not have indications of how people at large worshiped, if they did. Close study has revealed the activities of the royal wives as they worked in favor of their preferred temples and gods. These texts also show a remarkable openness to foreign or at least more recently arrived gods, and foreigners themselves appeared as donors and beneficiaries. This cosmopolitanism derived from the kings' concerns to control the hinterlands, which were threatening to the stability of the central government and eventually brought it down (Sigrist 1992: 222–46).

Some scholars have seen the reversion in the period to Sumerian language as showing some sort of ethnic difference in contrast to the Old Akkadian Period's use of Akkadian language. This may be because most of the texts came from the far south, where Sumerian was the dominant means of expression, although the spoken language itself may have died out even before this time. Our impression of the cosmopolitanism is tempered by later texts that criticized the god of the West, Martu, as a barbarian, and yet the dynasty certainly understood that employing and promoting foreigners was in its interest. It did so enthusiastically, especially with the Martu "Westerners," later called Amorites.

There are few contemporary literary texts, but the next period preserved many that referred to the rulers of the Ur Dynasty, and the second king, Shulgi, emerged from these royal hymns as an egocentric character who boasted that he once ran from Ur to Nippur and back in one day, a distance of 94 miles, or 140 kilometers, as the crow flies. The "righteous youth," as Shulgi's name meant, was perhaps a great athlete, but the claim of running such a distance is ridiculous. The documentation increased tremendously in the latter part of this king's long reign, indicating that he or his ministers wanted to get a hold on the flow of goods to religious organizations and to verify that the goods were in fact being used properly. No ancient ever explains such a motive, and from his royal inscriptions, no such motive is evident; only the scribal effort he called forth is clear.

One interesting text preserved from the subsequent Old Babylonian Period was a lament over the death of the dynasty's founder, Ur-Namma, who died in battle. This text may have been part of the mourning for the prince, and the unfairness of the death of such a creative individual must have emphasized the uncertainties of mortality for his contemporaries. Such a death was quite unfair – not just to the king but to his subjects, who had hoped to profit from his wise and productive leadership.

The Ur kings were the ones who restored the small but old site of Eridu, which by their time had been abandoned for probably five hundred years. They also embellished their capital of Ur, building the mud-brick temple tower or ziggurat that still stands there to a height of more than 12 meters, or 36 feet.

Ziggurats are known from a number of sites and may have been an improvement on the more ancient temple terraces. Those were big platforms of mud bricks on which temples were erected; presumably they were "pure places," as inscriptions frequently mention, and the terrace assured the ritual purity of the building. A temple tower was a bigger investment than a low terrace was as a support for a single temple at the top, but on ziggurats the temples have never been preserved, and they must have been related to the temples at the foot of the ziggurat.

Amar-Suena inscriptions 16 and 17 boasted of his having built a new dwelling for priestesses of the moon-god at the city of Karzida and emphasized that there had been no such dwelling earlier (Frayne 1997: 263–5). Thus, this marks a religious innovation, something that in general and certainly in later ages was to be avoided, but this king was proud of it.

The last king of the dynasty reigned twenty-four years, a long time, but he presided over the disintegration of his own authority everywhere except in his capital. By his sixth year, the record-keeping systems in all the provinces came to an end. Eventually he was removed by foreigners from the east and reportedly was dragged into exile, where he died. In later Mesopotamian thought, this sad fate qualified him as the one to blame for the downfall of the dynasty, just as Naram-Sin had been blamed after his death for the end of his dynasty. In Ibbi-Sin's case, the claim may have been more justified because he really was the last Ur king and had no successors. It is unlikely, however, that he lacked in traditional piety or concern for the usual old-fashioned

Mesopotamian gods. It is true that there are only five of his inscriptions preserved, against the many more known for the other Ur kings, but that probably correlates with his declining power, not with his lack of piety.

If the king was faulted for his behavior in later tradition, the few literate scribes also lamented this fall probably more avidly than they had been worried about the fall of Akkad. The laments were copied in the scribal curriculum and may represent feelings not especially at the actual fall of Ur but rather when cities were in the process of being rebuilt in the Early Old Babylonian Period a generation later. The problem the laments solved was that mud-brick temples had to be at least partly destroyed before they could be fully rebuilt. Destroying temples involved violating the basic values of Mesopotamian elites, and so one should be sad when doing it, but it was nonetheless necessary in order to reerect a more glorious temple. Because the rebuildings happened a generation or more after the fall, they cannot be taken as historical portraits of the fall, but they embodied the values of the elites and their esteem for cities, particularly for the temples that put the cities on the map for peasant and king alike.

Temples were always centers for redistribution of agricultural surpluses and places where the surpluses might be stored before they were needed. The Ur III archival texts also showed that they were places where unwanted humans showed up, to be exploited but also fed and clothed by the leaders of temples. The lives of the weaving women of Umma were brutish and short, and their children died like flies. Yet they were not begging on the streets, at least when they were working for the temple (Gelb 1972).

Temples were mud-brick buildings about 10 meters or thirty feet square, with flying buttresses to support the walls. They usually had two or three chambers, one behind the other, and in the most distant chamber, a statue of the god would stand. What happened in the temples was a lot like what happened in other great households. The god was awakened, given his break-fast, bathed, and later in the day given his dinner. Access to the god's statue was apparently limited, and so ordinary worshipers may not have been able to see the statue very often. The food that had been placed before the god was regularly removed and eaten by priests. Much of it had been supplied by the government, but the donations of individuals may also have played a part.

Many gods were involved in seasonal processions where their statues might emerge and go to visit other gods or, in some cases, go for a few days out to a "New Year's House," a subsidiary temple used at the spring equinox. On processions the public might catch a glimpse of the statues and thereby gain blessings. Some rich people had statues made of themselves in fulfillment of vows they made, and these statues might be placed before the statues of the gods, in the attitude of continual prayer. This involved holding both hands in front of the face, or in the case of stone statues for which this might be difficult to depict, as near to the face as possible or simply clasped together. The worshiper was protecting the face from the god's shining zap, the brilliant splendor that was felt to emanate from the divine statue. The inner part of a temple might be chock full of such votive statues or of smaller votive objects that people had dedicated, like the spooky eyes of the Tell Brak Eye Temple in central Syria.

OLD BABYLONIAN DECENTRALIZATION

The Ur state fell apart, and it, too, seems to have been cherished by its inheritors, but its inheritors ruled states that were smaller and centered on newer cities. These were not the same as the earlier city-states, and they were much less powerful. Politically the period was marked by an almost unrelenting competition among the states for power, especially as represented in the religious center of Nippur. Controlling Nippur meant a king could claim some of the ancient titles, including deification, and could get the Nippur priesthood to write royal hymns praying for his success and long life. The conceit was that there was only one king ruling at any one time who deserved that honor, although perhaps every one of them claimed some sort of deification, for that was what the later Ur kings had done. The reverence for that dynasty is seen in the list that catalogued the first kings of the city of Isin as actually being kings of the "turn of office," the term for dynasty, of Ur. Perhaps almost all the kings had started as officials of the Ur Dynasty; letters copied later indicated that this was the case at least for Isin.

We call the period Old Babylonian because Babylon after two hundred years came to the fore of those states and beat most of them into a new imperial amalgamation, although that lasted only a couple of reigns. Because later Mesopotamians looked back to this time as the end of a memorable epoch, the Old Babylonian Period produced literature and laws that were read in later times and that we still read.

One development that might have some religious implications was that all the rulers were connected in one way or another to the Amorite ethnic group that had infiltrated earlier Mesopotamia, perhaps both from the west, as their name means, and from the east, against which the Ur kings had built walls. The Amorites were not all dangerous invaders, and many had become high officials in the Ur Kingdom; they probably dominated the army, being considered the rough-and-ready barbarians whom, as the Chinese later said, one could use to fight barbarians.

Religiously the Amorites seem from their personal names to have worshiped somewhat different gods from the earlier ones. The moon-god became particularly important, and other gods could be given epithets as if they were family members, as in Hammurapi, "The paternal uncle heals," or perhaps Hammurabi "is great." This is another way of representing the generally benign relation of most gods to most humans, but it does have a down-home feel. The Amorites, although they retained their foreign names and maybe their extended family and tribal relationships, did not erect temples to their gods; they may have seen those gods as easily equated to Mesopotamian ones, to whom most were careful to show their piety, and they supported the old temples and priesthoods. Because there was mostly political disunity, kings may have had a tendency to favor their local city gods, but the pan-Mesopotamian gods continued to receive their ostentatious devotion, too. For example, Hammurabi wrote, "For the god Enlil, the great lord of heaven and earth, the king of the gods, my lord, I, Hammurabi, prince, favorite of the god Enlil, the beloved shepherd of the goddess Ninlil, reverent one, who heeds the god Shamash, . . . I built a storehouse which pleases him in Babylon, his beloved city" (Frayne 1990: 337). Any addition to Mesopotamian religious thought by the Amorites seems to have been minimal.

Some have argued that another important development of the Old Babylonian period was the increased interest in personal gods. The idea is that family religion focused, perhaps from an early period, on particular gods, and these gods came to be seen as parts of the family who would be more concerned than other great gods with the fate and progress of the family members. Study of earlier naming practices makes clear that this was not a new idea in the Old Babylonian Period and can be traced back to the very beginning of our understanding of the Mesopotamian naming tradition (di Vito 1993). We do seem to find, however, a proliferation of references to "my god" and "his god" in names without clarification as to whom the terms referred. The ever popular presentation scene on cylinder seals, as early as the Ur III Period and continuing into the Old Babylonian, showed the seal's owner being brought in by a god or goddess before a great god, seated like a king; both the introducing deity and the worshiper protected their faces from the zap of the great god.

We also see in this period a new kind of personal name, which has been described as indicating a greater "interiority" than earlier names. Names began to appear that did not express the happy optimism most names usually did. Instead, some names showed that individuals, or rather their parents, were unsure of their place in the world and needed gods' help to attain some sort of satisfaction. The names were identified on the periphery of Mesopotamia in this period, in Elam and in Syria, but these sorts of names became more common in subsequent periods and especially at Middle Babylonian Nippur, the religious center. They may have indicated a spreading of such feelings, or a spreading of the style of such names. The names include "I sigh," "Remove my burden, O god," "My hope is the god," "I cry (to the god for help)." The sentiments may not seem revolutionary, but the names show a much more personal feeling about the gods than was seen before and a continued concern for the fragility of human life (Oppenheim 1936).

The seminal figure of the period was Hammurabi, properly Hammurapi, but he has become too famous with a /b/ to dislodge it. Uniting the country almost to its Ur III borders between 1792 and 1750 BCE, his letters reveal him to have been very concerned about incorporating the old southern cities into his realm politically and religiously. It is because of Hammurabi that the god of Babylon, Marduk, eventually became the head of the pantheon of Mesopotamia. This certainly did not happen during Hammurabi's reign, however. His royal inscriptions showed instead a proper respect for the old gods of the old cities, and even personal names of the period did not particularly favor Marduk (Klengel 1991: 182–3). Although politically Hammurabi was trying something new for the period in uniting the various smaller states, he seems not to have been innovative in religion.

Hammurabi was the first ruler for centuries not to claim he was a god and to forego the accompanying temples and offerings that flattered some rulers since Naram-Sin. In line with this decision, if it was a decision, he did not continue the combined priesthood of royal daughters at Uruk and Ur. Some have speculated perhaps anachronistically about his dedication to a desert-bred simplicity, exactly the sort of claim that later Arabs would make about their dynasties, but for which in the ancient world there is little evidence. Hammurabi was the direct descendant of several kings who had had long reigns in the city of Babylon; it is not likely he was close to desert and tribal traditions anyway. Earlier kings with Amorite names had had no compunction at all about assuming the mantle, or the crown, of divinity. The old cities were not politically so strong as they had been when Naram-Sin needed to subdue them, but perhaps no one remembered anyway why kings had started to claim they were gods.

The legal implications of Hammurabi's long inscription, which its discoverers called a code, have been debated; it seems to be a collection of wise decisions that the king was endorsing and establishing not really as a modern code that would be referred to in court decisions, for it was apparently not referred to. It was, however, a demonstration of his leadership and also of his piety, and the prologue and epilogue showed that this was his main emphasis; between them stood the stipulations, 282 paragraphs long by modern count. The religious meaning is that the king was placing himself in the ongoing tradition of intervening in social and legal situations, or at least endorsing decisions in a formal way. The picture of himself that he wanted to convey was that of the "king of justice," who had shown concern for the poor and downtrodden and those who were dependent on the royal establishment. He was well aware that power and privilege sometimes rode roughshod over dependent people, and he wanted to mitigate that as much as possible – or rather, he wanted to be seen to mitigate that. He wanted to appear as a good shepherd of his people.

This image of the king may not actually be innovative with him or with this period. As in earlier times, Mesopotamian leadership needed to appeal to the downtrodden, or they would simply leave and go elsewhere, and so some concern for their well-being would always be obligatory.

We have stories about the use of omen-taking from earlier periods, but it was in the Old Babylonian that we get actual contemporary texts that describe its results. The basic idea was that one could ascertain the will of a god for a particular person by sacrificing an animal and looking at its entrails. Sheep and their livers were popular for this, but expensive, and texts from the period show there were cheaper ways of doing the same thing, with water and oil, for example. Perhaps these texts were the distillation of a much older oral tradition about what the observed meanings might be. Others were elaborations of earlier omens, however, and so we see already a proliferation of what might be called scholarly or secondary interpretations of observations. The question is what, if anything, this had to do with observed ominous things. There are liver models from the city of Mari on the Middle Euphrates and some other sites that have been viewed by modern scholars as connected to observation of livers in particular circumstances. They are little blobs of clay in an organic oval shape with writing on them. One says, "The omen of Naram-Sin when the land rebelled," but it seems more likely that we do not have in front of us the actual observed omen but a teaching device to get observers up to speed on what to expect (Snell 1974).

From the old Babylonian period came the first compilations of lists of omens, including technical descriptions of how the liver might look, and then brief declarations about what might happen to the person asking for the omen. This seems not to be the beginning but perhaps the fluorescence of a long tradition of regarding the world as a tablet on which the gods could write the future (Goetze 1947). It is good to remember, however, that this foreknowledge was not seen as absolute nor as unalterable. In fact, it was apparently assumed that, as in Gudea's practice, multiple omens would be taken, and if they clearly predicted bad things, counteractive measures could be tried, and human behavior and outcomes could be changed. Omens told you what the wisdom of the gods foresaw if present trends continued, but those trends could be changed (Rochberg-Halton 1982).

Priestesses had always been important in Mesopotamian religion, and in the Old Babylonian Period, especially in the northern city of Sippar, we see that an interesting group of them was the biggest money lenders in town. Their lives as revealed in archival texts and also in Hammurabi's legal collection illustrate the close integration of moneyed power with religious authority (Harris 1975).

The way their status was supposed to work was that rich families with lots of daughters would give a dowry to the daughters and make them become *naditu*s, or fallow women, for the god. They were to live, perhaps in relative seclusion, in the cloister that had been built for them. Supposedly, they were not to have children. The idea was to give them a leisured life and to protect their brothers from having to divide the inheritance into too many parts. The traditional way of dividing inheritance was to give all children equal shares but with the firstborn son getting a double share; this led inevitably to dividing land and other possessions into increasingly tiny parts. The brothers would have to share their lots with their sister while she lived, but in theory she would have no children to complicate their children's inheritance.

It frequently did not work that way. The *naditu*s used their money to invest in land and loans, and when they contemplated death, they not infrequently adopted other, younger *naditu*s as their heirs, preserving all the accumulated wealth for them and not including their brothers. The brothers could and did sue, but they did not prevail.

In Sippar, the names of the *naditu*s reflected their devotion to the sun-god and his wife, Ayya; perhaps the women had assumed those names when they were committed to the cloister. Charity was not among their goals, nor was any religious duty imposed on them in any way reflected in texts. They might have been ancient feminists in some sense, for they sometimes had scribes who were female, a rare occurrence in Mesopotamian history before them, although the goal may have been to avoid too much contact with the opposite sex. In Babylon the *naditu*s of Marduk included a royal princess, although those ladies were not so well documented as the Sippar ones (Harris 1975: 315–23).

The Old Babylonian Period was not a political unity except under Hammurabi and his son, and the political divisions may have fostered religious divisions. In a polytheistic system, however, there did not seem to have been desire on anyone's part to discredit the gods of other places. Some Amorite gods appeared in personal names, such as the god Lim in Mari on the Middle Euphrates, but most of those gods did not attain a high enough status to be revered in the building of temples, and so the Mesopotamian pantheon seems to have stayed relatively stable even though the city-god Marduk owed his eventual increase in status to the success of his city's kings in this period. Outsiders ruled, but they were aware of the ancient history that had gone before them and of the fantastic agricultural and political success that the Mesopotamian gods had brought to the land. Thus, the kings did not sponsor innovation.

In far northern Mesopotamia, this period is the one in which the governors of the city of Assur and their people made their independent voices heard. They were engaged in a lucrative long-distance trade into Anatolia, now Turkey. To this ore-rich area they brought Mesopotamian textiles and tin with which to make bronze, probably from Iran or farther afield, and they racked up profits of up to 100 percent on each trip. Some stayed in Anatolia, married locals, and became part of the cultural landscape, although texts show that they continued to consider themselves Assyrians. The religious situation must have been fluid, but the archival texts that document these contacts do not shed much light on it, although certainly there were bilingual and bicultural children who survived the five generations of contact and may have had some influence on later developments.

Back in Assur, we have inscriptions that reflect a concern for piety for the god of Assur, who was also called Assur. These inscriptions did not indicate it, but it seems probable that originally the god was the rock outcropping overlooking the river (Lambert 1983). His characteristics at this early period were sketchy, but the city leaders did not style themselves kings of Assur; one explicitly said, "Assur is king," while he was only the ENSI or city-governor, sometimes translated vice-regent (Grayson 1987: 12–13). In the short inscriptions it is hard to catch a glimpse of these rulers' programs; Erishum established judges, some of whom had, or were given, great names relevant to their tasks, as in Se-raggu, "Get out, criminal!," and Ashur-hablam, "Watch over the downtrodden" (Grayson 1987: 20). Sargon I of Assyria was the only one to apply the divine determinative to his name, and what this may have meant for him is hard to guess; perhaps it only meant he was named after the great Akkad king who had eventually been deified.

A new, more international era opened in the north with the establishment of Shamshi-Adad, an Amorite prince, in the Early Old Babylonian Period. He paid less attention to the god Assur and more to the older Mesopotamian gods, including Enlil. His inscriptions spoke of his tearing down dilapidated temples and rebuilding them. We know from other Old Babylonian texts that he established control of Mari and envisioned a northern Mesopotamian empire ruled by his sons. However, a later inscription by an otherwise unknown Puzur-Sin boasted of getting rid of the wall and palace of Shamshi-Adad in Assur long after his death because he was not of the "flesh of Assur" and thus somehow did not have the right to rule (Grayson 1987: 77f). This ambivalence about the relation to southern Mesopotamia would persist in the history of Assyria, and it included both the acceptance of southern gods and sometimes their assimilation to the god Assur.

The Old Babylonian Period was the one when we first see the establishment of what we call Hittite culture. Hittites arrived in Anatolia during the period of the Old Assyrian trade colonies and established themselves as rulers. The Old Assyrians' trade was closed down, but not apparently because of the new rulers. The Hittites spoke the first attested Indo-European language, related to most of the later languages of Europe. They presided over a multicultural amalgam that in its earliest period, the Hittite Old Kingdom, 1700–1500 BCE, included the people who lived there before the Hittites, whom we call Hattic. Their language and traditions continued under the Hittites, and in fact many if not most Hittite religious ideas seem to have been borrowed from the people who were there before them. The Hittites were frequently interested in political expansion, and their policy was to incorporate the gods of the people they conquered into their worship. They came to refer to this phenomenon as "the thousand gods of Hatti," and there certainly were a great many of them.

Another important ethnic group that had been in the north Syrian area at least since the Old Akkadian period was the Hurrians, and from these people too, the Hittites took both gods and practices. Because of the variety of data, it is hard to posit any particular development in the course of Hittite religion, although it can be argued that there was a different tone to texts from the Empire Period (1400–1200 BCE), which might reflect a greater emotional attachment to particular gods as a result of the ascension of rulers from the southwest of Anatolia (Taracha 2009: ix, 81). So straightforwardly political an explanation for religious change seems a bit simple, but, as we shall see, such arguments are not unusual in the history of religions.

We have preserved a great many texts that tell what to do to appease the gods and solve people's problems. These ritual texts dominate the library at the Hittite capital, and many show derivation from Hattic and Hurrian sources. Although such texts are known from later in the Mesopotamian tradition, we lack the volume of rituals we have in the Hittite material in these early times.

The rituals sometimes took the form of a story that gave a mythological origin for a problem. The Telepinu text described a drought and famine that may have been seen as an annually recurring problem, although Anatolia, unlike Mesopotamia, does get at least some rain in most seasons. The problems in the text resulted from the unprovoked anger of the god Telepinu, who had left his usual haunts in the city in disgust. The other gods had various animals go look for him, and finally the lowly bee managed to locate him. The god had to be awakened, and then he had to be pacified. The way to do this was to engage a god to carry out ritual actions of sympathetic magic to cool and calm Telepinu. At some point in the history of the text, however, another ritual was added with slightly different demands, and then finally another one (Beckman in Hallo and Younger 1997: 151–3; Taracha 2009: 156).

The ideas behind this and many similar texts were that malevolent events that affected humans derived from the caprice of the gods, but other gods and ultimately humans, too, were capable of affecting the causers of calamity. The acts advised included libations and other sorts of sacrifices. But why the multiplicity of the acts that were recommended? It may be that traditions from different places about ritual actions came together in the text or that some had been tried once and had not worked, and so others were devised. This fact seems to give to the rituals in general a tentative air that may accord with the general Ancient Near Eastern view of omens and responses to omens; bad predictions could be averted, and here is how it was done once, but these other things might work as well. It was important to the Hittite scribes to write them all down so that the knowledge could be preserved, especially if one or two of the ritual acts did not work.

There were rituals for all sorts of problems, not just environmental disasters. There was a ritual that designated a scapegoat, actually a ram, to carry off a pestilence (Gurney 1977: 48), and another that spoke of a substitute person for the king if some evil was foretold for him (Gurney 1977: 50). It is not clear what later happened to that animal or person. Birth rituals also seem to be important, and they apparently went back to Hattic models (Beckman 1983). Beckman writes, "It was of no consequence that contradictory practices were found in the rituals as a group; what was important was that the experts who aided the ladies of the royal court... have available to them as much information as possible" (1983: 249).

The plague prayers of the Hittite king Murshili II are important for understanding how the Hittites, and perhaps others, thought about the roles of gods in bringing misfortune. An epidemic had been unleashed in Hatti because of a group of sick Egyptian prisoners who had been brought into Anatolia. The king embarked on an ostentatious series of prayers and sacrifices that inquired about what he could do to abate the plague. Answers were obtained by looking at sheep livers for anomalous shapes and patterns and coming to conclusions as a result of yes or no inquiries. The upshot was that sacrifices to the river Euphrates had been neglected in the past, and so the king sought to carry them out. Eventually, of course, the plague did die out (Beckman in Hallo and Younger 1997: 156–60). In the king's view, chance magic influences had brought the misfortune, not the intentional impiety of earlier kings, but the gods could be invoked to help the humans overcome it.

Another kind of misfortune was treated in Hattushili III's text that we call his apology. He explained how his brother, who had been the king, was succeeded by his nephew, who, however, undervalued Hattushili. Hattushili felt that he was commanded by the goddess Ishtar to overthrow his nephew; the nephew had also alienated his own generals, and hostile northern tribes who had opposed the Hittites decided to support Hattushili for the kingship. Hattushili as king exiled his nephew and claimed his own progeny should rule after him.

This text is unique in that it argues that divine favor alone could overthrow an apparently legitimate succession. The nephew was the son of a concubine, but that was not an objection to becoming Great King of the Hittites; it was rather his incompetence and his ungrateful behavior toward his uncle that counted (Beckman in Hallo and Younger 1997: 199–204).

The Hittites flourished until 1200 BCE. They continued to copy old texts, which might go back centuries into their past. In the era of nineteenth-century CE Romanticism, when modern scholars thought that the spirit of the folk was somehow embodied in language, much was made of their speaking an Indo-European language, but now this aspect seems less important than the Hittites' willingness to learn religious practices from their conquered peoples and also the cuneiform writing system itself. A contribution to later religious thought in which they participated was the treaty form, which they elaborated in their dealings with lesser states and with Egypt (Beckman 1999). This, too, echoes down the ages, but except for the brief mentions in the Hebrew Bible, these people had disappeared from the way Europeans and Americans thought about the past until their language was deciphered at the beginning of the 1900s.

The Hittites learned much from their southern neighbors in Syria and in Mesopotamia, but they also preserved older ways of thinking that they found in Anatolia. The thousand gods were forgotten, but some of the ideas the Hittites wrote about continued to be of interest.

5

THE LURE OF EGYPT, 4000–1400 BCE

If those at the top are fond of the rites, the people are easy to direct.
              – *The Sayings of Confucius*, James Ware, translator, 1955, 96, item 41

The old king was brought in on a litter, looking frail and uninterested in where he was going, but the litter bearers plopped him down in front of the master builder, shaven-headed and naked from the waist up. The builder approached carefully, and when the king saw him, the builder bowed to the ground and greeted him formally, "May the king have life, prosperity, health!"

The king raised his head, shaded in the hot sun; he, too, was bald and wore only a light robe, but his face brightened when he recognized the builder. "What have you got for me today?" he asked.

"I have your beautiful area ready for the festival of regeneration, the jubilee, where you will be able to run back and forth to worship the sun-god," the younger man intoned.

The king looked at the polished stone of the court and the shiny new buildings rising on either side of it. The buildings had no innards and were only facades, but he could not see that and certainly did not care. The outward show was the important thing.

The king's face clouded, however, as he asked, "But will I ever be able to run again? It is difficult just getting into this litter."

"The sun-god rejuvenates us daily, your majesty, and he will do it for you more so when we have completed this court and this structure," the builder said.

"But of course you would say that since I am spending so much on this building and its setting," said the king, smiling.

"I do your will, majesty, as do we all," he replied.

"You try, I know; you try, all of you," the old man said, gesturing around him. The workers had all stopped working and were prostrating themselves toward him. "It's all very beautiful, and how it has grown since my first idea for it! Why I thought only of a low traditional tomb where I and later my officials could peacefully begin our journey to the West after death. But now, you have created something really different," the king said.

He struggled to get out of the litter, and the litter bearers and the builder helped him. He was a little man who clearly had been vigorous in youth, but he had come to the throne only in old age, and his weakness plagued him. Now, however, he stood up and threw his head back to look from the bottom to the top of the enormous series of steps that constituted his tomb, higher than anything human beings had tried to make before. He smiled in satisfaction. He may not have thought the sun-god would rejuvenate him enough to run through his jubilee court, but the sheer size of the tomb could not be kicked aside by later people. It would endure, and with it, his name would last, Djoser, "the pious one," as his parents had called him, although he now had other names and titles. The massive rough pyramid was now ready enough for him to be buried in, should he die. "I am very satisfied," the king punned at the builder, whose name, Im-hotep, meant "in him is satisfaction." Im-hotep bowed and smiled.

⋆ ⋆ ⋆

The Step Pyramid of Djoser, still standing south of Cairo, was the first effort to expand the low benchlike tombs of Egyptian kings and rich people into something more. It began as a bench tomb, but resources and time were available first to raise a couple more stories on it, and then to extend it toward the life-giving sun even further. Now it is 204 feet, or 62 meters, tall, and its jubilee court is nearly as elegant looking as it was in 2500 BCE. As with later pyramids and many other tombs, the king's body has not been found, and it was probably robbed of portable valuables in antiquity by other greedy and impious Egyptians.

Egypt and its thought seem to be accessible to us moderns, although it is not clear that we really understand it better than other ancient cultures. The attraction of Egypt may be seen in the several epochs of Egyptomania, when art, architecture, furniture design, and dress styles were borrowed from Egypt, from as early as the 1700s in Europe. Things Egyptian seem attractive and accessible to us; although we cannot imagine sleeping on those graceful stone pillows that are little racks for the head, we can comfortably sit in the Empire chairs Napoleon's court made popular in the early 1800s. The reason for the interest in Egypt was above all its proximity to Europe; travelers could go there fairly easily, and because the great pyramids were right outside Cairo, tourists see magnificent things.

FIGURE 5.1. Step pyramid. The earliest Egyptian pyramid was built for Djoser. It started as a grand benchlike tomb, but apparently the king's life and resources endured, allowing additions in several stages reaching to a height of 204 feet (62 meters). Around the pyramid tomb itself were many other tombs of people connected to the court; there was also a village consisting only of facades, which was used for ceremonial purposes, perhaps connected with jubilee celebrations that were meant to prolong the king's life. Photo by D. Snell.

Another aspect of the attraction of Egypt, perhaps subtler and less immediate, was that the major writing system was made up of recognizable pictures. This did not mean that scholars could easily read them, but it did give the false illusion of accessibility. I know a bird when I see one, even if the discovery of the Rosetta Stone, a trilingual, with one of the scripts a relatively clear Greek that could be read and understood, did not immediately unlock the secrets of reading (Adkins and Adkins 2000).

Going back to earliest times, seeing the Nile flowing through its desert and making green the surrounding banks must have seemed like a miracle to the first Neolithic hunters who thought of living there. Later Egyptians were deeply thankful for the Nile and thought of all other water systems as imitations of it. The Nile valley had been the way early peoples got out of Africa, and so it had probably always been known to human beings. Yet they had not stopped and lived there for long. Perhaps they dreamed of more luxuriant places, or perhaps it was simply too hot in the summer. Nevertheless, Egypt seems not to have participated directly in the domestication of plants and animals, although human groups who long before had moved beyond Egypt were the innovators in the rest of the Near East.

Archaeology has now shown that people were living in the desert oases from very early periods, and the problem of Egypt is that, because the Nile is a very narrow strip of river with its naturally irrigated valley, modern people still live where the ancients did, and so we may not have found all the settlement sites that were there. It now appears that people began to build houses and to stay in Egypt only from around 4000 BCE, well after the village economies of the rest of the Near East had been established.

From that early period, there was an assertion that people lived on after their deaths. People were buried with pots and trinkets, and sometimes the pots had food in them, and so the idea was that they were going on a journey and would have need of food. This seems to be the major idea of Egyptian religion, not unique to Egypt but unique there in its elaboration. The dead might need a great deal of stuff to provision themselves for the future existence. Grave goods and favorite foods were buried with the dead in many Ancient Near Eastern sites, but this never became a cultural industry in the way it did in Egypt. There is no easy explanation of why life after death might have been emphasized. Certainly the wide range of resources elites could use in Egypt may have been one factor. Because our excavations have mostly been excavations of graves, however, we may have a skewed view of what was important to Egyptians. Their material life may have been even more varied and impressive than their provisions for death.

The defining physical fact is that before dams were built in the 1900s, the Nile flooded regularly in June, and it flooded the whole river valley, depositing silt it had picked up farther upstream in Africa. It took a while for the flood to pass, and when it had, farmers had to lay out the fields all over again, but the fields were fertile indeed (Feeney 2003). So the villages had to be on higher ground and back in the cliffs of the valley above the flood.

The idea of death was that it was a journey just like the sun's daily journey, toward the West. The sun set, and so did we. Tombs therefore should be built in the west, and practically people would keep them off the flood plain and push them into the cliffs and hills beyond. In the classical Egyptian language, "to die" was "to go to the west," and the dead were called "The Westerners."

We glimpse ideas about the life in the West in tomb paintings. These show the buried person enjoying most of the enjoyable things Egypt offered to those alive – hunting, fishing, banqueting, dancing, and travel, especially in boats. Writing arose at about the same time as the Mesopotamians devised cuneiform, and there is some indication that the idea may have traveled across the Near East, although the systems were quite different. The indication is that early in the 3100s BCE, Egyptians seem to have gotten hold of some cylinder seals, the most significant object for defining Mesopotamia in its period of greatest influence. Egyptians built important buildings of their local stone but with the buttresses that were necessary in the baked brick buildings in southern Iraq; that is, there were partial walls protruding from the building that supported it like medieval European cathedrals. This fashion soon died out, but it may show an awareness of developments across the Persian Gulf. In fact, the rapid political union of all of Egypt may derive from a threat to the gold in the mountains to the east of the Nile from foreigners coming across the sea. The local leaders who responded to that threat were the leaders of the regions of the Nile nearest to the gold, upriver in what we call Upper Egypt, around the area of modern Luxor (Brewer 2005: 125–43; Watrin 2003).

The idea of proliferating grave goods seems in the earliest periods to have been closely connected to the power of the ruler of Egypt. Oddly, the ruler did not seem ever to have only one title; he was "he of the sedge" and "he of the bee," meaning the king of Upper Egypt, where the sedge plant, a tufted marsh growth, flourished, and of Lower Egypt, noted for its bees. The symbol for sedge reflected the plant: so did the one for "he of the bee,"

These two areas were referred to as "the two lands." Egyptian grammar had a dual number in addition to a plural, and the dual number made writing "the two lands" easy. It is not clear, however, that there had ever been separate rulers of each.

The death of the king must have been viewed as a traumatic and dangerous time, and there were many rituals connected to death and death's prevention. There developed a festival that we call a "jubilee" that the king could celebrate to show his continued vigor by running back and forth and spilling out libations of drinks to gods. The depictions of the king running were old and persistent. It became a custom that the king celebrated the festival in his thirtieth year of reign and then would repeat it after three years. The festival may have derived from similar sub-Saharan ceremonies of actually killing the old king and replacing him with a new one, but the Egyptian kings were hoping instead to be rejuvenated (Frankfort 1948: 33).

When the king did die, he was placed in an elaborate tomb in the form of a bench above the desert floor into which his coffin could be placed. Some of the early kings may have been buried with some of their human entourage, on a lesser scale but certainly with the same idea as the Mesopotamian Early Dynastic Ur graves (David 2002: 75). This custom was not widespread, and it was probably eventually replaced by the burying of numerous little statues of servants who would be able to wait on the deceased. Members of the elite did want to be buried near the tomb of the king, however. The earliest spells that talk about getting to the West seem only to concern the king, and there may have been an idea that one could only get to the West in the company of a king – hence, the interest in being buried in his proximity. Kings had command of the snazziest grave goods, including beautifully carved combs of wood and bracelets of semiprecious stone. Yet many tombs found by modern archaeologists are empty, robbed in antiquity. So the proliferation of grave goods was not a guarantee of actually bearing them into the next life.

We think of the Old Kingdom, 2575–2175 BCE, as a time when the focus of the entire society was on the eventual death of the reigning king. Tombs were getting bigger, and finally under King Djoser, they blossomed into a pyramid, with the benches piled on top of each other. The tomb was not just for the king; many others were buried near him. The planners seem to have had time and extra labor on their hands, and so they made the pyramid-shaped tomb even bigger, leaving it as the Step Pyramid, a huge monument to the king and his time.

This monument was connected to more building. Beside an entire town of facades (fronts of building around the pyramid), there was a temple that was intended as a continuing place of prayer for the king and his companions. Like later temples, it was endowed with agricultural villages that would support the priests, and the intention was for it to function forever in this way as a pious endowment. However, just as the tombs tended to be robbed by people who valued the goods more than the possible pain they might suffer if caught, the endowments did not necessarily last, although Egyptians in writings at least honored their ancient kings.

As noted earlier, the king of Upper and Lower Egypt was categorized as a god. In Egypt, there were no special crowns for gods, but the term *neter* was used to refer to supernatural beings. The idea of immortality was not included in the idea of the *neter*. The king died, and in fact in stories other *neter* could die. Calling yourself a god seems to us to be a blatant power grab to seize the religious high ground and trump any other political actors. Yet the achievement of holding Egypt together, however loosely, was one that any king could be proud of. He was extraordinary and felt to be more in tune with the powers of nature than other people.

The king was associated very early with the god Horus, a falcon of the northern marshes around the delta. The falcon, however, seems to have been worshiped everywhere and was a sky-god, pervasive throughout Egypt. When alive, the king's religious task was to be the main priest in all the temples of

Egypt, no matter what god was worshiped. Because that task was physically impossible, the king designated priests to represent him when he could not be present, and yet he did try to be present at the most important offerings. He was definitely the only god who worshiped other gods, and in that role played a part in the linking of his people to the realm of the extraordinary beings that were *neter*s. Some have seen in this royal role a remnant of the ideas about kingship known later in sub-Saharan Africa where the king was responsible for all religious acts but also for the weather and other aspects of good and bad fortune. A king who underwent too much ill fortune would find himself criticized and deposed. In historical times, we do not hear much of the hassles around succession, even when, as in the case of Hatshepsut in the New Kingdom around 1450 BCE, there clearly were such hassles among the elites.

The mechanisms for transportation to the West, where the dead lived on, were not acts of filial piety. The tombs of the kings were prepared during their lifetimes by the kings themselves, and if they were not ready at the time of death, it may be that the king was buried in an unfinished tomb or somewhere else altogether. Intact royal burials from early periods have not been preserved. Within a generation or two of Djoser's pyramid, other kings experimented with the gigantically monumental form. A king called Sneferu ("improvement") was credited with three of these giants and seems not to have been buried in any of them. One of them was abandoned unfinished perhaps because its angle was too steep to be stable, and another was bent, meaning it started off at a steeper angle and then was modified to a more gradual one. Another attained the angle of about 45 degrees, which became standard in later pyramids.

These grandiose tombs were constructed on a grand scale only in three or four generations around 2500 BCE and attest to the enormous surpluses the kings could command. They may be seen as make-work projects on which forced laborers might work when the Nile flood was high. The people who worked on them were fed and housed while working, and they seem to have been proud of their achievements. Perhaps they, too, gained a bit of power from the king to move into the West at their deaths. As before, many of the elite were to be buried near the royal tombs. The pyramids were probably not star observatories of any sort, as some moderns have speculated, but they may have been intended as ways to get the king nearer to the sun, who was associated also with Horus, the falcon god.

The great pyramids were produced by a family of kings over three generations, with the largest one being the oldest. They mobilized the resources of the whole of the Nile valley for a number of years. Most of the stone for them came from nearby, but the smooth white casing stone that finished them, now gone from all but the middle one, came from farther away. The engineering involved was always a work in progress. Probably ramps of earth were built up the growing sides of the pyramids and then removed when they were finished. Pyramids were the focal points of a mortuary complex that included temples in the river valley, and in one case burials of wooden boats that may have brought the king and his grave goods from wherever he happened to die.

The temples were endowed like other tombs, meaning they had farms that were intended to supply the needs of the priests and other servants to maintain the offerings for the sake of the dead king forever. One of the pyramids kept its endowment intact and the services going for more than a thousand years, and still the pyramids make a big impression on Egyptians and others who visit them and serve as symbols of national unity and purpose. This must have been an ancient reason for spending so much time and money on them.

After the great age of pyramid building, some pyramids continued to be built, although smaller and of less adept construction than the great ones (Trigger et al. 1983: 87–9). We may say that the ideology of royal burials did not change, but the resources available to make the ideology concrete diminished. Not every king could afford to build one, and the last one identified was associated with a king of the Thirteenth Dynasty, after the 1700s BCE.

Although it does not seem that ideas about death changed significantly, there was a change in the access to grave goods and to the spells that were associated with a successful transition from life to the other life that was death in the West. Whereas in the Old Kingdom it seemed that members of the elite could only successfully get to the West by being buried close to the king they served, this connection was severed by the First Intermediate Period, when the unity of Egypt was broken for the first time, and local leaders boasted in their tombs of their success in keeping the people of their areas fed and protected. When this period of disunity was ended by the rise of another centralizing dynasty, the twelfth in the later counting, around 1975 BCE, the grave goods and the spells were used much more widely. Some have called this development a democratization of death, but it may not truly be a change in how people thought about death because grave goods for nonroyal individuals were known from early periods. It does say something about the renewed prosperity and integration of Egypt, which allowed elites from many regions to obtain the things that before may have been reserved for kings and their companions. Even a nonroyal person could be identified with Osiris, the king of the realm of the dead (Scandone Matthiae 2001: 16; Smith 2009).

Another development for the first time with the Twelfth Dynasty is the single idea that moved outside Egypt and became influential elsewhere. For the first time, we have depictions of the "weighing of hearts," in which the essential part of the dead person was depicted in one side of a balance and on the other side was a symbol for order or justice, in Egyptian *ma'at* (Brandon 1969). Justice was known long before as an important aspect of royal behavior; the term derives from words for straightness and correctness. It was the way the world was supposed to work. Yet the Intermediate Period had shown that the king could not necessarily maintain the justice that would ensure the proper working of Egypt's institutions. Instead, local leaders needed to step in.

The people depicted in the "weighing of hearts" were not royal or related to royalty, although they were doubtless rich. Of course justice never did outweigh their hearts; they were always deserving of an honorable burial, and sometimes the god of the necropolis, the jackal-faced Inp, the Greeks' Anubis, a benign character for the Egyptians, tipped the balance in favor of the deceased.

The underlying idea was that individual humans made contributions to the justice and order of life in their own ways, but the implication also was that they had the freedom of will not to, and conceivably a human being could be weighed and found wanting. The weighing of hearts happened at the death of the individual and not before and thus must have been thought of as involving all the actions of the individual over the lifetime (Brandon 1967: 6–48)

The details of what one should avoid doing may be contained in the 125th spell of the Book of the Dead; this is a negative confession, claiming not to have done a series of deeds that strike us still as reprehensible and so may constitute a baseline of Egyptian morality. Among denials that we might not expect to find included mistreating cattle and slandering a slave to his superior. The Book of the Dead also emphasized the need to avoid putting unjust weights in a balance in commerce and the need to avoid hurting orphans, who might not have protectors to take care of them. Nor was the person to interfere in a god's procession or damage a grain measure used to give offerings (Simpson 2003: 269–77).

From the Old Kingdom and after, we have a set of texts that entered the scribal schools and were copied as ways to learn good language and that sought to teach correct behavior, at least among the elites. These were called instructions, and there was an ancient Egyptian term for them, *sb3yt*, related to teaching and learning. The audience usually consisted of young officials, on rare occasions even a prince. The advice seems practical and sensible; perhaps a bit of cynicism emerged when the high official Ptah-hotep in the Middle Kingdom suggested that sympathetic listening on the part of a high official was as effective as actually intervening in someone's problem. Yet the overall concern of the texts was to curb the possible abuse of power and to make sure that the elite young men were told not to take advantage of their positions for gain. The concern for the poor and downtrodden, and again orphans, indicated that decline in station was a real possibility, and the empathy of the rich young men had to be cultivated to make sure such people were not abused (Simpson 2003: 137).

The term for justice and balance, *ma'at*, did not frequently appear in instructions, but that idea may not have been far from the minds of the composers (Assmann 1990). The future bureaucrats needed to be aware of this balance and had to see how their behavior could upset or preserve it. The Middle Kingdom composition "Complaint of the Eloquent Peasant" was a comic commentary on the failure of some officials to take this idea to heart. There an illiterate foreign peasant, from west of the Nile Delta, castigated officials for robbing him and not redressing his grievances. However, the officials kept him talking not because they rejected his claims but because they wanted to record his eloquent speeches for the amusement of the king. To us this seems in itself unjust, but all was made right in the end, and the peasant had his goods restored and his vengeance wreaked on the offending official, whose own goods were confiscated and given to the peasant (Simpson 2003: 25–44).

The implication of the "Eloquent Peasant" was that the balance of justice could be upset by anyone in authority. The poor and downtrodden had a concrete sense of what was just and how they were being abused. They could appeal to the underlying principles of Egyptian civilization, and they would be right, even if they were not immediately vindicated. The young scribal trainee might be proud of his accomplishments and know that he was in line for a very cushy and important job. Nonetheless, he was more obligated than others to keep in mind the balance that made Egypt run, the *ma'at* that the king willed; but that had to be maintained by everyone, ruler and ruled, to work.

It has been argued that *ma'at* was such a basic idea in Egyptian civilization that it might be translated not just as "justice" but even "traditional religion." Before the fall of the Old Kingdom, it may have been seen as the essential characteristic of Egyptian life, one that was kept intact by the ritually and legally correct acts of the king. When the state fell apart, however, there was a crisis in thinking about *ma'at*; the king clearly could not guarantee it, and yet it was still needed. Practically, individual local leaders took charge, and although they did not often mention *ma'at* in their inscriptions, in retrospect one could see them as fulfilling some of the functions of the king in redistributing resources and in protecting the poor from exploitation. These events may have led later thinkers to see *ma'at* as more a private matter, to which every aware person had to be committed. It may become a term more for "personal piety" than for traditional religion. People had to exercise *ma'at* even if everyone around them did not, even if one was not an important part of the elite. Kings could help, but people could no longer depend on them to do much. The gods would judge each person alone by adherence to the balance that made civilized life possible (Assmann 1990).

The state itself appears to have had a religious and moral function. The state was to protect the weak from the strong, to redistribute resources and to ensure that the proper balance and justice was maintained. In the Old Kingdom, it seemed as if a single deified human being was in the process of accomplishing these tasks, but afterward, when the Old Kingdom state had ceased to function and county officials had taken up some of the royal duties, it was obvious that everyone had to contribute to keep those functions going.

Another aspect that became clearer in Egyptian thought was the makeup of the individual person, the elements that we might translate as "soul." We should not assume, however, that these ways of talking about the person, usually the dead person, were felt to be important in every single instance or even to exist in everyone. As texts became more available, however, we see that Egyptians wrote about different aspects. The 3ḫ, or *akh*, was a word for spirit that implied an active quest and might fade into ideas about spiritedness and vigor. The term was related to words for "useful" and in the plural might refer to the power of magic acts, the results of knowing the right spells to say. Most famously the reforming king named himself 3ḫ, active spirit, of the Aten, the god whose power he was interested in enhancing. The active spirit could last beyond death and was invoked in spells about getting the worthy dead to the West (Shaw and Nicholson 1995: 20).

Another term, *b3*, or *ba*, was depicted by a bird with the head of the deceased, although it, too, existed both when you were alive and after you were dead. This little fellow was usually shown as present in the weighing of the soul, and the birdlike image derived from the sense that this was the aspect of the human being that could leave and travel about in dreams. It could also return after death from the West and so perhaps the term approached other cultures' ideas about ghosts. Gods, too, had these spirits, which allowed them to move about freely (Zabkar 1968).

Perhaps most widespread was the term *k3*, or *ka*, which may be a more general term for personality and power of life, but again it was an aspect that survived after death. It was related to words for work and for power, and again the work might include arts and crafts and magic, including spells to induce healing and other kinds of success. It was to the *k3* of the person that offerings were supposed to be made after death. It was probably in the *k3* that the various perceived aspects of the person were felt to be combined; still, it is wrong to think that Egyptians did not see themselves as unified persons. They did, but they knew there were various aspects of themselves that might have different adventures, especially after death (Shaw and Nicholson 1995: 146).

* * *

In sum, we may say that the early developments in Egypt set the mold for later Egyptian religion and thought, and the norms for kings and elites were within the bounds of our own morality. The ideas about death were not widely shared in the rest of the Ancient Near East, even though Egypt's political influence was at times extensive. Perhaps we simply misread Egypt if we think there was an obsession with death and the life in the West because we have mostly found tombs because they were built where the Nile did not flood. Or perhaps the rhetoric of getting the dead properly buried hid a much more nuanced set of ideas about human mortality.

Although everyone hoped their relatives were going off to a happy continuation of their meritocratic materialistic successes in life, in fact laments showed that the dead were profoundly missed. The eventual reunion that might be hoped for in the West with your loved ones was not seen as a likely possible end to the sorrow, although dead and live members of the same family were depicted with each other in funerary sculpture (Sweeney 2001). So the ideas about death, so rosy and unusual as they are painted, may not have been exceptional after all. Everywhere, and not just in Egypt, grave goods were prepared, and everywhere all people hoped not perhaps for immortality but for a smooth transition to another, perhaps more shadowy and less satisfying, life.

6

THE GODS OF EGYPT

As mortals we are afraid of everything, but we desire everything as though we were immortal.
                    – de la Rochefoucauld (1613–1680), *Maxims*, 1959, 100, maxim 511

The prince had been out driving in his chariot, alone on the hard desert sands, and in the heat of the day he came back closer to the river, thinking to ask a peasant for a drink. Dismounting, he saw no one; he unyoked his two horses and let them graze on stubble while he walked over into the shadow of the huge old sculpture covered over mostly with sand. Only the head and ears and the head cloth depicted on the head were visible. He lay down and took his siesta, but during his light afternoon sleep, he had a dream.

In the dream, the sculpture came to life, showing the power of the lion that was its lower body and the wisdom of the face that was on its head. "I am all covered up!" the sculpture complained. "No one can see my beauty and my power, and the memory of me has become foggy. People cannot say which king I am exactly, and they call me all kinds of wrong names. But look, you, prince, are alive still and wise. You could have me cleaned up and restored to my former glory. You could proclaim my name so all Egypt would know it – Khafra, meaning 'the sun-god has actually appeared!'"

The prince awoke and stared up into the statue's eyes. He swore, "I shall try to do as you ask, so the glory of the former kings can again be obvious to all."

* * *

When the prince's father died and he became king in his own right, Amenhotep II (1427–1400 BCE) did clear away the sand and had a commemorative plaque made and installed on the sphinx so everyone who could read could remember the earlier kings, including Amenhotep II and his glorious predecessors. He wrote:

> He would spend time there leading [his horses] around and observing the excellence of the resting place of Kings Khufu and Khafra, the justified. His

heart desired to make their names live. But he kept it to himself until (he became king). . . . Then his Majesty remembered the place where he had enjoyed himself, in the vicinity of the pyramids.

This text is only the first of the later reactions to the sphinx (Lichtheim II 1976: 39–42). Among the most famous is the poem Ozymandias by Percy Bysshe Shelley (1792–1822 CE):

> . . . Half sunk, a shattered visage lies, whose frown
> And wrinkled lip and sneer of cold command,
> Tell that its sculptor well those passions read,
> Which yet survive stamped on these lifeless things,
> The hand that mocked them, and the heart that fed;
> And on the pedestal these words appear:
> "My name is Ozymandias, King of Kings;
> Look on my works, ye mighty, and despair!"
> Nothing beside remains. Round the decay
> Of that colossal wreck, boundless and bare
> The lone and level sands stretch far away.

The figures of the gods in Egypt have always intrigued outsiders. There are some who were usually depicted as human beings, but there were others who almost always appeared as animals, but with some human characteristics. They would walk, talk, point, and bless. There were still others, and sometimes actually the very same gods, whose depictions showed mixed characteristics of humans and animals, and sometimes of humans and of symbols. The great example of the mixing was the sphinx at Giza, a massive sculpture made in the naturally occurring rock outcropping representing the king Khafra but with a lion's body.

The sphinx was seen by early visitors as enigmatic, and it remains for us, too, part of the puzzle of Egyptian divine images. The sphinx itself was called "Horus on the Horizon," although the lion-bodied king did not seem to have much directly in common with the falcon god. Other sphinxes were called *šsp-ꜥnḫ*, "living image," and that word supposedly was borrowed into Greek as the word *sphinx*, the enigmatic animal of stories.

It has long been tempting to scholars to try to put these figures in a chronological order and to posit that the animal figures were earlier than the human ones, but such does not seem to have been the case. The animal figures appeared early and late and in fact may have gotten more popular in late Egyptian times. Sigmund Freud popularized the idea that some religious feeling derived from a human identification with particular animals, which were then forbidden to be killed; this is a combination of the South Sea island idea of the taboo along with the Native North American idea of a totem as a special animal (Freud 1938: 807–930), but in fact, the idea of the totem does not help explain Egyptian developments (David 2002: 314–15).

The ideas about the natures of the gods in Egypt seem similar to what was said earlier about Mesopotamia, and the work of Egyptologists was used there to generalize about the limitations in the gods of both cultures. Egyptian gods were not all powerful, all knowing, or immortal necessarily, and yet they were definitely extraordinary, and not only in the way they looked. As sometimes occurred in Mesopotamia, the living king was a god himself, and this did not mean that he did not die; it meant that he partook of extraordinary power and could affect the lives of other mortals in basic ways. From at least the Fourth Dynasty, the king was given some of the honors due to a god, and in later periods, he had temples built to him. Those temples, like others to other gods, were set up as pious endowments that owned land and the service of people set aside for their maintenance and use.

Many gods began as gods of local areas, as municipal gods as the Egyptians said, *niwty*, "city one[s]," and some may have been intimately linked to the local environment. The falcon god Horus was revered in the delta, although also far upriver; he was seen as "lord of the sky," who could control creatures through his activities as a bird of prey. Very early he was associated with the king and so became a god revered up and down the Nile. Later the lord of the sky was associated with the sun. In a sculpture, the impressive figure of Khafra, the builder of the second great pyramid, appeared with the falcon Horus behind the king protecting him.

Far upriver, the god Khnum, conceived of as a ram with a human body, was a god of the first waterfall that interrupted boat traffic on the Nile, at Aswan. He came to be worshiped elsewhere as well and was also associated with the sun-god. He was connected with the Nile flood because it always came first to Aswan as it moved down the river, and the "Famine Stele" recounts his success in overcoming a period of low Nile floods in the Ptolemaic Period (Simpson 2003: 386–91).

Gods began to be worshiped in particular places, but many jumped beyond their local allegiances and became part of a larger family of gods who might be worshiped in various periods from one end of Egypt to the other (David 2002: 57). In this leap, it is not so clear that political developments played a large role. Aswan, for example, was always strategically important but never a political capital.

Kings enjoyed associating themselves with the lord of the sky, both as a falcon and as the sun, and those gods remained important through Ancient Egyptian history. Less clearly understood was the rise of Amun, the "hidden one," from the Middle Egyptian city the Greeks called Thebes (Egyptian: *W3st* "Scepter-town"). Depicted as a human, he inspired the devotion of rulers who embellished the huge temple complex at Karnak north of Thebes and turned it into a country-wide shrine, where they vied with predecessors in contributing to the wealth and size of the buildings and the priesthoods.

Amun may have replaced the warrior god Montu as main god of Thebes, although Montu did not himself disappear. Thebes became more important over time. The kings usually came from such upriver places, even if they ruled from Memphis, where the Nile met the delta, near modern Cairo. Amun, who was first seen in names in the Middle Kingdom, was joined with the sun-god as Amun-Re, and he became the royal god of all Egypt – the very opposite of a hidden god. He was praised as a creator of the world as well as its sustainer through his appearance as the sun (Wilkinson 2003: 92–7).

Other gods were never seen in animal form, like that most important of the gods of the dead, *Wsr* meaning "the strong one," which the Greeks heard as Osiris. This god was depicted as a person, but a dead one, wrapped in bandages and ready for burial, and yet still, miraculously, alive, for his color was green, the color of vegetation. He was the father of the living king, and when the king died, he was felt to become Osiris and to reign forever among the dead in the West, who were euphemistically called "the living." The living king was very involved in preparing his father to enter the West and carried out the proper rituals that would allow him to enter there successfully (Scandone Matthiae 2001).

The gods of Egypt probably did not equal in number the imputed thousand gods of the Hittites of Anatolia, but they certainly were numerous. Also, their characteristics could change among their various forms, although usually their sex remained the same.

A major goddess at least from the Fifth Dynasty was Isis, "the [sacred] place," who was the mother of Horus and wife and sister of Osiris. She was not identified with any particular place or city. Her popularity, which ultimately spread into the Greek and Roman world, derives without doubt from her fulfilling the roles of female nurturer. She also had a gift for mastering magic. She was seen, too, as the chief mourner for kings and other mortals. In her maternal role, she was assimilated to Hathor, a goddess of motherhood who frequently appeared as a cow or as a human being with features of a cow, such as floppy ears (Wilkinson 2003: 130–45).

Another goddess is of interest because of the lack of personality she displayed, and she did not appear in stories or myths that might flesh out her character. She was *ma'at*, personified balance and justice. She was not independently worshiped in her own temples, although she did show up in other gods' shrines. Yet, as we have seen, she may have represented the very essence of Egypt as a civilization, the idea that the state existed to help redress the balance between the powerful and the powerless. She was sometimes represented as merely a feather, perhaps with the understanding that a light feather could make a difference on the scale of judgment between a life well lived and an ill-spent one. She appeared in the scenes of the judgment of the dead, where the deceased person's heart was put in the balance against her. Although she usually was shown as a lovely woman, sometimes with wings, she could also be depicted as a woman whose head had been replaced by a feather. She was a personified idea, and an important one, but she did not appear in the family stories of the gods (Assmann 1990). In a New Kingdom papyrus illustrating the judgment of the dead, the deceased person's heart was weighed against a tiny figure standing for *ma'at*. The goddess herself stood on the far right, sporting only a feather for a head. To the far left were Osiris, king of the dead, sitting on a throne, and behind him stood Isis, probably as the chief of mourners; the sign on her head is the sign of "place," representing her name, *3st*.

The problem of evil continuing to exist was addressed among the gods in two ways. In the worship of the sun-god, he was seen as proceeding across the sky in a boat during the day, and after he sank into the land of the West, he was attacked by a snake, called Apopis, against which he had to struggle all night. Nonetheless, he always emerged from the struggle triumphant.

The other evil figure was more ambivalent; the god Seth, depicted as a human torso with an ambiguous but clearly animal head, was Horus's brother in some stories, but he was seen also as his murderer. He was associated with the desert and other environments the Egyptians found dangerous, and yet sometimes he could be enticed to rejoin the family. Some kings of the New Kingdom used his name as the god element in their names, and he once blessed the new king, Ramses III, right along with Horus, his falcon-headed brother.

Foreign gods, too, were worshipped in Egypt. Amenhotep II, the prince who enjoyed going to visit the pyramids and the sphinx, was especially attached to the Syrian god Reshef, a god of plague and the netherworld in Syria but perhaps identified with the god of war Montu in Egypt (Fulco 1976: 30–2).

FIGURE 6.1. The Sphinx. The statue of Khafra was part of the valley temple complex that was built for the pyramid. Here the ruler installed priests and aids who were supposed to commemorate his life in perpetuity, funded by pious endowments that he had left in the form of farms and people who were to contribute to the upkeep of these ceremonies. Photo by D. Snell.

The Nile itself was not deified, although Hapy was a human personification of the inundation, the most important function of the river. In general, there does not seem to have been much change in the ways Egyptians thought about their gods. Seeing them as having human characteristics cannot in itself be taken as a sign of progress, and many remained either mixed beings, like the sphinx, or usually had animals representing them (David 2002: 2, 35, 51).

Like Egyptian hieroglyphic writing, these gods look accessible and understandable. Some, like Anubis, the god of the cemetery and embalming, the jackal-headed man helping with the scales in the judgment scene, seem sinister to us, although he was seen as benign to the ancients. Old cities had complex pantheons that tried to tie together many gods, and temples might be built to house families of gods. The major gods were revered in most places, and within such a diverse polytheism, most people could find something worth revering and petitioning (Wilkinson 2003).

7

THE AKHENATEN DREAM, 1350–1300 BCE

In our natures we approximate one another; habits put us further and further apart. The only ones who do not change are sages and idiots.
— *The Sayings of Confucius*, James Ware, translator, 1955, 109 item 2

The priests were quite confused. No one had explained to them yet what they were supposed to do here, in the new city that the king had quickly built. They had been rousted out of their usual homes in villages in the region and marched together, forced by the king's burly thugs, to new houses in the new town. They had been told to bring along only their basic priestly garments, none of the more elaborate vestments some festivals might require, and definitely no leopard skins, which apparently in themselves offended the king as symbols of the very old order.

So the men, mostly old, stooped, and generally incapable of reading the hieroglyphs on walls around them, had been herded into the square before sunrise and now stood expectantly, unsure about whether they would be suddenly assigned roles in the new ritual or whether they had just been brought to witness whatever was going to happen. Or would they, perhaps, be slaughtered wholesale, as it was rumored some priests had been who had resisted the king's orders? They murmured such questions among themselves as the eastern sky brightened noticeably. There were hundreds of them stretching along the road that led from the houses to a spanking new temple.

But what a temple! It was not like the dark cavelike temples in which people worshiped Amun, the hidden god who had created everything. Nor was it like the huge halls devoted to the god of the sun. It was, they could see through the gateway, a large roofless courtyard open to the sun and devoid of any offering tables or sacrificial altars. There might not have been even a statue of the god at the end. So what did the king propose that they do there? Sing praises to some of the other gods in the form of hymns they had learned since childhood? Or did he want something completely different?

There was a sudden hush in their questioning when down the road there appeared the king in his chariot, driving slowly and acknowledging the bows of the crowd. He was a strange-looking fellow with droopy cheeks and lips, and his none-too-attractive torso was naked except for his elaborate necklace of gold. Perched on his head was an old double crown, symbolizing his control of Lower Egypt and of Upper Egypt, too. He smiled as the priests and other onlookers flopped onto their bellies as he approached; he raised his left hand, apparently to bless them as he slowly drove along toward the temple gate.

That was not the oddest thing about the king and his chariot, as the priests realized when they snuck glances at him as he passed. The oddest thing was that he had with him his goofy-looking wife and apparently all of their six little girls, who were laughing and prancing in the narrow chariot. Why had he brought them at all? Was this supposed to be a solemn religious occasion? The priests did not understand. Of course kings had always had women and children, but they did not bring them out in public; that would have been unseemly. It might also have undermined their images as divinities of absolute power. This king did not care about that, it seemed. In fact, he seemed to be enjoying himself as a very human father. Right before he drove into the temple, in fact, he raised one of the little girls, no more than three, and planted a big kiss on her cheek for all to see, looking very pleased with himself.

After the chariot had passed, the priests stood up and looked at each other in bewilderment. Then from inside the temple, just as the first rays of the sun began to touch the river valley, they heard a hymn sung loudly and clearly in a language so close to the vernacular that they could almost understand what was being said, so unlike the ancient and incomprehensible hymns they had spent their youths memorizing. The singers inside intoned, "You rise in perfection on the horizon of the sky, living sun disk, who determines life. . . . " And in fact the sun quickly rose and began to bake the day and the people still waiting along the road.

* * *

After centuries of placid religious development in Egypt, a king came to the throne who attempted to change almost everything. He wanted to emphasize one god over all the others, and in fact suppressed the worship of other gods, except for the role he reserved for himself as intermediary between the people and this one god. He reigned in the New Kingdom, sometimes called the Empire Period, in which Egypt had successfully intervened in Asia and Africa and spread her garrisons and trade influence farther than ever before. The New Kingdom kings were by any measure successful in maintaining

Egypt's infrastructure and her army and naval power. The reform or revolution was not, as far as can be seen, a response to a loss of perceived power and influence.

The reformer came to the throne of his fathers and took the name Amunhotep, "Amun is satisfied," the fourth of that name. Amun was the head of the pantheon in the New Kingdom. The reformer was not content with the status quo in religion, however.

His motives for change derived from the experiences of earlier kings. In piety when they had military or other successes, they donated lands and the people who farmed them, as well as goods to the temples, and the temples of Egypt of course kept those things. Temples were redistribution centers and places for charity for those in need, and there was probably always more need than resources. These practices, however, meant that more and more land, in Egypt and even abroad, was under the control of the temples. If the king wanted to pursue any initiative, he would have had to beg resources from the priests. The priests were in theory his representatives and appointees, but there was a tendency for priesthoods to be passed down in the same families, and such inheritances were disrupted only in unusual circumstances. So the king's power was limited. Such was the economic motivation for trying to close down the Amun temples and priesthoods. We know, for example, that the temple at Karnak employed more people than the king himself (David 2002: 202).

This was probably not the entire motivation. There may have been an aesthetic reason as well, although this is hard to gauge. That is, the old gods may have been seen as stodgy and incapable of change. The king had focused his devotion not on the sun itself, which had long been a major member of the pantheon but on a god of the sun's rim and rays, the parts of the sun that touched the earth and gave life to people and to all other things. This was the god Aten, whose name meant sun disk. It was a god worshiped earlier but as a minor aspect of the sun itself. The aesthetics the king chose to emphasize included the pervasiveness of light and the openness of shrines and apparently even of human feelings.

The approach has been called "the religion of light," and the depiction of the king, his family, and his courtiers and successors was very different from earlier images (Hornung 1999). Instead of stolid strength, the king had himself shown as paunchy, showing some female as well as male characteristics, and, in a break with all earlier kings, as a family man who doted on his children. Most striking are the sculptures, several found incomplete in a sculptor's studio, of the king kissing a child. This approach must have scandalized informed opinion because the previous norms for art were to ignore the king's human life and entanglements. Kings had loved their children and families, but why show it? Perhaps this intimate art was somehow intended to reveal the blessing of the sun's rim.

To us the sculptures and reliefs from the period seem more naturalistic, but they follow a formula just as earlier art had. This formula was interested in what we would call the humanizing detail; old people were shown as wrinkled and old, and most interestingly the ancient avoidance of any sense that art might depict movement or instability gave way to a new idea that movement might be the most interesting thing happening. The view of immobility as a symbol of strength yielded at least in part to a sense that change was not entirely a bad thing (Groenewegen-Frankfort 1987).

There was innovation also in language. The norms of grammar and writing had been set in the Middle Kingdom, after 2000 BCE, and scribes studied hard and long to be able to imitate the old models. The spoken language was changing, though, and under the reform, it became permissible to show some of these colloquial elements in writing. One new feature was the use of infinitives instead of conjugated verbs. Most interesting is the use of the word for "one" as an indefinite article and of a word meaning "this one" as a preceding definite article, "the." Other nontraditional spellings indicate that scribes were being given some, if not much, freedom to depart from earlier norms in writing. The language development seems of a piece with the artistic move toward a certain realism.

The king took a new name several years after he began to rule, and the new name made him Akhenaten, "The (active) spirit of the Aten." He also undertook to build very quickly, and with shoddy materials, a new capital in Middle Egypt but away from the city of Thebes where earlier New Kingdom kings had ruled. He called the city Akhetaten, "The horizon of the Aten." Of the few Egyptian cities we have been able to study, it seems the most planned, but with new elements. It, like other cities, was centered around the temples, but the temples were quite strange in contrast to earlier structures.

Akhenaten's capital had several temples, itself a bit odd if the point was to emphasize the power and supremacy of one god. The temples were not huge, dark piles like the temple at Karnak, which in antiquity was a dark place in honor of Amun. The sun shone into all of Akhenaten's temples, and probably his houses, too. The king did not want to fail to acknowledge the power of the Aten, but he also had a temple to *Ma'at*, the goddess of personified justice, perhaps because she did not really threaten the idea of the supremacy of the Aten.

The shoddy construction derived from the speed of construction, facilitated by using light and easily portable stones that could quickly be slapped together to form walls. There were also large ceremonial boulevards where the king and his family paraded to acknowledge their faithful subjects. The subjects for this city were probably handpicked bureaucrats who were not likely to complain or protest against what the king did.

Elsewhere the opposition was not so docile. In fact there was considerable anger among the elites against the king, but he was not directly attacked during his lifetime. Only after his death were there efforts, only partly successful, to obliterate his monuments. He was eliminated from the list of rulers, doubtless because his emphasis on the Aten was seen by later Egyptians as the height of impiety because he failed to acknowledge the existence of the other gods.

Was what Akhenaten trying to do really innovative? Earlier thinkers had exalted particular gods in their praise of them, sometimes to the exclusion of other gods, but they did not make statements saying there were no other gods. There is a story that in the Second Intermediate Period, 1750–1600 BCE, one of the Hyksos rulers, the "kings of foreign lands" who controlled the delta at least, had chosen the god Seth as the main god of the state; this idea probably derived from later reflection about Akhenaten. There is no contemporaneous evidence the Hyksos emphasized any god (Assmann 2002: 228). The queen Hatshepsut had complained that strangers had misled Egypt and directed the land without knowing the sun-god, but there do not seem to have been precursors of Akhenaten's reforms. The god Aten had been worshiped before, and Akhenaten's father especially seems to have been devoted to that god.

Some modern scholars have suggested that Akhenaten was a monotheist and of course have then attempted to trace some connection with Moses, the Israelite leader probably of several generations later. The connections seem stretched to Moses, but the idea of monotheism deriving from Akhenaten depends on what you think monotheism is. If it is the exclusive worship of a single god, it is hard to see that Akhenaten's approach really embodies that because he reserved for himself divine status as an intermediary. This role was a lot like that of earlier Egyptian kings, who were themselves gods (Allen 2006).

Akhenaten did, however, strive to shut down the earlier religious establishment, not just in his own capital but throughout the country. This must have involved throwing people out of their jobs and curtailing their livelihoods and centralizing in the king's own hands the power that the locals were used to wielding. Because there was no recorded dissent during Akhenaten's lifetime, he must have had the backing of the military to do what he wanted. The resentment of his policies persisted, however, so that when the dynasty had problems with succession, the old norms were eventually reasserted.

Even among people who may not have minded a king having more power, there may have been resentment of what one scholar has called Akhenaten's "fundamentalism." Under his regime, everyone was forced to worship a specific god in a certain way; in theory, old locally diverse patterns were supposed to disappear. As in any reform that derives from the top and tries to move down among the people, acceptance was perhaps not widespread, and the benefits of adherence to the new norm were not so clear to people outside the capital. There might have been new priesthoods that people wanting to get ahead could join, but by definition, because the king wanted more economic control, they would not be so powerful and all-pervasive as the old Amun priesthoods (Hornung 1999).

Akhenaten's view of death was particularly innovative. The great hymn to the Aten, preserved in the tomb of one of his followers, said that death was falling asleep. There was no talk of the sun's proceeding on a ship through the night to reemerge the next morning, as earlier texts suggested. The world nightly without the sun was depicted as sinister and dangerous, a kind of practice for death each day. Burials, too, were different; the deceased was not trying to prepare for a journey to the West but to rejoin the sun during the day. Our understanding of the approach to death is limited, but it is obvious that the innovator was trying to make ideas in some ways the opposite of what had been practiced before. This approach cannot have been a comfort to anyone, and that seems to be a basic requirement for a religious change to have much appeal (David 2002: 245). Here especially the new religion was felt to be dangerous to the future well-being of adherents in the afterlife; buried as the king advised, one could be sure not to reach the West, to live happily forever with the old gods, who were not supposed to be worshiped now.

The movement has been compared to the Soviet leader Michael Gorbachev's *perestroika*, the "restructuring" of the Soviet establishment, which led eventually to the dismantling of the whole Soviet Union (Hornung 1999). It was different in that Gorbachev's program did not involve any particular new ideology, although it certainly rejected the old one. The Soviet leader may have thought of it as Akhenaten did, a clarification and simplification of a pervasive system. However, Gorbachev hoped to combine aspects of the West's market economy and freedom of expression with the union of nations that he led. It is perhaps too early even now to say whether Gorbachev succeeded or failed, but Akhenaten's changes seem to have moved in the other direction, toward restricting what Egyptians could do, not allowing them to do other previously traditional things.

James Breasted popularized Akhenaten as "the first human being in history," meaning that he seems to have been, at least in his self-representation, someone who decided what he wanted to do and how without too much regard to tradition. He was a self-made man, and this appealed to ancient historians and the public in the 1930s (Breasted 1934). Breasted's assertion assumed that earlier people were entirely bound by tradition, and that is unlikely.

Akhenaten rebelled against earlier norms, and because he was the king, he could impose his or his coterie's ideas on the rest of the country. Nonetheless, his personality remains as elusive as that of other ancient personages, and prolonged study of his monuments, texts, and art has not led to a consensus about his goals and achievements. He remains for us an interesting figure, but his idea of a radical simplification of the pantheon and a radical curtailing of the powers of the gods' priests, although they seem attractive to us monotheists, may not lead directly anywhere. The narrowness of his demands can be seen as quite oppressive if a worshipper was not on his side.

His legacy in Egypt was mixed. Through obscure successors, especially a son or son-in-law, Tut-ankh-Amun, we can see the material magnificence that must have accompanied Akhenaten's reign. Soon after his death, however, the old gods were again revered, as Tut-ankh-Amun's name indicates, meaning "living image of Amun." The ultimate inheritor was a general named Horemheb ("Horus in festival," again using the name of an old god) who restored many aspects of the traditional religion. Later kings apparently led the effort to forget about this interlude entirely and to erase the "heretic" king from the king lists and obliterate some of his monuments.

Yet in the realm of art and of language, the changes associated with Akhenaten had important echoes. Kings went back to being depicted as ideal beings, and family life was again not a theme on which they dwelled, but there was some effort occasionally to show some of the naturalism that Akhenaten had preferred. The old were sometimes old, and dance and movement were actually depicted in tomb painting. Art of the later New Kingdom could sometimes be lively and engaging in a way it had not been before.

In language the colloquialism that had been allowed probably retreated a little, but some of the features that were associated with Late Egyptian did become more and more common. In the context of women's laments for the dead especially, texts written down continued to reveal a bit more about how Egyptians actually talked (Sweeney 2001). Both art and language might have changed without Akhenaten's other innovations, and we cannot ferret out the ideological connection among all these aspects. Later, however, Egypt was definitely different in how it represented itself and how it sounded.

8

PRACTICE IN EGYPT

Today old age has begun for you, and potency has left you. Think about the day of burial, the passing over to an honored state.

– Tale of Sinuhe (in Simpson 2003: 62)

They were all confused to be taken out of the classroom, and they thought their songs were not really ready for public performance. Still, this was what they had been practicing for, some of them actually for years. The little girls were wearing their long white formal robes, and each had flowers placed in her hair. They were supposed to sing a mourning song as the high official heaved into view, and their hair had been let down so they would appear to be in mourning.

But they were not unhappy. The king had died years ago. They were simply being educated to keep up the mourning rituals so that his soul could be made happy in the West. To achieve that end, ladies had to sing at least once a day; it was an easy job, they were constantly told. They did not even have to grind grain or do any of the other tasks that women usually had to do. They did, however, have to get the songs right. So they waited patiently in their fine clothes, the first words playing through their minds.

This display was a rehearsal that had been called for in a letter the steward of the mortuary temple had just gotten this morning. A high official was coming, and he had been told to get all the pretty girl-children "to stand as a jubilating crowd" when the official appeared.

* * *

We know about this event because the letter is preserved (Wente 1990: 77). Mortuary foundations were established all over Egypt to honor the souls of all sorts of people by the Twelfth Dynasty, around 1800 BCE, when this letter was written. The financial arrangements might not last too many generations, but the idea was that they should last forever. The success of Egyptian agriculture was such as to make that imaginable, even if later generations developed other priorities for the use of the land and the people set aside for foundations.

Because people are still living all over Egypt in about the same places they were in antiquity, it is hard to find sites that were not tombs to see what people did that was religious in their usual life. One place that has been excavated is the site of Lahun in northern Egypt. Lahun was probably built as a worker's village for people working on the nearby pyramid of Senusret II, near the entrance to the Fayyum Oasis. Senusret II reigned about 1877–1870 BCE in the Egyptian Middle Kingdom, and the town he founded lasted another hundred years; obviously the pyramid had been finished, but offerings kept on being given to the deified but dead king. It is not known why the site was abandoned (Szpakowska 2008: 14, 144).

Lahun shows us that religious acts were happening in many places, especially if the ritual stands for offering small amounts of bread or other materials were used in the houses in which they were found. Many houses had them, and they may have been associated with family rites praying for fertility and general defense against evil (Szpakowska 2008: 135).

The gods who were revered were Hathor as a lady who stood for love, beauty, and fecundity, and Sobek, a crocodile god who may have been able to protect against natural forces. Anubis, the god of the cemetery, was also revered, as of course was the deceased Senusret II (Szpakowska 2008: 138).

Because the mortuary temple of the king was a major focus for the town, there were records of how the priesthood staffed the temple. There were four groups or watches of priests who served for a month each in succession. They were probably expected to be farm laborers the rest of the time. Also there were dancers and singers who might be brought in for special occasions. The singers were native Egyptians, but the dancers were Asiatics or Nubians. On the whole, the temple was staffed with fewer than fifty people at any one time, and its activities were mostly done in secret, with only the highest priests having access to the actual statue of the god (Szpakowska 2008: 139, 141, 144).

The inhabitants of Lahun carried out a pilgrimage, however, where normal people might catch a glimpse of the divine. The pilgrimage headed down to the Nile and downriver many miles to the Old Kingdom cemetery of Abydos, where the tomb of the early king Djer had become identified as the tomb of Osiris, the god of the dead. Festivities there may have included ritual battles, and they may have culminated in the joyful resurrection of the god (Szpakowska 2008: 145–6).

We see also how religion worked on the ground especially in another very odd village community that was occupied for a much longer time, for most of the New Kingdom, from 1550 through about 1100 BCE. Deir el-Medina ("The Monastery of the City") in its modern name was a community of artists who were paid to work on the tombs in the Valley of the Kings and of the Queens opposite Thebes in Middle Egypt. These people did not have to work as farmers the way most Egyptians did. They were supplied with food and other goods by the state, and they were valued for their artistic prowess and their dedication to the job of making the elite look good and being able to go to the West after death.

Some of the artisans were literate because they had to work on tomb inscriptions, and we have from this strange village a large collection of objects that allows some insight into how these uncommon people thought about religious issues. They may not have been representative of their age and time, and yet we lack similar information from other times and places.

The concern for death and grave goods was important to the Deir people. They spent money and time on their own tombs, and they were experts at doing so. They commemorated their family gatherings and parties, depicting the life they would hope to lead in the West. There was time for such things because the work schedule included holidays for about half the days of the year. They could get a lot done on their own projects. This seems likely to have been in contrast to most peasants in Egypt, although the yearly summer flood brought some forced inactivity for them for part of four months of the year.

Reception rooms in Deir houses may have been where visitors were received and where the owners slept, but some also had wall paintings of the god Bes, the ugly hippopotamus god who was benign to human beings. A second room, much larger, sometimes had statues and false doors with inscriptions in honor of ancestors. Even a kitchen might have a niche for a divine figure (James 1984: 231–4).

Bowls inscribed with letters to the dead relatives were sometimes left in graves. Although embalming had been perfected by the New Kingdom, Deir bodies were not necessarily embalmed; the cost may have been too great. In the course of the funeral, which might take days, the dead had the mouth ceremonially opened so as to be able to speak again and thus take part in human interaction. It was hoped that both women and men in the West would become Osiris, just like the kings of old, meaning that they would assume a place of honor in the afterlife. The dead might be supplied with real food and drink, but they would also be endowed with pictures of such things in abundance. More opulent tombs had small chapels, like those of elites in earlier periods, where the living could come to give offerings to the dead and to commune with them. The tombs were maintained and supported because the dead were felt to be part of the living community, still able to help or hinder its development (Meskell 2002: 182–7).

Although there are many prices recorded in texts from Deir el-Medina, only the grave goods can be classified as having a religious function. Coffins may have been priced separately from their decoration, and ranged from 10 to 200 *dbn*, or weights, in value. The decoration was cheaper, 8 to 65 *dbn*. One of the little dolls standing in for slaves cost only 1 *dbn*. You might need a copy of the Book of the Dead, which would cost as much as 100 *dbn* (Janssen 1975: 216, 224, 243, 246).

The *dbn* was a weight of 90 grams of copper; it was one of three moneys used in the New Kingdom. To compare, oxen ranged in price from 44 to 141 *dbn* apiece, so the tomb expenses seem modest. Coffins were bought fairly often among other goods, and though this cannot mean that they were cheap enough for every workman, still they were not out of everyone's reach (Janssen 1975: 524, 537).

It is hard to gauge the religiosity of the workers in this village, but their names invoke a number of the great gods from Amun to Montu, god of war, Horus, and Khnum, the god of Aswan at the first cataract, and also Osiris, the king of the land of the West (Janssen 1975: 594–601). Perhaps the popular religious tradition that the names might represent was not distant from that of the elite tombs on which the artists worked, or perhaps we are misled by the village's long-standing contact with royal tastes.

Artists, as my friends who are artists never tire of reminding me, are always in tension with society, trying to get commonly accepted taste to see things in a new light. The innovations the Deir artists practiced are harder for us to see than those of our contemporaries, but they were chosen for being the best and most creative at their tasks. As elsewhere, there was a tendency toward nepotism that may have blunted innovation, as in any institutional setting.

The dying artists hoped themselves to reach the happy West and to join their royal masters in enjoyment of the benefits of the dead. The unique placement of their village, physically and economically, allows us to see their successes in preparing for that end.

9

THE INTERNATIONAL AGE, 1400–1000 BCE

If religion was a thing we all could buy, the rich would live and the poor would die.
  – Wolfgang Mieder, ed., *A Dictionary of American Proverbs*, 1992: 503 item 5

The princess had traveled months from southern Babylonia, mostly by cart, sometimes by river barge. She had had the choice of a sea voyage from Byblos, and because she had never been on the sea, she chose that. Now it was seeming like a bad idea. She had been nauseated by the tossing and turning on the sea, and one of her slave girls had died and simply been tossed into the deep. She had wept for days, between fits of nausea.

Her chaperone, an old crone who had once been married to an Egyptian and spoke that language, had been very concerned. Now that they were gliding up the placid Nile on the way to the capital, she was barking orders to the slaves to make the princess presentable. She did not feel very presentable. She had left almost everything behind just because her father had made an alliance with this odd and distant land, and she was the token of it. Her sisters had been married off closer to home, but she was the pretty one, and Daddy wanted to make an impression. She did not feel pretty now, but she put on the eye makeup the Egyptians were said to like and dressed in her best gown. An Egyptian chaperone had joined the party as they came into the river, and she was babbling with the Babylonian one about what they should do with her hair. The princess did not care. She just wanted a bed that did not rock back and forth and maybe some food that was recognizable, onions with fish maybe. Surely there must be some onions with fish in this supposedly rich land.

When they finally got to the capital, she was feeling better. The boat eased into its berth, and the princess was pleased to see that the entire court had come down to greet her. There were all sorts of bands and soldiers, although none of the men seemed to wear any clothes on their chests. Then she saw the man who must surely be the king coming down to the boat. He was older than she, but not really past his prime, and she realized with a start that she did not mind his not wearing much on his chest. She smiled modestly and bowed low to him as he came aboard and guided her ashore. He seemed smitten with her. Daddy would be pleased.

✱ ✱ ✱

Akhenaten's innovations were perpetrated at an unusual time in Ancient Near Eastern history when there was unprecedented contact among the writing civilizations of the area. The regions in contact stretched from Egypt through Syria to Turkey and southern Iraq, a rough triangle with sides about 900 miles (1500 kilometers) long. The concrete symbol of that interaction is the numerous synchronisms one can document among the rulers of Egypt and those of other lands, including the Hittite area, the Mitanni Kingdom of northern Syria, Assyria, and even Babylonia. The interaction of the rulers of those areas can be traced in the amazing set of more than three hundred letters found at Akhenaten's capital and called now after its modern name, the Amarna letters.

Like most letters from the ancient world, they were not dated, and sometimes their contexts and order remain obscure. They show the kings jockeying in an ostensibly friendly way for gifts from each other and especially for the gift of a daughter of another distant king in marriage. It seems that the Egyptian king did not allow his daughters to marry abroad, but most of the other kings had no such compunction.

These international marriages were, however, only one sign of increasing contacts among the cultures of the period, and this interaction included some discussion of religious ideas. There seems to have been a conscious blending of religious views that usually seems justified, as when the Hittite sun-gods were equated with the Egyptian sun-god. In one letter, the Mitanni king, for example, hoped his daughter would be perceived as lovely and worthy of the Egyptian king, invoking Shaushka, his goddess of love, and Aman, Egyptian Amun, to "make her the image of my brother's desire" (Moran 1992: text 19: 24, p. 44).

Most interesting is the Mitanni king's letter accompanying an image of the goddess Shaushka, which he sent to Amenhotep III. The Syrian king wrote that the goddess, Shaushka of Nineveh, had asked to take a round trip to Egypt, perhaps to visit the Mitanni king's daughter, now a wife of the Egyptian monarch. The Upper Mesopotamian king told how in past times both Egyptians and Mitannians had honored the goddess, and doubtless would again. In the last line of the letter, the king wrote, "Is Shaushka for me alone my goddess, and for my brother not his goddess?" This amazing assertion implies a certain universality for the Upper Mesopotamian goddess, at least in the eyes of the king who ruled her area. A note on the tablet in Egyptian hieratic is not clear, although it does indicate that the king received the letter (Moran 1992: text 23, p. 62). The hieratic does not indicate what the Egyptian reaction to this mission really was, but the Mesopotamian king assumed that it would be seen favorably and that the theological idea he asserted – that the goddess was to be revered both in Upper Syria and in Egypt – was obvious. The background to this temporary gift eludes us, as well as the end of the mission, but the letter clearly represents an act of international trust and an assertion of fraternal devotion to the same or similar gods.

The differences among the gods were acknowledged in the letters, but the gods were invoked to protect both Mitanni and Egypt. The Mitanni king wrote, in his own Hurrian language, "may the gods guide both of us together . . . we wish to love one another in brotherly fashion and close attachment. As man loves Shimige [the Hurrian sun-god] on seeing him, so do we want, between us, to love one another. . . . And all the lands that exist on earth, that Shimige shines upon" (Moran 1992: text 24: iv: 117–25, p. 71).

Other kings invoked their own local gods to protect the Egyptian king, as the king of Byblos called on his own Lady of Byblos (Moran 1992: text 68, p. 137). In that case, the Lady of Byblos was identified with the Egyptian mother goddess Hathor (Stadelmann 1977: 630). It probably is not significant, however, that the most interesting examples of sharing gods came from the Syrian area. Perhaps it was a general assumption among the informed diplomats, courtiers, and scribes (Helck 1977: 643).

Incidentally, there is no sign that the foreign kings knew anything about Akhenaten's religious innovations or had any reaction to it. In fact, the king of Mitanni, referring doubtless to the international situation, wrote, "Nothing whatsoever is going to be changed from the way it was before" (Moran 1992: text 29: 68, p. 95). Egyptian kings in any age were not overly concerned with what foreigners thought, and this may explain the apparent neglect of foreign kings as seen in their complaints in the letters (Murnane 2000: 107).

We tend to think that ancient polytheisms were rooted in their own places, and their gods sometimes were seen as intimately connected to the fertility and success of their particular regions. However, these kings at least sometimes had a broader vision, not edging toward the exclusivity of Akhenaten himself but asserting the logic that a great goddess in one place must be powerful also in another. The idea seems a sensible extension of the greatness of a particular god. As the geographic awareness of elites grew with the technology of writing and the creation of a community of international interest, there may have been little theological reflection on the power of one god in other cultures' areas, but there was a roughshod beginning of universalism. This idea would become more important in the first millennium.

In the Hittite area, we know that there was intimate interaction on the level of the intellectuals since there were visiting professors of cuneiform literature that came from Babylonia to Hattusas. This may have been the mechanism by which lexical lists came to the Hittite capital, and yet there were not lists of gods found there, and so systematic identification of Hittite gods with others was not, apparently, a by-product of the exchanges (G. Beckman, personal communication, spring 2008).

Another aspect of internationalism that marked the age may be seen from Assyrian archives in northern Iraq. Babylonians thought Assyrians were upstarts, but Assyria's military prowess allowed it to eclipse and then replace Mitanni in Upper Syria and to become a full actor on the international stage. The state's interest in the exploitation of foreigners extended from extorting agricultural tribute to deporting prisoners, but the personal names found in documents showed an increasing diversity. This may mean that Assyrians of various statuses in their jobs as soldiers and administrators in the West were exposed to different gods from the usual Assyrian ones (Fine 1952–3, 1954: 116–34).

This is also the period, in the late second millennium, when the personal names that show greater interiority, or self-awareness, became more common not only on the fringes of Mesopotamia but also within it. The people who used Akkadian in their names preferred in some instances the names that indicated close relations to the gods and looked to the gods to lift from them their feelings of inadequacy. Such names included Ana-ilia-atkal, "I trusted in my god" (Clay 1912: 203). Names could become little self-contained prayers that represented the person as in need of divine guidance and protection (Oppenheim 1936). A seal inscription reads, "O Sun-god, judge, . . . of sky and land, who knows well my conduct, have pity." Another preaches, "Do not rely on people. They are exalted; they are neglectful, the people, but rely on Marduk; you will get good things" (Limet 1971: 70, 118).

GILGAMESH FOR ALL

The phenomenon of the stories about Gilgamesh, the Early Dynastic king of Uruk who had adventured perhaps to the east and to the west and who had met the hero of the flood, became an international saga in this period. We

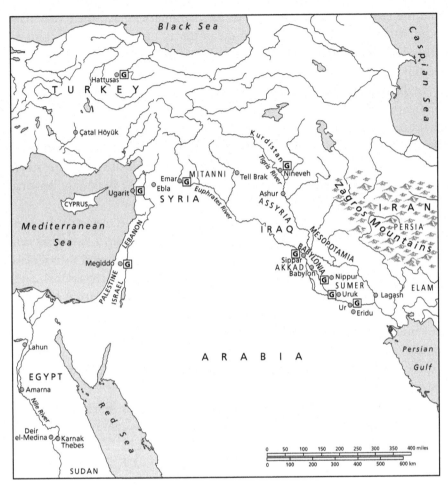

MAP 9.1. Places with copies of the Gilgamesh epic.

find copies of the poem as far from southern Mesopotamia as the Hittite area and also in Israel. The interest in the poem in the west might derive from the idea that the first adventure of the hero was toward the west, into the cedar forest of Lebanon.

The stories had first been told long before and were part of a cycle of legends about Early Dynastic kings of Uruk who may have lived as early as 2700 BCE. There were more stories about Gilgamesh than the other kings, and he appeared as a god of the underworld in early times (Vanstiphout 2003). By the Old Babylonian Period, there were tales about him in both Sumerian and Akkadian, and by the Middle Babylonian Period, these were reworked and combined into a multitablet series. This was happening to other extended compositions, including collections of omens. It meant that scribes were collecting, evaluating, and synthesizing similar material to form large collections to be copied together. These extended compositions transcended the limits of a single clay tablet and created much larger and more complex pieces. Making series of tablets appears to be an innovation of the period and must indicate considerable editorial activity was taking place, even though the texts of classical compositions from the time are paltry in contrast to what preceded and what followed in the first millennium.

The ancient king of the long poem probably had not borne the name Gilgamesh when he lived. The name may mean something like "the old (has become) young," an idea in keeping with the theme of the whole story, or it may have just meant "heroic ancestor," an epithet more than a name. The tale was a critique of unbridled kingship, and this theme may have spread its popularity. At the beginning of the work the Early Dynastic king was young and vibrant but immoral and out of control, having intercourse with young brides before their husbands. The elders of Uruk implored the gods for help, and the gods created a rival and companion in the form of an untamed wild man who ran the steppes, that is, the areas between the cities, and protected animals from the civilized hunters by springing the traps. His name, Enkidu, "lord of the Pure Place," indicates to any Mesopotamian hearer that he would certainly die and go to the horrible place of death, euphemistically called the "Pure Place" (George 1999: 223).

The hunters conspired with Gilgamesh to trap the pesky wild man with a prostitute, who introduced Enkidu to sex. After that, Enkidu found the animals no longer accepted him, and so he was forced to learn about civilized life, how to eat bread and drink beer. The prostitute invited him to Uruk.

There Enkidu encountered the king and wrestled him to a draw. Then the two, recognizing their complementary powers, became friends and, ignoring the counsel of the old men of Uruk, decided to go on a long trip to the cedar mountains for wood. Arriving successfully, they found Humbaba, the scary guardian of the forest, whom they killed, and they took his wood back home to Uruk.

Bathed and freshened up, Gilgamesh met the goddess Ishtar, who asked him to marry her. Strangely, he refused on the grounds that she had not treated her earlier lovers well. She offered him eternal life, but he turned her down, and she stomped off to demand the death of one of the heroes from her divine father.

Although the earlier parts of the poem seem to be critiques of royal abuses, this vignette criticizes the idea that gods and humans could or should have sex and marry to ensure fertility. This is what modern scholars call the sacred marriage, and it may have been behind some of the Early Dynastic imagery of kingship. It appears in the early Old Babylonian Period in poems including the name of a king of Isin around 1900 BCE, and it may be implied in the love songs associated with Inanna, the Sumerian goddess identified with Ishtar. Such poems are known from the Old Babylonian Period in Sumerian language, but there is no indication the sacred marriage was a widespread practice (Renger 1972–5).

Gilgamesh's critique implies that refusing to participate would not in fact damage fertility for everyone else and that the promise of the goddess could not be relied on anyway. There is a similar rejection of a goddess's advances in a poem in Ugaritic language from north Syria from around 1300 BCE; again we do not know about sacred marriage practices there (Pardee 1997: 346–7; Pardee 2002; Wyatt 2007: 66–8).

Gilgamesh's refusal was ironic in light of the subsequent action of the story. The gods decreed that Enkidu should die, and he did so after being forewarned in a dream; he experienced a traditional good death, where he was able to assemble his friends and acquaintances around him and bless them, or, in the case of the prostitute, curse them. Enkidu reversed his curse, however, when he was reminded that she had been the one to introduce him to Gilgamesh and to all his subsequent adventures (Ariès 1982: 5–92, 590–1).

Gilgamesh was inconsolable when Enkidu died. He would not allow the corpse to be buried until it began to decay. After it was taken from him, he behaved as if insane, "running the steppe," just as the wild Enkidu had done before he learned about civilization. Gilgamesh was confronting the fact of his own death; he would die just as Enkidu had, and he decided to try to find "life," or immortality, for himself. He traveled to distant places and fixed on the idea of finding the hero of the Mesopotamian flood. This worthy fellow had been given immortality, along with his wife, as a reward for their having lived through the flood by obeying the god of wisdom and freshwater who opposed the destruction of humans by the other gods. Perhaps Gilgamesh could learn how to gain eternal life from him.

In an Old Babylonian story, Gilgamesh met an ale-wife, or barkeeper, in his wanderings. She inquired about his goals and gave a speech that seems for moderns to encapsulate the lesson of the poem. She said that the gods had reserved eternal life for themselves, but humans could make the best of what they had, be kind to those related to them, live and be merry. Barkeepers were among the wise in Mesopotamian society, and their roles of giving counsel as well as loans were important in the community. We may assume that the poem's hearers probably thought the barkeep was right, but to accept limits without striving against them was not very heroic.

Gilgamesh of course did not take the woman's advice, and in the later composition, her speech was deleted. This omission seems crucial to us, but it may accord with the Mesopotamian cultural style of not wanting to generalize. For example, they knew of the so-called Pythagorean Theorem, that the square of the sides of a right triangle is equal to the square of its hypotenuse, but they did not state this as a generalization. Rather, they gave lots of examples, from which the student was to derive the idea of how to solve such problems. Perhaps the barkeeper's speech was seen as simply too explicit and too simplistic to include, especially long before Gilgamesh's adventures were over.

Gilgamesh reached the flood hero's island and asked him to explain his story, and the flood survivor did. It was obvious by the end of the story that his eternal life was a fluke granted by the gods and not something that even a careful and pious person could duplicate. The flood hero did offer to give Gilgamesh some hints if he could stay awake for seven days. Instantly, however, Gilgamesh fell asleep and only awoke after seven days, showing how very human he was despite his mother being a goddess.

The flood hero's wife took pity on him and encouraged the hero to tell Gilgamesh where he could get a plant that would not give eternal life but would return the old to youth, only to grow old again, but definitely to prolong life. Gilgamesh retrieved that plant, and interestingly, in light of his earlier selfishness, he decided to bring it back to the old people of Uruk and not just use it right then himself. This may show his maturation as a king and a person. As he returned toward Uruk, he neglected to guard the plant carefully, and a snake stole it and molted its skin, becoming young again. This story is a trivial explanation for the snake's apparent ability to become young again, but the theft underlines the irrelevance of such drug interventions. Becoming young again does not nullify death; it merely delays it.

Thus, the hero returned to his city without any concrete achievements, although, as the beginning of the poem says, he had acquired "knowledge from before the flood." Coming back to his ancient and proud city, Gilgamesh asked the visitor to inspect how beautifully made the walls were and how artfully laid out the city was. He precisely quoted a few lines from the beginning of the story, creating a chiasm or repetition of themes that underlined the compositor's idea of what Gilgamesh and other humans could achieve. They could create magnificent edifices for protection and benevolence, but they could not get eternal life.

There has been discussion about whether the Gilgamesh poem should be seen as an epic, an extended poem about important themes showing interactions between humans and gods. The gods were not in general so intimately involved in his story as they were in the Greek epics that defined the genre for Western literature. Yet the theme of Gilgamesh does seem more lofty and important than the anger of Achilles or the wandering of Odysseus.

The epic must have been put together in the Middle Babylonian Period, perhaps as early as 1300 BCE. It is best known from the later library collected by the Assyrian king Assurbanipal in the early 600s BCE. Because there were not very many copies in any one period, it may not have been so popular among scribes as other works. Yet its being read across the writing world in several states and down the millennia suggests that some people in each period may have found it attractive. For us it embodies the Mesopotamian quest to understand the position of human beings in the world – limited in their potential, unable to achieve immortality, and yet capable of creating enduring achievements. The walls of Uruk are still perceptible on the Iraqi landscape, although the river that made urban life possible there has moved away. The site is 42 miles (68 kilometers) northwest of the modern town of Nasiriyah.

Elites were in contact, but the international structures and the states on which they depended were fragile, as later events showed. Ideologically, too, there may have been a weakness that is obvious only in hindsight. In their rhetoric, earlier rulers had said they were good shepherds to their people, concerned for their well-being and willing to intervene in economic and legal matters for their welfare. The kings of the Old Babylonian Period may not have had a consistent economic policy, but their so-called freedom edicts had decreed moratoriums on some kinds of debt and promulgated more general statements about good and fair administration. The legal material that we call codes may have usually been an exposition of that royal concern.

The states of the later second millennium did not show such interest in their downtrodden subjects, however. In the Amarna letters and elsewhere, the urban dissidents who took to the steppes and mountains were characterized as bandits, although they could also be used as mercenary soldiers in a pinch (Bottéro 1972–5). The concern for justice seems to have receded from royal consciousness in many areas of the Ancient Near East. The literature of advice in Egypt and elsewhere commending social justice continued to be read, but perhaps only by the scribes who copied it and not by kings.

The distance between ideology and action always existed, of course, and what kings said reflected ideology and might or might not have been expressed in their actions. This distance may explain at least a bit of the fragility of the states of the Ancient Near East when they were threatened.

The causes of collapse may be found in climate change, leading to a period of less rainfall and invasions by foreigners envious of the states' wealth. The evidence for the desiccation is anecdotal, but it is certainly a strong possibility. What inscriptions complained of was movements of foreign peoples (Redford 1992: 244–5).

The Egyptians called them "Peoples of the Sea" and complained that they had left "their islands," perhaps Aegean islands, and attacked the Egyptian delta, not once but twice in a generation, in the late 1200s and in the 1170s BCE. Egypt managed to repulse them, but then used some of them as mercenaries in Palestine, as their coffins there show. Some became known as the Philistines of the first millennium. Other groups may have been scattered across the Mediterranean. Geographic names indicate that people from Sardinia, and perhaps even the Achaeans, or later Greeks, were involved (Stadelmann 1984: 814–22). The Homeric poems, composed only in the 700s BCE, may have preserved some memories of these disruptions from the point of view of the disrupters, but they were also colored by memories of later ages.

Palestine was changed by these events, and further north the city of Ugarit was attacked from the sea perhaps by similar groups. Its state and its writing system disappeared around 1200 BCE, although its language and culture may have continued without the state. In the Hittite area, a letter mentioned the Aḫḫiyawa as perhaps threatening the coast, and again it may have referred to Achaeans or Greeks. The details are sparse, but the Hittite state collapsed, although there were people from the south of Anatolia who continued to speak a Hittite dialect and use the hieroglyphic Hittite script that had flourished alongside the imported cuneiform.

Further east the states did not fail, but there were ethnic movements that rulers found disturbing, particularly the advent of the Aramaeans. These people were first heard of as nomadic desert dwellers who traded with Mesopotamians, but, perhaps impelled by the withering of their traditional pastures, many of them sought refuge along the rivers and among the settled populations. The Assyrian state reeled from their pressure but persisted under a series of proud but weak kings. Babylonia, too, was ruled by less powerful kings who may have been making accommodations for the newcomers.

One of those was important in the history of religions. Nebuchadnezzar I was king of Babylon from 1124 to 1104 BCE. He managed to campaign into Elam, the state to his east in Iran, and to retrieve from there a statue of Marduk, the god of Babylon, which the Elamites had snatched away earlier. He was rightly proud of that achievement, and he may have commissioned a poem that celebrated the return that became known as the creation epic, *Enuma elish*, "When on high," in Akkadian. Copies of the poem are all from later, and we will examine its place in Mesopotamian religious practice in later times, but it originated here, amid the weakness and chaos as the international age fell apart.

10

GODS AND PEOPLE

We already participate in the still rather imperfect life of the universe through morality, science and art. Religions are the abbreviated and popular forms of this participation; therein rests their sanctity.
    – Ernest Renan, Dialogues 126–7 (in H. Peyre, *Sagesse de Renan*, 1968, 38)

He had awakened early, as he had planned. He climbed up to the roof, and the patient lamb was still where he had moored her the night before, drowsing near the scattering of grass that grew on the roof. She looked healthy; the gods would care about that.

He looked out over the city again, and all was calm and dark. Only his keen eyesight could discern the two-story buildings near the greater temples and the meandering streets leading down to the river. Because he was in a large city, however, some people could be seen beginning to go about their business, some with small oil lamps to light the way. He did not need a lamp; he only needed his knife.

He drew the lamb over toward the edge of the roof; she seemed to fall back asleep as he laid her down. Then he drew himself up and assumed the attitude of prayer, with both hands in front of his face, which was turned to the wheeling stars overhead. He had been paid in advance by the minister of the king himself; that official needed to know whether it was propitious to begin negotiations of peace with the neighboring kingdom, and he wanted the answer read in a still pulsing sheep's liver. The official was himself still asleep, of course, but the liver expert prepared himself to pose the question.

After his proper prayer, he bent down, ended the lamb's life, and pulled forth her liver. Yes, it seemed to indicate, according to the lore he had learned, it was propitious to proceed.

* * *

We have preserved a poem that reflects these events, beginning with a description of the quiet and dark city, saying that the great gods too had gone away for the night. And the sun-god, invoked as a judge, also was not available. But the diviner called on stars and the gods represented by them and asked them, "Stand by me! In the extispicy I perform, in the lamb I offer, place the truth!" (Foster 2005: 207–8).

A key question is how people, of both high and low status in Mesopotamian society, communicated with gods and how in general they managed to interact with them. How gods were thought to be evocable and what they might do if invoked helps to define what we mean nowadays by religion. The gods were felt to be potentially present in a variety of ways in the lives of the peoples of Mesopotamia.

Our category of prayer seems to be a basic one, and many kinds of compositions qualify as prayers – invocations of gods by people ranging from kings to illiterate peasants, although the illiterate were not likely to have their prayers recorded. There is the added problem that, as is so frequently the case in Mesopotamia, there seems not to be a general word for "prayer." The Akkadian is *ikribu* (Oppenheim 1960: I, 66), but in Sumerian, several words indicate specific genres that may help us understand the range of emotions and motives (Falkenstein and Von Soden 1953: 20–6). The Akkadian word is equated to SIZKUR, perhaps a more general term. The sign SIZKUR, consists of a sign for "calf" with "grain" inside and was also equated to *niqû* "sacrifice, libation." This seems to indicate a fairly concrete view of what was going on, at least in the writing system. That is, the one providing the SIZKUR was the person who was about to give an offering to the god; the verbiage that has been preserved for us may not have been the most important thing, but the offering may have been.

The words show, however, that people who prayed in Mesopotamia saw the gods as powerful and capable of helping them in diverse situations, and they thought that the gods liked flattery and acknowledgment of their great power. Despite what was said earlier about the possible role of personal gods, it does not appear that they were needed to address the great gods verbally. Nonetheless, high social status, like being a king, could of course ensure a hearing for your prayer.

This communication, rooted in physical gifts being given to the gods, exudes a sense of Mesopotamian religion as an instance of the Latin formula *do ut des*, "I give so that You might give." There is sometimes an indication of calculation of what a particular favor from the god might be worth. To emphasize the occasional selfishness of Mesopotamian prayer seems to make our own prayers seem more selfless than they are; people do not do religion *not* to get some benefit. However, we think of the Book of Job's question,

"Does Job fear God for naught?" The implication was that he ought to serve for no expectation of reward, and there are similar ideas in Mesopotamian thought.

FATE AND DECREES

Probably the most important aspect of the Mesopotamian worldview about the relations of gods and persons is the idea of the divine decree. We sometimes translate NAM-TAR ("thing cut" in Sumerian) and *šimtu* ("thing put" in Akkadian) as "fate," but it really did not mean that everything was preordained by the gods. What it meant was that the norms – the general structure of how the world worked – had been preordained. The greatness and power of the gods were concentrated in their having set up the systems in which people functioned, but this did not include the individual outcomes for particular persons (Rochberg-Halton 1982).

Most interestingly, there seems to have been no idea of luck or chance having an influence on what happened to a person. Everything proceeded from the interaction of gods and human beings, and people were busily making their own futures. Those futures were not inevitably determined. Gods were capable of intervening to change things. Bad consequences of earlier actions could be influenced by events induced by the human beings.

There also seems to have been no concept of the necessity of things happening as they did. The gods manipulated everything, but their actions could be affected by humans. This is rather a refreshing difference from the classical Greek view of the world; fate was predetermined at birth, and everything followed from that fate; only dire necessity made people conform to that path. Human beings could adjust their receiving attitudes but not what happened. Hence, perhaps the Greeks had a need for the theatre of tragedy to give models of how one might accept cruel fate (Dodd 1951: 6–8). The Greeks worried about whether human acts had any meaning at all given that people seemed not to have any power. The Mesopotamians, however, assumed their actions did have results, and they could avert bad things that might be decreed by gods.

DIVINATION

To change the future involved two problems that not every human being could hope to solve. The first was to know the future, and the second was to affect it (Veldhuis 2006).

The Mesopotamian answer for knowing the future was the study of omens. How early in Mesopotamian history this became a systematic effort is not known. We have references in the late third millennium to rulers' having omens taken, but we do not begin to get collections of omens until the early second millennium. The heyday of collection and exposition was the first millennium, when Assurbanipal's library revealed many omens.

The connections between omens and experience, rather, between what was observed to be ominous and what subsequently happened was not always obvious. The early assumption of modern students was that there was a kind of empiricism in omen taking and keeping. As we have noted, we have a series of clay models of sheep livers from the Syrian site of Mari in the early second millennium. They have different shapes, as real sheep livers can have, and they have explanatory commentaries written on them. Some of them mentioned earlier kings and said things like, "When Ibbi-Sin's land rebelled, this looked like this" (Rutten 1938: omen 7). Ibbi-Sin lived years earlier, but perhaps the oral tradition was passing down actual data of observations. Or perhaps not, because there clearly were observational clichés that were being repeated. In later periods when we have the large collections of omens, not on clay models but in plain prose on clay tablets, there is a certain logic and a tendency to be formulaic in them. What is on the left is good, and what is on the right is bad; presumably this is the opposite of what one usually experienced in life, but it was the usual scheme in omens. The function of the models was in teaching novice observers what to look for, and the collections may have been dictionaries for consultation in unusual circumstances – again a kind of teaching tool.

One omen would not, however, be enough in all circumstances. We know kings kept taking omens until they received the answers they wanted. All kinds of things might void an omen; someone present might have been ritually unclean, or the wrong spell might have been said. It was a risky business, and it might not reveal what you really needed to know. It was a science, in the European sense of a body of knowledge but perhaps not in the English sense of an empirically derived set of conclusions.

It could be costly. If you were going to sacrifice a sheep at each moment of uncertainty, the neurotic person might spend quite a lot of money and sheep to get the answers. Luckily there were different ways the gods might instruct human beings about the future.

In omens we make distinctions, which may not have been in the minds of the ancients, among what was public and private and what was induced and observed. There seems to be no logical reason for the usages of the observed world that the Mesopotamians made, and yet there were cost differences, and people made their choices based on the gravity of their situations and their own resources.

By "public," we mean problems that confronted the king or the whole state and country, problems such as rebellion, famine, and disease. These problems were addressed usually by expensive measures like sacrificing a sheep and looking at its liver. By "private" we mean problems that seem to be relevant only to a nonpolitical individual, regardless of status or wealth. These distinctions may not always hold, although they are useful ways to think about omens.

The other dimension of omens is whether they were observed or induced, whether you simply saw something unusual going on or whether you tried to get something going that was supposed to produce an ominous result. It was cheap, usually free, to observe things, but interestingly that did not necessarily mean that such things were felt to apply to only the private sphere.

A cheap way to induce an omen was to throw oil on water, and it seems that most of the results catalogued for the process did apply to the problems of ordinary individuals; yet we have an instance that might be seen as applying to kings. A text reads, "If I throw oil into water and the oil divides itself into two, the sick person will die; for the campaign: the army will not return" (Guinan 1997: 423). The sense here is that if one were inducing this omen in a matter of an individual's sickness, it would mean the worst thing, and for the state occasion of an army sent off to battle, the result would be disastrous as well.

The expensive process of cutting up a sheep led to results for the king and state. An example is "If there is a ḪAL sign at the emplacement of 'the well-being' [a part of the liver], the reign of Akkad is over" (Guinan 1997: 423). The cuneiform ḪAL sign was a fairly simple one, just two wedges in a line, but it also stood for a word for "secret," and also for the "seer" of secrets, the interpreter of omens. The fall of Akkad was an infamous state event in Mesopotamian history, and definitely public.

Cheap observation of an omen was the theme of the long series "If a city. . . ." An example is "If there is black fungus in a man's house, there will be brisk trade in the man's house; the man will be rich" (Guinan 1997: 424). And you would have thought that the fungus was a pretty bad thing.

Looking at the stars was free, but interpreting what they meant seems to have been a major expense for kings, and the subjects that were interpreted were public ones. In "When Anu and Enlil . . . ," the series of tablets dealing with omens in the sky, you read of state matters, as in "If there is an eclipse

of the moon in April and it is red, there will be prosperity for the people"
(Guinan 1997: 423–4).

The attitude of the receivers of omens is rarely known, although Assyrian
scholars did discuss omens they were trying to interpret in letters to their
kings (Oppenheim 1967: 160–9). One reads, "As to Your Majesty's inquiring
of me: 'Is there anything unusual in the sky that you have observed?' I am
very attentive, and who am I that I would not have reported to the king had I
seen anything? But nothing unusual has appeared. . . . " The king, in this case,
Esarhaddon, king of Assyria from 680 to 669 BCE, was actively concerned with
omens, so much so that some modern scholars have seen him as obsessive,
but perhaps we simply have the letters showing royal concern from his period.
Because his royal father had been assassinated, Esarhaddon had good reason
to keep on his toes.

Astrology in Mesopotamian tradition was for public purposes, things
affecting the king and the state, and it was a revelation of what the fate of
the situation was, what the gods had determined. Sometime before 410 BCE,
this idea, that the stars revealed what the gods had determined, was applied
to individuals, and we begin to have horoscopes dealing with people's private
futures. These texts were not trying, like the Greek horoscopes, to find the
unalterable cast of a person's life based on stars visible at birth, but the basic
idea may be the same, that astrology could be applied to individuals' lives
(Rochberg 2004: 202–7). This development leads to today's inane astrology
columns.

EXORCISM

If a person had managed to identify a future evil, the next step was to attempt
what has been called "mastery of the future," meaning that you needed to
perform a ritual that would avert the bad event and substitute something
better for it. The rituals that have come down to us are probably only the
tip of the iceberg in terms of what was actually done, and they are perhaps
not representative because they did attain a written form. Nonetheless, they
may be seen as important assurances that the bad things predicted might
not happen and they can be seen as a stabilizing factor in the mental life of
Mesopotamians. Assurbanipal, the last powerful Assyrian king, probably tried
to have as many as possible written down so that they could be available into
the future (Maul 1994: 225–6).

An example addressed the sun-god; the person prayed, "because of the evil
of ill[-portending] fungus [seen] beneath a stone, look wi[th favor upon me!]

I have knelt at your feet, . . . the evil of the sack of [wicked] machi[nations] avert from me! May that evil not approach!" (Caplice 1974: 347). Unlike the earlier-cited example, the fungus may not be the bad thing that might happen. It was just the portent of it, but there was definite hope that with the right words, the great god might remove the threat if not the fungus. These words were to be accompanied by a number of ritual acts (called "its deeds") that included censers, torches, and holy water, the offering of bread, dates and flour, honey and ghee, a butter-like substance. Beer was to be offered as a libation. Did you need to do all of this to make the words work? Maybe not, but it was probably better to be safe by doing too much.

On other occasions, the prayers for intervention might be rather general. An Old Babylonian incantation asks for cattle to be relieved of a disease: "Let the face of the cattle be bright again, Let Sumuqan (a god of cattle) rejoice, let the herbs rejoice, let the trail resound with merry bleating" (Edzard 1997b). The petitioner promised to give the great gods "lots of little sun disks" if they in fact managed to cure the disease. This incantation applied to something that had already happened, and the averting of the evil would be pretty obvious to a shepherd or sheep owner, although the disease is not easy for us to identify.

A word for incantation means "undoing, releasing," and indicates that the omen could in fact be undone (Rochberg 2004: 201). You could not count on being able to obtain the right incantation that would alter the course of what was predicted, although that might change by itself. Kings especially were keen to employ numerous incantations so that they might be able to hit on the right one. As a scholar pointed out some time ago, for the Mesopotamian king, "Everything that surrounds him is a trap. Contamination is so easy," and stumbling into evil is always possible (Dhorme 1949: 262).

The Mesopotamian with a problem could and probably frequently did become a Mesopotamian with a plan, and there was continually the hope that the problem might be resolved and dissipate either by itself or because of the intervention of the gods. Nothing was determined, and anything might happen, but people were subject to many vicissitudes, diseases, and misfortunes. The gods might not smile on you, but they always could.

It also seems that over time some gods dropped out of the pantheon and were no longer paid much attention. In fact, in every period there were only about thirty gods who had hymns addressed to them, and perhaps there were about that number who had active temples where a staff attempted to minister to the gods' care and feeding and going on trips. Neo-Babylonian Babylon had about fifty temples, and maybe a thousand smaller shrines. So when we look at the lists of gods, of which there are many versions, we must understand them as scholarly elaborations of how the world worked, not necessarily depictions of deities that really mattered to a broader public (Foster 2007: 169, 200; Lambert 1957–1971).

The greatness of the gods may have increased over time, but our perception is that the number of gods decreased. This does not mean that we edge into monotheism in Ancient Mesopotamia, but we find recurring instances of claims in hymns that the powers of one of the great gods were exclusively theirs.

11

THE LORD IS ONE — ISRAEL IN ITS ENVIRONMENT

Not separating the fate of humanity from that of their small race, Jewish thinkers were the first who worried about a general theory of the development of our species. — Ernest Renan, *Vie de Jesus*, 141

It had begun innocently. The earnest young Jew, born in Babylon but educated in the traditions and languages of his people, had simply never met a kindred soul among the Babylonians themselves. But he was at a party once, a sprawling outdoor picnic with hundreds of guests who had brought their own food and were in a festive mood, celebrating the coming of the New Year at the spring equinox. Jews did not celebrate the equinox, but they did go to parties. As he was seeking a place apart to relieve his bladder of the beer he had drunk, he happened to see a tallish man with a prematurely graying beard just like his, and an alienated look, as if he were slightly annoyed with the traditions going on around him. On impulse, the Jew approached him and asked him what he did.

The man could not reply because he did not know Aramaic or, of course, Hebrew, but he had friends around who could, and so the two began a conversation of rather limited breadth helped by the occasional Aramaic translator. It seemed the Babylonian was a scholar as well, steeped in his tradition, but seeing no way to make any money out of preparing cuneiform tablets for people, he studied the texts that dealt with the stars. He was not sure how, or if, as it turned out, the stars affected human life, but he was fascinated by their movements, in which he sought regularities.

Later, as the Jew grew proficient at the Babylonian language and the Babylonian at Aramaic, it developed that the star-watcher was crackerjack at mathematics and was working on equations that might relate to the movements of the heavenly bodies. They got along famously, and they visited each other's families. At some point, they began to discuss their religious traditions. The Jew was amazed at the seriousness with which the Babylonian thought about his gods, and he was baffled by the punishments that seemed to be meted out to the innocent. The Jew did not doubt for a moment that the Babylonian's gods were ridiculous and false, but he was not quick to criticize them in his friend's presence, although he was not hesitant to suggest that his own God was actually in charge of the entire universe, which He had created. If so, the Babylonian countered, what does your God say about me and mine? What are our roles?

The Jew had gone away perplexed; this was not a question his tradition had addressed. Later, when he had formulated an answer, that Jews were supposed to be witnesses, "a light to the nations," his friend was not interested, and they grew apart. The problem remained in the Jew's mind, however, and in the mind of anyone who took monotheism seriously.

* * *

Another group that was thrown up by the movements around 1200 BCE was the one that became the Israelites. Their origins were depicted in the Bible, the collection of books held to be divinely revealed scripture by Jews and Christians. Revelation itself is a historically conditioned idea, however, the origins of which need to be explored and not simply asserted.

What we know about early Israel outside the Bible is quickly sketched. First, there is an archaeologically attested explosion of the number and size of villages in the hill country of central Israel and the Palestinian West Bank after 1200 BCE. This population growth was much larger than could be accounted for by natural increase. It is not easy to say where those people came from. Their pots and their techniques of terracing the hills so crops could be raised there, and the cisterns they dug to catch the sparse rainwater, were all known earlier in the region. The Bible says there was an immigration from Egypt, but there is no evidence from Egypt of any such movement. The period before 1200 BCE, though, was one in which there was a great deal of interaction between Egypt and Palestine, and so it is not unlikely that groups from Western Asia had come into Egypt and later had left it. Still, if there were ex-Egyptians in the hill country, there were also probably people who had lived in the Palestinian cities but wanted to withdraw from that centralized and controlled life. The Bible in Joshua 24 indicates that some places chose to be included in the Israelite group without having been conquered, but there were also stories of violent conflicts, initially and in the next century, where the Bible depicts a lack of central authority among people assumed to be Israelite.

Interaction with Egypt can be seen in the several Israelite figures of priestly status who bore Egyptian names, including Moses (short for a name such as Thut-mose "Thoth has given birth"), Aaron ("His [a god's] name is great"), and Pinhas ("the Nubian, the southerner"). These names do not help date the stories about their bearers, but they support an assumption of continued close association with Egypt.

The earliest mention of the name Israel appears in the Egyptian king Merneptah's victory stele commemorating events around 1209 BCE. In it his scribes did not use the sign for foreign lands but instead used the sign for people; Israelites were seen as a distinct population, but not yet as an organized foreign land. The Egyptian king claimed to have destroyed Israel along with many other groups.

In the period after 1200, Egypt was entering the long and incoherent Third Intermediate Period, when its unity was in question and its ability to intervene in Palestine was slight, but descendants of one of the Sea Peoples, the Philistines, had formed cities on the coast and later were shown in Bible stories afflicting the fledgling Israelites. However the Israelite polity was developing, it did not need to worry much about outside intervention from Egypt, and the Hittite power in the north had dissolved completely.

The Bible constitutes a unique testimony to some of these processes, but it is one that is difficult to use. Although it contains many old texts, the bulk of it comes from later times and was influenced by the development of centralized monarchies. Also, we have no early copies of it or its parts; the Dead Sea Scrolls of the first century BCE and the first century CE include copies of fragments of every book except Esther, but they also have other texts that did not enter the Bible. We have a complete copy of the Hebrew Bible, the Old Testament, only from the tenth century CE. This preservation was due to the sense that old things should be kept and copied over when they became dilapidated but that reverence was not a guarantee that later concerns and ideas did not enter into the copying. Biblical scholars divide about how much later thought affected earlier writing, and in any story, there may be evidence of later hands.

Narratives of the development of the Israelite state and religion are likely to remain speculative, but to retreat into the doctrines of believing communities today seems to me to be a betrayal of the historian's task. We shall proceed to weigh theories and evidence in a way that seems most plausible; others will certainly differ.

The religious world in which those people in the hill country lived was one dominated by a pantheon of gods probably headed by the god who brought rain, called Baal, "Lord," in the Bible and in the earlier Ugaritic texts. He was associated with other symbols of fertility, including especially the bull, the tractor of the ancient world, who made ploughing so much easier than if it were done by hand. Baal had a court and a family, especially a sister who in Ugarit had searched for him when he disappeared, as he tended to do in the long dry summers. There was another female figure called Asherah, "the happy one," or perhaps "the [sacred] place," who was associated with fertility and represented by a tree or just a stick stuck in the ground.

Worship of these deities could take place anywhere, and they preferred blood sacrifice, possibly including human sacrifice, but frequently settling for sheep and other animals. These would be killed, and the fat would be burned on an altar, but most of the meat was shared among worshipers. Any sacrifice, as elsewhere in the Ancient Near East, was an occasion for a party. Later critics of Israelite religion claimed that such rites also included sexual excesses and drunken orgies, but other evidence for that is slight. Our guess is that most of these gods and ideas had been taken over from the earlier populations, whom later Israelites called Canaanites, people from the low country along the coast and the valleys who were alien from the Israelites.

The development of the Israelites' ethnic self-consciousness and then of their state is tricky to follow. A very early poem preserved in Judges 5 told of a conflict with the kings of Canaan about trade routes. Perhaps the kings had tried to charge significant tolls to people journeying in the hill country. The response was to call on leaders of tribes to oppose the kings. A recurring theme in the poem was how some tribal groups responded positively to these pleas, but others did not. Judges 5 showed that some Israelites had a sense that there should be ethnic unity, but in fact there was not. It may be significant that the "clans of Reuben" criticized in the poem ceased to exist at some point in Israelite history; maybe they drifted away or were folded into the larger tribe of Judah.

Over the next two hundred years, this loose coalition of tribes was threatened, especially from the west by the Philistines, and it was that pressure that led to a plea for a king who would have powers to organize resistance in a more systematic way than any of the tribally based leaders, called "judges," had had. The stories about the kings do not clearly show any religious preference on their parts. There is not much evidence of ethnic self-consciousness either, because they employed people from various Canaanite groups, including the Hittites, maybe refugees from Anatolia, in their armies.

Religiously some Israelite thinkers may have been moving from polytheism toward henotheism. That means that they acknowledged the existence of many gods, but they emphasized the importance of one for their own group. This development seems to share something with the idea of the personal god that had been current earlier in Mesopotamia, as well as with hymns that exalted the powers of particular gods over others.

The god was called Yahweh, "he who causes to be," although he was perhaps at first not particularly a creator god. He was a god identified with mountains in the south, including Seir in what is now Jordan and Sinai in the Sinai Peninsula of Egypt. In later times, it became taboo to say the name of Yahweh, and in pronunciation the consonants were given the vowels of a Hebrew word for Lord, the term used for Yahweh in most modern translations of the Bible. If you say the consonants with the vowels for Lord, you get Jehovah, a fine-sounding name in English that has no independent existence in Hebrew.

The henotheism of early Israel is perceptible in the Ten Words or Commandments in which the Lord demands, "You shall have no other gods before me," showing there were such gods around. Later stories indicate there was tension at least between some Israelites and some Canaanites, and although sacrificial practices may have been similar among them, there was a revulsion against child sacrifice. We see this in the story in Genesis 22, where Yahweh provided a ram to replace the boy Jacob. Later prophets also decried the tendency of Israelites to sacrifice their firstborn children. The whole custom seemed absurd to later Jews and Christians, but in a time of high infant mortality anyway, it may have seemed a safe bet to give the god the first child; more would be on the way, although they might not survive either (see Chapter 14).

One attractive idea about how monotheism evolved comes from the late Israeli scholar Yehezkel Kaufmann, who argued that these developments happened at the very beginning of the Bible story with Abraham as early as 2000 BCE. Kaufmann noticed that in the other religions of the Ancient Near East, the realm from which magic came seemed to be above and beyond the gods. People could tap into the power of magic not by being pious or moral but just by knowing the correct spells, the proper things to say. In stories even great gods also used spells to extract power from the realm of magic, but in Israel those concerned with worship of Yahweh alone wanted to ban the use of magic, not that they denied its obvious power. Kaufmann suggested that the reason for this antipathy was that Yahweh himself was the power of magic, beyond and above other gods. His acts could not be controlled by the use of sacrifice; he did not need anything humans could give. His embodying magic explained the dislike of magical practices among the adherents as well as the sometimes irrational or demonic acts attributed to Yahweh, like the destruction of the little priest who touched the Ark of the Covenant to steady it (2 Samuel 7). That poor fellow had simply connected too closely to the uncontrolled power of Yahweh and had died for it (Kaufmann 1960: 79–80).

The number of people concerned with Yahweh may have been small to begin with, and as social complexity became greater, there may have been divisions derived from religious differences. Certainly that is the way later biblical texts depict the situation. Kings arose in Israel as permanent military leaders, and the state organization they elaborated included priests. The second king, David, in a list that may be old, appointed some of his sons as priests, but later priests may not have been directly related to royalty, although they were certainly servants of the king (2 Samuel 8:17–18 has the sons, but 2 Samuel 20: 25–6 does not, nor does Solomon's list in 1 Kings 4:4–5).

The interest in worshiping only one god may have grown over the first half of the first millennium BCE, but later texts show kings as largely irrelevant to that movement. Other gods existed but were inferior, and this one god was a "jealous god" who was felt to forbid worship of others. This bid for exclusivism may echo Akhenaten's devotion to the Aten, but there were no systematic attempts to close down shrines devoted to other gods in early Israel.

King David's conquest of a previously foreign city in the heart of the hill country, Jerusalem, and his establishment of it as his capital allowed him to update earlier practice and perhaps to install a priesthood under his thumb. Those priests, however, the sons of Zadok, may have been there from time immemorial. They may have only gradually assumed an Israelite identity, because that identity was slowly developing at the same time. David's military successes made being an Israelite desirable, and his son's construction of a showy temple may have increased the economic stakes in favor of adherence to the court's religious preferences, if any. There is almost no archaeological evidence for these reigns, however, and the kingdom dissolved into two parts around 925 BCE, with the north being the larger and more prosperous but with an unstable dynastic tradition, and the south still with kings descending from David.

Most interesting for later developments were figures known as prophets. The ones about whom we have stories and writings attributed to them were fierce critics of the status quo and of the royal government. They came from both the northern and the southern kingdoms and may not have had much contemporary influence, but their followers wrote down and copied their words, and so they come down to us. They represented the old idea, seen in Old Babylonian Mari in the west of Mesopotamia, that divine powers could speak to people in authority through almost any human being. In Mari the messages conveyed by these ecstatics usually concerned a warning to the king not to neglect particular temples. These messages might be seen as self-serving if the people were attached to those temples (Nissinen 2003). In Israel some of the prophets may have been temple employees too, but their messages were much more critical of the status quo than those in Mari. In Israel, Isaiah and Jeremiah were priests, and Amos was explicitly not.

Some prophets, like Amos and Micah, rejected the old forms of sacrifice – not in favor of new forms but stressing the call of Yahweh to personal concern for the poor and neglected. The prophets railed against rich people who neglected their fellows and enjoyed luxuries. Sometimes it was the kings who were criticized, but in general the message was to the political class, rich people who affected decisions taken by the state. Some have seen the prophets as a response to a social crisis that included increased speculation in land by rich people, "adding field to field" (Isaiah 5:8, Dearman 1988: 39–42). Because there are essentially no economic data from the period, it is hard to say whether this idea is right; later tradition assumed that the prophets were speaking truths from Yahweh and haranguing their contemporaries into better behavior.

Many of the prophets threatened that the Lord would intervene to the detriment of the rich and their states unless there was reform. Later texts say that in the north there were no official impulses toward religious change, but it was from the north that a book came that we know as Deuteronomy, and it had a high respect for prophets in general and may reflect some of their teachings. Virtually ignoring kings, the book can be placed in the north because of its geographic references (Deuteronomy 27), but it was a retelling of Israel's early history with an emphasis on how that history was to be understood by the current Israelites.

Prophets threatened doom and destruction, as did Deuteronomy, and, reading the international situation, they were right to be worried. Assyria after 883 BCE had begun to expand its tribute-taking into the west, and coalitions of small states including the northern kingdom of Israel were unable to stop it for long. In 722 BCE, in response to rebellion against its tax burden, Assyria attacked the northern kingdom of Israel and dismantled it, deporting thousands of its leaders to northern Syria. They were settled there as peasants, and they were not heard from again as Israelites. These were the ten lost tribes; they were not lost, but the Assyrians had successfully scared them into no longer resisting Assyrian plans. Although the Assyrians had no particular religious policy toward conquered territories, they did manage by deporting people to make them forget their earlier traditions, at least in the long run (Cogan 1974).

The effect of this northern exile on the southern kingdom was profound. The kings were chastened into obeying the Assyrian tax collectors, and intellectuals began to ponder their old traditions and look to what was left of the earlier prophets to try to understand why the northern kingdom had fallen. The answer for them was that the pleas of the prophets had been ignored, and the Lord's wrath had eventually struck. The Book of Deuteronomy may have come south along with some northern refugees, and a century later, the "book of the law of God" was discovered in the Jerusalem temple itself as it was being refurbished (2 Kings 22:3–13).

Even before the book was found, King Hezekiah had tried to rid worship of some foreign elements, and King Josiah in 622 BCE rent his robes when he had the book read to him. He was in mourning because no one had been doing what Deuteronomy prescribed, and he assumed that it did in fact reflect the Lord's will. His reforms included elaborate efforts at purification of worship, elimination of old but tainted traditions, including the statue of the snake in bronze that was connected to stories about Moses and the "chariots and horses of the Sun god" that stood on the temple roof (2 Kings 22:14–23, 27).

The other aspect of the reforms was centralization of religious observance. This meant that local shrines were to be abolished and brutally destroyed. The priests who had served there were to come to Jerusalem and join the retinue of the only legitimate religious center, the temple of Jerusalem. This requirement, quixotic in its exclusivism, meant that the king would have complete control of religion and also of the offerings that came in to sustain the priests (Claburn 1973).

These measures must have disrupted normal life in most of the southern kingdom, and they did not outlast Josiah's early death in battle. He was nonetheless remembered as a valiant reformer who had done what the Lord wanted. Later kings did not pursue these efforts, probably because the population did not support reforms, but religiously inclined intellectuals took Josiah's efforts seriously and must have been busy collecting, editing, and copying old texts including those of the prophets. Prophets living at the time were still critical of the elites and concretely predicted that Assyrians and others would be back to send the south into exile, too.

The Assyrian state fell apart from 630 to 612, but southern Babylonians took over the remnants of the empire, punishing rebels with deportation, just as the Assyrians had done. By 598, they had exiled some people from the southern kingdom, Judah, to Babylonia, and after another futile rebellion in 587, more leaders from Judah were sent east. This is the exile that mattered, although it may not have been so big as that of the northern kingdom. It included kings and prophets and priests and people who must have carried with them the old traditions of Israel, sometimes orally and sometimes in written form. All sought to make sense of the loss of the land, but the surviving reflections do not make the normal polytheistic deduction that the Lord had been bested by the gods of Babylon. Instead the survivors felt they were being punished by the God of Israel for generations of wrongdoing. Unlike the exile of the northerners, it seems likely that the southern exiles were settled close to each other, perhaps because their numbers were small. The prophet Ezekiel implied he was able to stand before them all and argue with them. His ideas were controversial and did not appeal to everyone who heard him (Ezekiel 18).

One of the exiles whose name is not known but whose work was attached to that of the prophet Isaiah began to make consistently monotheistic assertions – that is, he was denying even the existence of other gods. The motives for such ideas seem counterintuitive. This Second Isaiah, as we call him, lived in a community acutely aware of its past, probably because of the skills of the traditionalists in conveying to Babylon their memories and their books. The northern exile had warned them to be ready, and they were.

The Second Isaiah rejected all the attractive aspects of Babylonian poly-theism, but he was troubled by the role non-Israelites might play in a consis-tently monotheistic world. This was an issue that the presence of foreigners had raised before but had not been dealt with in a systematic way. This prophet, perhaps inspired by friendships with non-Judahites, or non-Jews as we may now say using the English term, argued that other gods did not exist, and therefore the God of Israel had to care for all the peoples of the world. Israel was to be "a light to the nations" to explain their religious errors and to bring them as junior partners into the worship of the one true God (Isaiah 40–55). He did not speak in detail about conversion and what this might mean, and that only became an issue later. He did, however, lay the framework for all later monotheists. In Christian terms, the black babies in Africa deserved to be evangelized and convinced of their role in the one God's plans. The response among Jews of the prophet's time to these ideas is unknown, but their relevance subsequently became clear. Perhaps these con-cerns arose from a scholarly friendship such as that imagined at the start of this chapter.

In 539 BCE, the Persians invaded Babylon and initiated a religious policy of self-determination. People who had been exiled by the earlier empires were free to return. Jews in Babylon had made good lives for themselves, and many had no interest in going back to a homeland most of them had never seen. Some thought, however, that the renewal of God's blessing in the land meant you had to be in the land of Israel, and by 520 BCE a small party had immigrated back to Jerusalem and begun reestablishing its walls.

In another generation, more Jews came, and under the priest Ezra and the Jewish governor who had become a high-ranking Persian official, Nehemiah, they established their small community within what they saw as a sea of alien peoples, some of whom had been resettled by the Assyrians. Others claimed to be Jews who had stayed in the land and not been exiled, but Ezra especially felt that such a pedigree was not enough to establish a person as a true follower of the one God. Jewish leaders asserted that only returners from exile were part of the true community. They were worried about religions that could assimilate other gods as they had seen in Babylon.

The rejection of Jews who stayed in the land of Israel led eventually to the self-consciousness of the Samaritans, who claimed to be the true inheritors of the old traditions. They venerated only what came to be the first five books of the Hebrew Bible; their textual traditions continue to be of interest to scholars, and the community still exists in the West Bank. The tensions with the Jews who returned from exile were continuing.

The most controversial of the decisions of the Jewish leadership was the rejection of mixed marriages, meaning marriages between men who were descended from the exiles and women who were not. The leadership felt that such unions undermined Jewish cultural unity – the children would speak "the language of Ashdod," a coastal city – and threatened religion. Ezra's efforts to force divorces were controversial and extended; the court of inquiry he started was not deciding easy matters, and there might even have been degrees of assimilation among the women being questioned. Some Jews rejected these efforts entirely and apparently left the community (Ezra 9:15; Nehemiah 13:28).

This emphasis on trying to secure the purity of the Jewish tradition was understandable because the community saw itself as small and threatened, and each defection was a loss to it. Leaders felt that only an emphasis on the rigidity of tradition could guarantee a future, and so we see, perhaps for the first time, the exclusion that has protected the Jewish community from innovation down the centuries. Although not attractive to people living in societies that stress multiculturalism and assimilation of minorities, the argument for such exclusion can always be made. It is in the mind of all grandmothers when they ask, "Why are you dating that _____?" where you can fill in your own out-group. The grandmothers, like Ezra, will say that if marriage ensues, the out-group member will not understand our traditions, and what about the children?

The emphasis on exclusion proceeded along with the universalism that Second Isaiah proposed, as in his assertion that the Lord has "given you as a covenant to the people" (Isaiah 42:6b). Ezra would argue, however, that the true understanding of how the world works could only be extended to the rest of the world if it were securely handed down. The idea of conversion was formulated in this postexilic period, although details on when and how are lacking. The Book of Ruth has sometimes been taken as an argument against extreme exclusion; there a Moabite daughter-in-law became the mother of the family of King David, saying, "Your people shall be my people, and your God my God" (Ruth 1:16b).

Personal names for returners from exile have been preserved in lists in Ezra and Nehemiah, and they overwhelmingly had Yahweh as the divine element. This contrasts to Israelite naming patterns in earlier periods and may show that in exile the idea of monotheism became more widely accepted among Jews (Snell 2000).

Another recurring idea that had echoes down the centuries was the hope that God would reestablish the kings descended from David. This view was embodied in the so-called dynastic promise given to David early on by a prophet ("And your house and your kingdom shall be made sure for ever before me [God]; your throne shall be established forever" (2 Samuel 7:16)). It may have inspired several generations of Jews after the exile. Many preserved prophets, although alienated from actual kings who reigned in their times, asserted that God would supply better kings later, as the specially appointed ones (*mashiah*, from which we get *messiah*) of the Lord. A couple of shadowy figures did appear in the stories of the returners, but none established a dynasty of kings or governors, and so the predicted restoration remained theoretical in Israel. When Israel did seize independence under the Maccabees from 164 to 63 BCE, those priestly rulers were not seen as likely kings in the tradition of David, and so the lure of a messianic figure continued to be one in which desires of all kinds could be embodied.

Here for the first time in Ancient Near Eastern history, we see a break with polytheism and a systematic rejection of its principles if not its practices. Later Judaism, as we may call it, still sacrificed to the Lord in the old way, but it rejected all the other gods, and, although its leaders admitted that the powers of magic existed, Jews were not supposed to use them. Particularism would alienate polytheists, and monotheism would seem to limit the ways of thinking about divine powers.

The attraction of monotheism was its simplicity. There was among Jews to be no more concern about alienating gods who were previously unknown. Health and sickness came from only one source, the Lord. This view put the problem of evil in a new light. In polytheisms, evil came from a person's offenses against gods and powers that might be unknown. The response had to be the effort, through spells, rituals, prayers, and personal piety, to placate whichever gods and powers had been offended. With monotheism the response might be similar, without the spells, but the source of evil could only be the one God. The question of why the Lord would bring misfortune is in a monotheistic system unanswerable, but it did give rise to a rich literature that has echoed down the ages. The inclusion of some of this literature in the Bible has made it a much more subtle and worldly-wise collection than it might otherwise have been. The good do sometimes die young. The resolution of this problem in the assertion of reward and punishment after death was not considered in Judaism until the last two centuries before our era.

12

THE TURNING

Reflective explanations always have something lacking when we try to apply our timid procedures of analysis to the revolutions of creative periods which decided the fate of humanity. — Ernest Renan, *Vie de Jesus,* 139

Everyone knows about the foolishness of those kind of people – yelling, actually yelling at the priest. How do they get away with making that kind of scene? And to say that the old sacrifices were not working, why that was almost a sin in itself, wasn't it? Who is to say the old sacrifices aren't perfectly good? Certainly from ancient days our ancestors have managed our activities in these ways. The big ceremonies, did they not seem to connect to the needs and wants of the divine? In the past, they seemed to.

It is true that we live in unusual times, times in which the bloody Assyrians do tend to come over the hill to take people away to who knows where. But to say that God does not want sacrifice is just not warranted. What would God want if not what He has always wanted? What is all this about justice, anyway? The poor are always with us, and there's not much we can do about it, is there?

Then the gall of that guy arguing that he was not really a professional prophet at all! To insult the king by saying in public that his wives would be disgraced and he carried into exile! We've never heard such impious excesses before.

* * *

Such may have been an upper-class Israelite's reaction to the events seen in Amos 5 through 7. Amos was a volunteer prophet who rejected the practices of the old-time religion but asked for individual action.

The prophets of Israel were a part of an international development that has had profound implications for later human history in the writing civilizations. They were figures in what has been called the Axial Age, a period in the middle of the first millennium BCE in which religious ideas in some places turned on their axes and headed in a new direction. The momentum of this turning is with us still.

The German-American philosopher Karl Jaspers was not the first to notice the chronological coincidences, but he was the first to formulate ideas about what the results of these changes were. The facts are simply told (Jaspers 1953: 1–60).

Confucius lived from about 551 to 479 BCE in central China. Involved in politics early in his life, he moved about looking for kings to turn into philosophers but soon gave up. He then taught ways for anyone, or at least literate men, to become philosophically happy. This involved the study of ancient poems and an emphasis on family virtues. The teacher did not want to speculate about gods or heaven, feeling that such things were not within human ability to understand.

The Buddha ("the enlightened one") was born Prince Gautama in northern India around 566 and died around 486 BCE. Perceiving how unjust poverty was, he embarked on a spiritual quest that led him to reject the idea of eternal rebirths based on one's past sins; people could break out of the rebirths just by becoming enlightened.

Pre-Socratic Greek philosophers lived from around 550 to around 400 BCE and taught a wide variety of things. The innovative aspect of their teaching was that they did not accept older tradition as a sufficient explanation for the perceived world. Although they were not empirical in a modern sense and in no way formed a single school of thought, they did emphasize the rule of human reason in coming to decisions. Not all of them rejected the gods or the ways the world had been depicted earlier, but all were ready to question received opinion.

Zoroaster may have been the earliest of these Axial figures, living around 1000 BCE somewhere in Iran. Books containing his wisdom come only from much later, and his date and teachings remain disputed. He apparently disapproved of earlier Indo-European religion, perhaps as reflected in traditional Hindu India nowadays, and asserted that right-living people had to take sides in a world divided between good and evil.

The Hebrew prophets flourished from before 750 and perhaps there were prophets into the 400s BCE. Some had books that have come down to us, but others did not. Like the Greek thinkers, they did not constitute a school or agree on one line of approach, but they came from the Yahweh-alone groups and argued for a purification of religion. Most emphasized the responsibility not necessarily of the king but of the rich and influential people and the punishment that the one god would mete out on the basis of behavior that slighted the poor and the weak within society. Some explicitly rejected sacrifice as a way of pleasing God; instead, kindness to the weak was more important than religious action in the sight of Yahweh.

These thinkers were contemporary but were not aware of each other. Some seem to have responded to chaos in their societies. Again, there may have been a mild desiccation along the temperate zones in which writing civilizations flourished. Confucius lived in the Spring and Autumn Period, 722–481, when earlier Chinese political unity had been shattered. His teachings exuded nostalgia for a time of peaceful unity. The Buddha was at the top of the elites of his North Indian society, but he was struck by the injustice that other people had to become beggars. Zoroaster's social situation, like his date, is vague to us. The dimensions of the crisis the Hebrew prophets confronted are hard to define, but the prophets' alarm is obvious. The pre-Socratics, coming from several cities, many on the Ionian coast of Turkey and so menaced by the Persian Empire, may have sensed various threats to their societies.

The responses to crises varied. Confucius seemed the least political and the most conservative. He refused to speculate about gods but asserted that the ancients had become virtuous by studying and learning old poems, and that was the discipline he suggested to his contemporaries. The Buddha was the most innovative in that he rejected the old ideas of eternal rebirths into different statuses and beings based on one's previous sins. The Buddha's idea was that one could simply step out of the cycle of rebirths by realizing one could, but instead of taking advantage of this enlightenment and enjoying himself, he taught others how to step out of the cycle of rebirths.

We may generalize about the teachings of all of these figures, even though that may not do justice to the variety of their thought. All emphasized the individual and the individual's actions as determinative for blessing in this world. Communities could be misguided; states were ephemeral and not necessary to the individual's well-being, in their views.

A corollary of the emphasis on the individual was the call of these thinkers that their hearers change their lives and take steps to conform to the thinkers' messages. The actual action called for varied, or there might be no one particular action called for, as in the case of the Greek philosophers. Again, these calls might force the individual to separate from the group and even to reject previously sanctioned religious behavior. Trying to follow the way of the Axial Age thinkers might have been difficult and painful for followers; they were not recommending easy ways to live, simply better ones.

The ideas of these thinkers amounted to a withdrawal from traditional religions received from earlier antiquity. Some have called what was going on the creation of secondary religions, meaning the major traditions that have been passed down since. They are secondary in the sense that each was reacting against something older, criticizing it and modifying it for a new day, with a more explicit emphasis on individual choice and behavior (Wagner 2006).

As a group, these men argued that the individual alone could find and do the right thing, regardless of what the community might do, and regardless of the success or lack of success of the state. This explicitly contrasts with early ideas in Egypt and Mesopotamia about how the state, or perhaps in early periods just the king, was in charge of holding the world in good order, of dealing with the crises of the poor and meting out justice and trying to enforce virtue. In Egypt the state might have been thought of as existing to do just that, and although the situation is less clear in Mesopotamia, and of course there were more states functioning, it is probable that redistribution of resources was always an important function of rulers there. The Axial figures were saying, however, that the state could not be relied on to be enough, and most of them were living in times when the stability and power of states were called into question.

There is some irony in the fact that most of the thinkers after their deaths had states founded with their thought at the hearts of state religions. The pre-Socratic Greek thinkers avoided this fate, but after their deaths, the other thinkers all became part of state-sanctioned religious practices. The irony is that these men were not interested in that kind of authority, and many would have argued that the virtue they sought could never be imposed on anyone but could only emerge from individual decisions taken by independent thinkers like themselves. They were all mavericks, and their independence of thought is still obvious. However, state structures have their own logic, and wrapping the state in religious sanction has always seemed like a good idea to rulers seeking legitimacy, even if there were logical problems with doing so with the thought of mavericks. Logical consistency has been a concern of philosophers, but not of state-builders.

The states that embraced these new religions included all subsequent Chinese states taking on Confucianism, most notably the precedent-setting Han Empire, which lasted from 202 BCE to 220 CE. Perhaps the first Buddhist state was that of King Ashoka in northern India from 274 to 236 BCE, but many others followed as the religion moved into Southeast Asia and Japan. Zoroaster's influence on the Persian Empire, ruling the Near East from 539 to 330 BCE, is disputable, but later the Parthian Arsacids, dominating from 171 BCE to 223 CE, and Sassanians, reigning from 223 to 651 CE, both apparently claimed to be Zoroastrian, and striving for religious purity may have been part of the propaganda of the Sassanians for overthrowing their predecessors. In the Axial Age religions, you could claim your enemies were only superficially following the true religion and use that as a reason to unseat them. This process sometimes led to an ossification of traditions and their adaptation into sets of ideas to keep the ruled in their places, but such were not the goals of the thinkers themselves, who deplored oppressive political authority.

The Hebrew prophets were used by later Jewish traditionalists to affirm their state structures, but the words of the prophets remained loose cannons in the tradition despite efforts of priests to get things under control after the return from exile in the 520s BCE. God might still speak to others, probably not with totally new requirements, but religious enthusiasts were mostly not seen as supportive of authority figures. Later, Judaism sought to limit new prophecy and to contain mysticism, which may have been seen as related to prophecy. In fact, only the Maccabean state, flourishing from 164 to 63 BCE, offered a way to independence for Jews, and its success was limited, especially in the eyes of contemporary religious people. The kings, when the Maccabees became kings, were too tainted by Greek politics to be unequivocally endorsed by religious thinkers.

It is reasonable to assume that in other traditions and in other periods there were critical thinkers who called assumptions into question, the village atheists whom some anthropologists have identified, although the term need not imply they really were atheists. The Axial Age thinkers were successful in having their ideas remembered and to an extent replicated. The key elements may have been the challenges to the current structures of societies. The Axial Age thinkers were responding to things that many people were seeing, a crisis of confidence in the institutions and ways of thinking of each society. They proposed answers that appealed to leading thinkers beyond the governments of their days. All preached a message that, regardless of institutions, individuals were called on to assert their own values, an appealing idea to the disgruntled in any age.

The existence of groups of disciples willing to spread the messages cannot be verified for each of the thinkers, although it seems likely that these persons were the most important factor in the preservation and perpetuation of the Axial Age ideas. As ever, the existence and role of disciples is least clear with Zoroaster, but Confucius and the Buddha had famous students. One of the Hebrew prophets, Jeremiah, had a secretary who perpetuated his work; others had similar friends, without whom we would not have their books.

Egypt and Mesopotamia were notably absent from the list of societies affected by Axial Age ideas. There may be several reasons for this. One was the success and prestige that each area enjoyed, even in the first millennium when some of the old power centers were weak. Although Egyptian kings might not be able to intervene in distant conflicts as they had earlier, priests still served the traditional shrines and basked in the obvious glories of the pyramids and other monuments of the past. The very success of earlier ages may have kept Egyptian elites from imagining that reform was needed. Yes, there were foreign kings ruling over them, but there had been foreign kings before, and the Egyptian civilization had eventually either assimilated or expelled them. The old gods would succeed again, given enough time and religious support from the populace.

In Mesopotamia, the north had strong and successful kings in Assyria through the first half of the millennium, and then the Babylonians flourished in the years of the middle 500s BCE, which elsewhere were the core era of Axial Age thought. Political success may have masked the need for reform and kept Mesopotamian dissenters out of the limelight and away from disciples who might have carried forth their words.

One interesting exception may have been the last independent Babylonian king, Nabonidus, who reigned from 556 to 539 BCE and was deposed by the Persians. In Babylon, he came to be regarded by the priests as demented because he did not participate in their ceremonies as tradition demanded. Instead he seemed unusually devoted to the god of the moon, of whom his remarkable mother had been a priestess in the far northwestern city of Harran, in present-day Turkey. He rebuilt the temple there with much fanfare and perhaps did not give the old gods the attention their priests expected.

Also Nabonidus left Babylonia to live for several years in central Arabia, conquering the oasis of Teima and establishing a Babylonian city there. This behavior has been explained in various ways that seem to reduce the likelihood that he was insane. Perhaps he was seeking communion at Teima with the moon-god in another old center of lunar worship; but if so, why was he so brutal in suppressing the local inhabitants? Or maybe he was trying to open up a southern camel-borne trade route to avoid the taxes levied by the Persians, who had taken over the northern tier of the Near East. He was interested in building in the far southern city of Ur, then still perhaps on the Persian Gulf. Nabonidus himself wrote that he was avoiding a famine in Babylon by removing himself and his numerous members of the court from the city; but does one go into a desert to avoid famine? Perhaps he was working on a new formulation for Mesopotamian religion, but because many of the texts we have were put together by his enemies – the Babylonian priests and the Persians themselves – the taint of insanity has stuck.

In the biblical Book of Daniel, Nabonidus's mental state was transferred from him to his more famous predecessor, Nebuchadnezzar. Daniel asserted that the Babylonian king was cured by converting to Yahwistic monotheism, an unlikely upshot that nevertheless may reflect his desire for new thinking. In the Dead Sea Scrolls, there is a Prayer of Nabonidus that shows that the insanity motif had once been applied to the correct Babylonian king by Jewish writers. Because there were no successful disciples and no preserved writings apart from the opaque royal inscriptions, Nabonidus's thinking did not have an impact on later ages or change how Mesopotamians thought about society and the gods (Beaulieu 1989; Vermes 1987: 274).

Akhenaten was perhaps a better candidate for an Axial Age thinker, in that he did try to bring about a reform in religion, even though he lived 850 years before the other reformers. However, he did not share with them the concern for the individual as an independent actor, except of course for himself. This distinction seems important because he did argue that the received Egyptian religion was not enough to ensure proper living in the world, much as the later thinkers did. Like Nabonidus, if he had any disciples, they were unsuccessful in propagating his ideas.

Some modern scholars have suggested that other later reformers should be thought of as Axial Age figures, including Johanan Ben Zakai, the leader of post–Second Temple Judaism, Jesus, and Muhammad. A case can be made for their originality, and they persisted in stressing the importance of the individual and individual decision in doing what God wants; just as clearly, they saw earlier religious ideas as imperfect and capable of reform. Yet none seems so innovative in his teachings as the earlier thinkers, and each acted as an elaborator of the basic Axial Age themes, which continue to reverberate in our times.

One aspect all of these thinkers shared, except Akhenaten and Nabonidus, was that proper thought and practice was not dependent on governments and indeed might be better pursued without the interference of authorities. This means that the resulting traditions were all mobile and capable of adaption; they were not attached to particular dynasties. They traveled with their learned adepts, who could be free of worldly attachments and free to criticize worldly affairs. Authority structures would be built on them, in Christianity most notably where the bishop of Rome, the center of the Roman Empire, came to predominance, but this was not so prominent a feature of the other traditions. In fact even the Christian tradition was capable of breaking out of political structures, even before a Protestant Reformation burst the papal bonds.

The Axial Age sensibility did not pervade everywhere even in the writing civilizations. Most Egyptians and Mesopotamians felt exempt from any need to reform religion. From this period on, however, there would be pockets of the various disciples of the Axial thinkers with explanations of events and of the human condition that seemed increasingly plausible to their fellows, and these thoughts would give form to the ways we think now.

Jaspers in his formulation thought that he was witnessing in the Axial Age the creation of the modern consciousness and the modern person. This idea seems unlikely because there probably always was dissent from tradition. Systematic dissent that was widely accepted was new and it placed at the heart of these traditions time-bombs of ideas that could go off at any moment, inspiring new waves of reforms (Armstrong 2006).

THE PROBLEM OF THE INDIVIDUAL: RIGHTEOUS SUFFERING

The Axial Age interest in the individual person recalls the attention that had been paid to the issue of the person who seemed to be conforming to the gods' notions of what humans should do but who was not receiving the rewards for good behavior. Some of these texts came from before the Axial Age and may have gained currency during it, for they undermined the main idea of human wisdom, that what goes around comes around and that acts have consequences. This perception is still in general true, but in particular the texts assert that human reward and punishment were not laws of physics but more like probabilities of biology.

The earliest of them is a late Old Babylonian composition that has been called "The Dialogue between a Man and His God" (Foster 2005: 148–50), beginning with the line, "A young man implored his god as a friend." The man lamented that he was suffering and assumed it was because of a fault of his, but he did not know which fault it might be. The god intervened and "gladdened his heart, He ordered the restoration of his good health to him." The moral was that one must never forget one's god. The god was not named, and it seems to have been a personal god, but there was also a social element to this piety, because the man was enjoined to "anoint the parched, feed the hungry, water the thirsty" (lines 62–3). The text certainly did not undermine the idea of retribution for bad deeds, but it may have presented a model for proper religious behavior, and it stressed the role of the individual. He sinned, and he had to throw himself upon the mercy of his god; having done so, he found himself healed.

A later text, "I will praise the Lord of Wisdom," has an acrostic that gave the name of the writer as Shubshi-meshre-Shakkan ("O Shakkan, make wealth exist!"), known as a high official in the Kassite court, from the early 1200s BCE. Although no manuscripts are that early, the composition may be from that time (Foster 2005: 392–409). The god Shakkan was a god of animals living in the wild. The long poem praised Marduk, the god of Babylon, who by the 1200s was a prominent member of the pantheon. Marduk understood what the other gods were thinking, but they could not understand his thoughts (i, 30). As a royal courtier, the author found himself reviled by others and not favored by the king. He feared that his misfortune might derive from his inability to see what the god really wanted; he might be doing something unpleasing without knowing it (ii, 34–5). The sufferer's ills became physical and not just social; his body seemed to be giving out too, and divination did not clarify the source of his disease (ii, 109–11). Finally in a dream the sufferer saw a young man who promised to purify him, with an effective incantation (iii). Later a young woman healer appeared in a dream. The sufferer was restored by Marduk himself, the god who had afflicted him. The restored courtier gave a feast for the Babylonians at his own tomb, emphasizing that Marduk could restore to life, and Marduk's consort, Ṣarpanitum, could too (iv). As in the earlier composition, the author did not blame the god for exacting punishment but was simply relieved to be free from disease and despair. There is a somewhat earlier composition from Ugarit in North Syria that shared some of the clichés we find in "I will praise the Lord of Wisdom" (Foster 2005: 410–11), indicating that these sorts of compositions had a certain currency among scribes at least.

A hymn in Akkadian and in Sumerian together begged help for someone who had been punished for unspeakable sin (Foster 2005: 723–4). Similarly another petitionary hymn admitted, "All human beings there are harbor sin" (Foster 2005: 724–5, line 14).

A poem from the first millennium, "The Babylonian Theodicy," considered these cases in a philosophical way and tried to come to a generalization about the roles of humans. An orphaned man, the youngest child, lamented to a friend that he had no success, but the friend responded, "The humble man who reveres his goddess will gather wealth" (Foster 2005: 914–22, line 22). The sufferer asserted his own piety, which had not resulted in wealth (916). The friend rejected his complaint, noting "the purpose of the gods is remote as the netherworld" (line 58). The sufferer countered that reward and punishment did not follow as they should piety and impiety (917, line 75). The dispute continued to the end, with the friend affirming that reward was forthcoming for piety and punishment for impiety, but the sufferer denied that. He ended with the prayer that the god and goddess "take pity" on him, especially "the shepherd Shamash," the sun-god, associated with justice (922, line 297). In this composition, the sufferer did not accept blame for wrongdoing, although he held open the possibility that he had sinned. The only way out was to implore the pity of the gods.

In a late text, "The Dialogue of Pessimism," a master examined the advantages of various courses of action, and his slave subserviently agreed each time. Immediately, however, the master changed his mind, and the slave agreed with that view, too (Foster 2005: 923–6). This patter exudes relativism, even about religious sacrifice because that may make the god too dependent on the worshiper (925, vii). Even patriotism was rejected because the rewards for it did not last (ix).

These sorts of compositions certainly provided the background to the biblical Books of Job and Ecclesiastes. Job is perhaps to be dated in the period after the exile of the Jews, although set in an earlier but indefinable early time, and the author may have tried to obscure his questioning of reward and punishment by providing a happy ending (Tsevat 1966). The mood was definitely like the Mesopotamian compositions, questioning the automatic-ness of divine interventions. Whatever Job's ending may mean, the God of Israel, like those of Mesopotamia, did not mind a questioning spirit in followers. Job's friends in the epilogue were definitely rebuked and condemned for not speaking the truth, but Job had been trying to speak the truth.

A similar mood is seen in the Egyptian composition "The Man Who Was Weary of Life," sometimes understood as a conversation between a man and his *ba* or enduring spirit (Simpson 2003: 178–87). It dates from the Middle Kingdom, 1975–1640 BCE. Certainly the weariness derived from the prevalence of injustice in the world, but the resolution did not involve reconciliation with the gods. Rather, the text advised enjoying the present possibilities even if they did not attain the perfection that Egyptians imagined after death.

These compositions remind us that the emphasis on the individual was old in Ancient Near Eastern thought, but it may have come to the fore in the first millennium when adverse conditions, political and climatic, may have made questioning justice more important. The adversary's question at the beginning of Job set up the situation for these thinkers: "Does Job serve God for naught?" (Job 1:9). The sufferer, whether self-righteous and sure of no wrongdoing like Job or an abject sinner as in the Mesopotamian works, ought in fact to be reverent (in Akkadian: "fearful") toward gods, even if no reward was ever forthcoming. This became the preferred role of human beings in the Axial Age, and the emphasis continued to be on the individual and the individual's behavior. Community responsibility may have been important earlier, but, although the old cities were proud to assert their communal rights and exemptions from taxes and labor duty, it was the individual person who was the important unit in first millennium thought (Snell 2005b).

These texts do not themselves embody the Axial Age developments, but they seem to have been a prerequisite for them, although most stemmed from Mesopotamia, where there was no successful Axial Age figure. They emphasized the life and thought of the individual and assumed the individual's sufferings were what counted, to gods and to others. The sunny certainty of earlier traditions was under attack especially in the first millennium BCE, but there probably always had been thinkers who doubted such upbeat readings of reality, however attractive such readings might seem. In rejecting, at least temporarily, the power and success of spells and incantations, and of other traditional means of knowing the wills of the gods, these texts did not question the validity of the gods or their power, but they did undermine confidence in tradition at least among some scribal dissenters.

Earlier thinkers may not necessarily have thought in communal terms. There was in Hammurabi's laws communal responsibility for a city near which a robbery was committed (Roth 1997: 23, 83), but it does not seem likely that this implied the responsible parties did not see themselves as having individual lives and responsibilities. Still, the thrust of the Axial Age was to be more explicit about the limitations of human understanding and to be open to the empirical observations that goodness was not always rewarded or evil punished.

This insight opened the way for a new subtlety in Ancient Near Eastern tradition and made sure that its manifestations in the future could not be just assertions of the glories of obedience to human representatives of the gods and the states. These bits of dissenting literature hardly meant that kings and priests had shed their power and legitimacy, but they do show there was another way of looking at the world. Sacrifice and traditional religion might not, in fact, be enough to free the individual from sin and disease.

13

THE GOOD GOD AND THE BAD GOD

Only religions know how to respond to death. No doubt that's what they were invented for. — André Malraux, *Lazarus*, 1977: 114

A simple idea, the old man thought, is a dangerous thing. People do not like me, and they do not like their old gods criticized. They want everything to continue absolutely as before, but thoughtful contemplation of the world and its light does not allow that. The manifold problems of the silly proliferation of the gods are so clear that only a fool would be able to gloss over them. Yet he lived among fools, it seemed, and his role of priest did not simplify matters. The simple people still came to him and begged him to heal and consult omens. He was weary of explaining to them how limited his own poor powers really were. It was tempting of course to lie to them, but that was not the Truth, and the old man had spent his life devoted to the Truth and fighting the Lie.

The Truth was that there was both evil and good everywhere, closely competing with each other for the minds of people. He had first seen this so many years ago, and he was weary of repeating it.

He walked into the fire sanctuary, where the sacred flame burned, bowed to the ground, and began his old prayer to the Great Lord who could guide people to Truth, covering his mouth with his cloak so as not to pollute the pure fire. There was commotion outside, however; he had not noticed it before, but there was shouting, the clashing of swords, and the sounds of horses dying. He turned to look at the door, and an outlandish vaguely central Asian-looking man stormed in, his sword already bloody. He walked up to the praying prophet and effortlessly lopped off his head, then looked around to see that there was not much to steal in here, and so he turned and stormed out.

* * *

Such is the traditional story of the death of Zoroaster, at age seventy-seven (Yamauchi 1990: 419).

It is not wise to complain about how little we know about Zoroaster. His is not a situation unique in the Ancient Near East, but the later importance of ideas attributed to him makes us wish we had at least the little headlines we get in the biblical prophets' books identifying the reigns through which the prophets lived. We may doubt those dates, but at least they are a basis for discussion. We lack even that for Zoroaster.

Zoroaster lived perhaps as early as 1000 BCE or as late as 500 BCE, and his sayings were passed on orally and only written down much later, not unlike the Christians' New Testament. As with any canonical process, later ideas may have been interpolated, and it is only after 520 BCE that Persian kings mentioned Ahuramazda in their inscriptions. He was the wise lord, who was one of the two creative deities in the Zoroastrian system (Kent 1953: 116–57). This was not a monotheism because another lord, Ahriman, was always present and was the evil leader of all the bad spirits. Ahuramazda also led other spirits who were beneficent to humans.

Zoroastrian thought, however, did attack the primary logical problem of monotheism, the existence of evil in a system in which there was only one creative god. Judaism posited that evil as well as good proceeded from its God, but Zoroastrianism did not and set up an eternal struggle between opposites – truth and the lie, light and dark, order and falsehood. The role of the individual was to ally with the good god and trust in his protection. Evil was palpable and threatening, and Zoroastrians did not imagine that the good people would always find the protection they sought, but they did think that seeking the good was always the right thing for the individual to do. The Zoroastrian texts assume in fact that good people will not be rich (Skjaervo 2005: 20).

One unclarity is the tradition's connection with earlier Iranian religion. That was presumably a polytheism somewhat like the later Hinduism seen among speakers of other Indo-European languages on the Indian subcontinent. There animal sacrifice was a central duty of householders, and ritual purity was a goal; the gods would not be happy to accept sacrifices from people who were not ritually clean. Ritual purity should not be confused with personal cleanliness but probably meant abstaining from some normal practices. It seems that Zoroaster rejected most of these ideas, but he did retain the ritual use of intoxicating drink, which had been important in the earlier tradition. He tolerated a priesthood that probably existed before him, called the Magi in later tradition, that was not really very magical. The prophet was nonetheless depicted as a reformer who was trying to regularize religion and simplify it so that it would be accessible not just to religious practitioners but to everyone.

The prophet saw his enemies as embodiments of the bad god, and his vision of the future was that there would be increasing conflict that would end eventually, after much suffering, with the triumph of the good god. His was not a creed of resigned contemplation but rather an active call to personal reform.

As in the earlier Indo-European traditions, Zoroaster saw fire as a purifying element, and subsequent worshipers revered flames. His followers felt they should not pollute flames, nor the ground itself, with dead bodies, and so his followers exposed their dead to sun and scavenging animals until only the bones were left, and those might be buried.

The prophet was probably dead by the time the Persian kings embraced his tradition as their state religion. In the polytheistic context, his approach is unusual, and Persian kings seem not to have stressed this aspect of their state religion, if in fact they were Zoroastrians at all (Jacobs 2006: 214, 219).

Persian kings ruled almost the whole Near East after 539 BCE when they took Babylon and administered a multicultural empire, and their religious policy as publicly expressed was one of toleration. They probably had calculated that they were not going to gather large numbers of converts for Zoroastrianism, and so they opted to give lip service to support for any and all religions. The stories about the restoration of the Jewish temple come only from Jewish sources, but they seem to be in general accord with other evidence of Persian religious policy. Perhaps the Persian kings did not really authorize large expenses from their tax revenues to be spent on the Jewish religious establishment as in Ezra 6: 8, but they were likely to have encouraged undoing as much of the Assyrian and Neo-Babylonian policy of deportations as was practicable and desired by the populations that had been displaced over the centuries. Most people born in new lands would not have wanted to leave, and so it cost the Persians little to support their freedom of movement. In the case of the Jews, it is likely that a much larger number of Jews stayed in Babylonia than returned to the land of Israel; Babylon remained a center of Jewish life and learning until the creation of the state of Israel in 1948 CE when Jews left Iraq in large numbers.

Zoroastrianism remained a disputed orthodoxy in Iran until the coming of Islam in the 650s of our era, when it gradually began to recede as a dominant tradition. We know of the contests about the meaning of Zoroastrianism through later texts and also the dynastic histories of the Persian kings of late antiquity. After succumbing to the conquests of Alexander the Great in the 330s BCE, Greek kings ruled the area, replaced around 247 BCE by local dynasts, the Parthians descended from Arsace, and thus called Arsacids, "sons of Arsace," who may have viewed themselves as protectors of the Zoroastrian faith, although other Iranian traditions continued to be practiced under them. These princes, opponents of the Roman Empire on its eastern frontier, were replaced about 224 CE by another group from southwestern Iran who saw themselves as defending the true Zoroastrianism, the Sassanians. Then, too, other gods were worshiped, and particularly the old goddess Anahita continued to be important. There were not many inscriptions from either dynasty, and so it is hard for us to understand the different emphases they may have put on the traditions (Schippmann 1990: 92–7).

Interesting is the advice given by a Sassanian king to his son on the intermingling of state and religious authorities, conveyed in an Arabic-language manuscript:

> Know, my son, that church and state are twins, and one cannot exist without the other. For religion is the basis of the state, and the king is the guardian of the religion. Be responsive to the needs of religious people. If you neglect and oppress them, among the people of religion will appear secret leaders from among those whom you have tyrannized, deprived of their rights and humiliated (Frye 2000: 22, quoting Grignaschi 1966: 49).

This seems to indicate a tension between what we would call secular and religious authorities, and the ironic thing is that it foreshadows the Iranian Revolution of 1979 CE.

When the Muslims came, they viewed Zoroastrianism as a pagan worship of fire and did not dwell on its characteristics. Demographically Iran was quick to convert to Islam, quicker than Syria, Iraq, or Egypt, if one can judge by the later biographical dictionaries (Bulliet 1979).

Zoroastrianism did not cease to exist, however. It remains a minority tradition within modern Iran, but moved also into India, where the Parsees (literally: "Persians") continue to practice it. Later developments and contacts with Islam and Christianity have made Indian Zoroastrianism more and more monotheistic, and Parsees now would assert that such has always been the case (Yamauchi 1990: 395–466).

The great contribution of Zoroaster's thought lay in the dualism, the assertion of a good god and a bad god, which it advocated; this was attractive also to the more explicitly monotheistic traditions. The Iranian prophet in seeking a simplification of his own tradition had posited two great groups of divine beings and had accounted for the existence of evil by the persistence of one of those groups. The mechanisms for the diffusion of these ideas to the monotheistic traditions are not known, but it seems that sometime in the late first millennium, there was contact with the Zoroastrian ideas and that this contact led to Manichaeanism, a Jewish and then a Christian heresy that flourished in Iraq, which saw the power of an evil opponent to the monotheistic god as much greater than had been the case among earlier thinkers. The name Manichaen came from an early teacher, Mani, supposedly called "the living," *ḥayyaʾ* in Aramaic, who was martyred after 240 CE by a Sassanian king (Asmussen 1969).

In the Book of Job, "the Satan" had been a member of god's court and was probably to be understood as an adversary or prosecuting attorney, or in other references in the Bible just as an enemy. In writings after the close of the Hebrew Bible canon, the power of this figure increased, and although the view that God had created all things was not rejected, the evil power was seen as great. The Gospel of Luke worried that "The ones along the path are those who have heard; then the devil comes and takes away the word from their hearts, that they may not believe and be saved" (8:12).

Later monotheistic thinkers rejected this dualism as wrong when it denied some of God's power, but it was comforting to think that some of the evil perceived in the world came from primordial causes. In the New Testament, the early Christian community saw the figure of the devil as a crafty opponent to god's purposes who could be overcome only with difficulty. This thinking was not restricted to Christians, and already in the Dead Sea community and among other Jewish thinkers, the world was divided between the good and the bad, and the choice of individuals was crucial in guaranteeing not only the success of the side of the good in this world but also in the afterlife (Bianchi and Stoyanov 2005).

Another aspect of Zoroastrian thinking is the idea about the judgment of the dead, which was seen as an ordeal by fire to occur at the end of time. This would mark the ultimate triumph of the Wise Lord and the conquest of the bad god. The prophet called on people to be saviors themselves, to fight on the side of the good god and to lead the forces of good in the final battle (Boyce 1992). The ultimate reward was to be the resurrection of the body, a concept that was also attractive to later traditions (Boyce 1979: 29).

The dualistic ideas have been seen by orthodoxies that arose in Judaism, Christianity, and Islam as heretical distortions of the real position of evil, which was taken as a reality but hardly a force equal to the one God. Still, this view has had a millennia-long attraction, especially among people who have felt themselves persecuted by forces too powerful to oppose. In some circumstances, it has given rise to a quietistic resignation that gave solace to sufferers. Orthodoxies by definition have some sort of power, and so they have not found themselves well served by Zoroastrian ideas. They have preferred to think there was much one could do against evil in the world.

14

THE LANDS OF BAAL

All distant lands, you make them live, for you set a Nile in the sky that it may descend for them and make waves upon the mountains like the sea to irrigate the fields in their towns.   – Prayer to the Aten, in Simpson 2003: 282

The mothers were always upset, but what had to be done had to be done. The white-clad priest lifted the newborn from the arms of his reluctant young father, and the baby jolted awake as the priest held him aloft and turned about for all to see: a healthy young baby boy, now wearing nothing at all. The baby began to cry, as did the old women who had come with the young man, not yet twenty, who was the father.

The priest swiftly carried the baby up the steep altar where the flames were already licking the wood. It used to be that the baby was simply laid on the pyre still alive, but this priest was skilled and did not like overmuch mess. He had a small knife in his sleeve, and as he got near to the fire, he skillfully and quietly slit the baby's throat and then laid him on the pyre. His flesh was gone in minutes; his bones would be collected later and buried quietly with the others.

The priest did not relish these days of sacrifice, but he understood why the young couples resorted to these measures. Half the children born died in the first year, so why not get the protection of the god who ruled the city by giving up the firstborn? It was a small sacrifice to make, and although lots of people did not like it, and not all couples resorted to it, the priest felt it was an act that would, in the broad course of things if not immediately with the next child, bring the god's blessing.

* * *

Such must have been the proceedings among people on the coast of what is now Lebanon and around the Mediterranean where the cities sent out colonies in the first millennium BCE. Their enemies always made fun of it, and the prophets of Israel decried it too when they encountered it, but that in itself must have meant that the argument for attaining successful birth and childhood was an appealing one to fathers and mothers afflicted with infant mortality rates much higher than we experience nowadays anywhere in the world.

The western Semitic-speaking cultural area was part of greater Mesopotamia for most of the ancient history of the Near East. Ebla in western Syria was the first place where a Semitic language was written with cuneiform script, and even though that language may have changed as it descended to the second millennium, similar languages and, more importantly, cultural traditions, persisted in the region. Its cultural uniqueness became clearer in the second millennium, and it was a hotbed of experimentation with writing systems and possibly other kinds of institutions, too.

Here in what is now Syria, Lebanon, Israel, and Jordan, the agricultural basis of life was rainfall, and the god of rainfall, known simply as Baal, "Lord" and "owner," was the head of the pantheon. In mythical stories, he lived on the mountains, which caught the rain coming in from the Mediterranean and made sure it spilled some of its life-giving power on the land around.

The religious situation in Ebla appears to have been different from that in southern Mesopotamia in the same period, the late Early Dynastic, around 2400 BCE. Ebla lived from intensive sheep raising and processing the resulting textiles. The gods that were mentioned in the extensive texts from Ebla seem of three sorts, at least from our perspective. There were gods who were known from southern Mesopotamia, like Enki "Lord Earth" and Ashtar, southern Mesopotamia's Ishtar, goddess of love and war. There were also gods who become more prominent later but were not then prominent in southern Iraq, like the many "lords" of various places, who were later combined into the one "Lord," and the god Rashap, or Reshef, a god of the desert drought and destruction, a warrior associated with death. Then there were the gods that did not fit into either of those categories, who in fact constituted the majority of the gods mentioned (Pomponio and Xella 1997: 313–15, 527–38).

The most important god at Ebla, both in terms of the amount of material dedicated to his worship and the number of attestations in personal names was a previously unknown god Kura, who seems to have been a special god of the king and his family. Because he was the only one in Ebla who was called "father" in names, his paternal characteristics were important. His spouse, Barama, was also unknown elsewhere. Next in importance may have been Adda, later Adad or Hadad, the god of storms, and the god NIdabal, well attested, but whose name we cannot securely read, and that is why we write the ambiguous element all in capitals. Incantations from Ebla invoke many gods who were not Sumerian and seem to reflect the local tradition, not the Mesopotamian (Pomponio and Xella 1997: 52–4, 83–8, 247, 285–8; Xella 1988: 352; Younger 2009).

Although Ebla texts must be dated to the century 2500 to 2400 BCE, and most Syrian sites had writing again only a millennium later, there appear to have been some continuities, especially with the city of Ugarit. Not only did some of the same gods receive worship, but the custom of revering royal ancestors with offerings was found in both places (Xella 1988: 354–8).

Ugarit was a city near the Syrian coast that was a center for trade; cuneiform texts were found there from 1400 to 1200 BCE. It was in the Hittite political sphere, but its religious life was not particularly Hittite. The city is important because of the variety of writing systems used in it, and this variety allows us some insight into religious traditions from various cultures.

At Ugarit, besides Hittite, there were texts in Sumerian and Akkadian, mostly copied in scribal training, but also Akkadian was used as the official language for recording legal acts. There were also texts in Hurrian that may have descended from local traditions given that earlier there were a lot of Hurrian-speakers in the area. There were also texts in a script known from Cyprus, a script we cannot yet read, but the texts seem to be short economic records.

Of most interest was the script used to write the local language, a variety of West Semitic we have dubbed Ugaritic. This language had linguistic affinities both with later Hebrew spoken to the south and with Aramaic, the dominant language of the first millennium. The script itself was a simplified form of cuneiform but with new signs, and it represented single consonants with any vowel. This was not really an alphabet with single signs for each significant sound, but it was a system that recorded each consonant, and that system may have been the most important mental breakthrough toward the simplicity of an alphabet (Daniels 1990: 729–30). Ugaritic script did have three signs that differentiated vowels when they followed a glottal stop, the sound we make when we begin a sentence with a word starting with a vowel, a sound that was phonemic in Ugaritic but is not in English.

Another element of the Ugaritic script that points to later developments was the fact that we know the order of the signs thanks to practice tablets that have survived, and it was the order with which we are familiar in later Hebrew and that is essentially the same we still use in our European alphabets. There are some other important continuities from Ugarit to the present, and these have inspired much modern study.

The texts that come to us in this Ugaritic script include rituals and letters and also extended poems that may have had a ritual use, but it is hard to see what the context of these mythological pieces may have been. They show an ordered pantheon revered in Ugarit, including El, a fatherly creator god who in the texts seems not to have played an active role. The executive of the gods of Ugarit was Baal, the lord of the rain, and yet his power was far from absolute. He was opposed by two figures, Sea and Death, and although he eventually overcame both, it was a close thing in which his sister Anath, who mourned him and then revived him, was a key figure.

Baal died fighting the Sea, but the stories show that he then rose and fought again. The resolution of the battle was indecisive, but the Sea was set in its limits. It appears that only here does one actually find a dying and rising god who might reflect seasonal change, but the season is the winter of the angry sea, not the summer of parching heat. Baal is also the only dying god who is called a savior in Ancient Near Eastern texts and so seems to foreshadow developments in Judaism, although of course in the Bible the God of Israel confronted Baal and his religion. The dying and rising god persisted into Phoenician thought as well (Xella 2001b).

Mortals in the texts the Ugaritic scribes copied were kings who lacked sons but who miraculously got them in the end. In the poem about Aqhat, the hero rejected the demand of the goddess of love and war for his bow, advising her that the craftsman god could easily make her one. This lack of cooperation with the goddess seems similar to Gilgamesh's attitude, and the consequences were as grave.

In most of the Ancient Near East, we do not know which devices defined poetry, but in Ugarit we can see that parallelism and repetition were important, when "El laughed, and stuck out his tongue, spoke up and said...." This parallelism was also a feature of poetry in Hebrew later, and even some of the parallel words appeared both in Ugarit and in the Bible, again arguing that there was a continuity in culture.

In personal names there seem to have been fewer Ugaritic gods than at Ebla, but that could be a function of the volume of the texts. The god of the sea appeared in names, as well as his opponent Baal and the creator El (Gröndahl 1967: 78–85). A continuity between Ebla and Ugarit is that both conducted worship of the kings' ancestors (Xella 1988: 354–8).

Hurrian influence seems to have been important at Ugarit, and this may have colored some of the practices. The centrality of the king as a religious actor blotted out the memory of the acts of others, and the cult of ancestors was clearest for kings and less clear for lower-class people, although it probably existed among them too (Wyatt 2007: 62–6).

The city of Ugarit succumbed to the movements of the Sea Peoples, which ended the international age around 1200 BCE, but there were certainly some

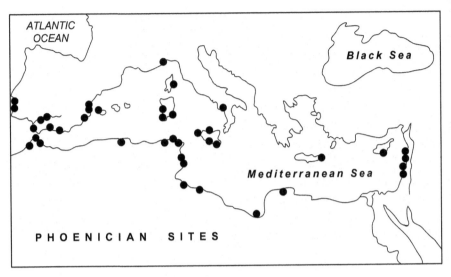

MAP 14.1. Phoenician sites in the Mediterranean.

cultural continuities in Syria and Lebanon. The Ugaritic writing system ceased to be used, but somehow the basic idea of it, and the order of the signs, was remembered, to emerge after 1000 BCE in a new script, the Phoenician. This script was a variation on Egyptian signs used by workmen in the Sinai Peninsula in the second millennium, simplified and endowed only with phonetic, not logographic, value. The signs stood only for sounds, not for whole words or ideas. Some of the signs might owe something to classical cuneiform and some to Ugaritic cuneiform, but they allowed the writing of any language that conveyed meaning mostly in consonants, as the Semitic languages did.

The term "Phoenician" was what the Greeks called the coastal peoples; they would have referred to themselves as citizens of particular cities, Tyre, Sidon, and Byblos, for there was no single Phoenician state. The Greeks knew the Phoenicians as purveyors among other things of a much-valued purple dye that they got from mollusks that grew on their coasts; it was called *phoenix* in Greek, and so its traders were labeled. This term may echo the Egyptian term for a people of the area, the *Fnḥw*. Phoenicians spoke a language related to Ugaritic and were engaged in the sea trade in which their ancestors had thrived, moving goods around the eastern Mediterranean and into the West. They brought more than dyes. They also brought some new ideas that caught on with those with whom they traded. The simple writing system was one, and the Greeks borrowed it, using some of the signs they did not need for the vowels that were significant in their language, creating a system that did try to represent every sound that made a difference in meaning with its own sign, a true alphabet.

It has also been argued that Phoenicians spread with them economic complexity that may not have been there before, including pricing products in gold and silver. Because the areas they visited had been illiterate before them, it is hard to judge whether this really was an innovation, but it may have been. Whether they brought Ancient Near Eastern wisdom also remains doubtful (Brown 1981).

In the course of their travels, we know from shipwrecks that they moved wine and oils and ingots of tin, a key ingredient in making copper into the tougher metal of bronze. In some places, iron smelting became more important after 1000 BCE, maybe because tin was harder to obtain.

Another aspect of Phoenician travel was planting colonies. Some were only meant to be temporary trade emporia, built on islands off the coasts or on easily defensible peninsulas, like Cadiz in southern Spain, one of the Phoenicians' more distant settlements. In other places, Phoenicians were less worried that they would be attacked, and they may have involved themselves in the production of local products that might be of interest back in the central part of the Near East. This colonial expansion, whether contemplated as long-term settlements or temporary trading posts, included export of aspects of Phoenician religion, and because these areas visited were also dependent on rainfall agriculture, the Phoenician gods seemed relevant there, too.

The gods previously honored continued to be important, perhaps especially a form of Baal called Melqart "King of the City." The word "king" for a god went back in the region all the way to Ebla sources (Pomponio and Xella 1997: 458–65).

Gauging the popularity of a god from inscriptions is difficult, but it is known that Melqart was popular, along with other gods not otherwise known. Eshmun was a god of healing on the Phoenician coast, and a god like Pmy (we do not know its vowels because of the Phoenician script!) might come from foreigners the Phoenicians visited because it was found only in the western Mediterranean (Benz 1972: 233–5, 391–2).

Architecture of temples in the first millennium appears to have developed toward structures with more public access than previously. This may reflect a trend toward making religious observance more accessible and understandable to common people (Oggiano 2006), a trend we definitely see in the Deuteronomic writings in Israel as well.

The aspect of Phoenician religion that proved the most controversial in the ancient world and subsequently was the custom of child sacrifice. Hebrew thinkers found it repulsive, and yet its continued attractiveness inspired the prophets to oppose it down the ages, and they labeled "passing a child to Melqart" as particularly evil, even done in the valley running beside the hill of Jerusalem (Leviticus 18:21, Jeremiah 32:35, 2 Kings 23:10, Micah 6:7).

The ideology behind child sacrifice was that in a time of high infant mortality, if parents voluntary gave up the first child to the gods, they might make sure that at least some of the rest would live to adulthood. Phoenicians never wrote about these matters, and so we may be merely guessing about what they thought. However, the persistent criticism of neighbors and the archaeological evidence from their most famous colony, Carthage, "New City" in what is now Tunisia in North Africa, demonstrates the practice continued into the late period of Phoenician culture. The custom lasted at least until Carthage's destruction by the Romans in 146 BCE, and Phoenician culture and language continued beyond that (Harden 1962: 74–5; Tubb 1998: 140–6). Apparently not every family felt compelled to human sacrifice, or there would be many more graves of infants in urns at Phoenician sites.

In this last period when Carthage was the great enemy of Rome, there is little information from Carthage itself, and Phoenician literature has disappeared on the perishable materials on which it was written, except for a few paltry royal and tomb inscriptions. The latter are short but plentiful, and their large number argues that Phoenicians may have enjoyed a high literacy rate. The most detailed descriptions of what Phoenicians did came from their enemies, who saw them as the antithesis of everything good and just and Roman, as in Titus Livy books 21–30 on the two Punic or Phoenician wars (Radice 1965: 16).

One other aspect of Phoenician thought seems important, and that is their feeling that their gods definitely were not associated only with one place. The King of the City could be found wherever there was a city, and the lady Tanit was known in the west and felt to be the same as Astarte in the east (Harden 1962: 87–9). Astarte was the same as Ishtar of Mesopotamia, and the goddess retained a celestial aspect, equated with the planet Venus (Wyatt 1999: 111–12). This mobility and adaptability of the Phoenicians was useful in their travels, but it may have contrasted with earlier ways of thinking, where the gods of a place were relevant only to that place, as in the story about the deportees to northern Israel being concerned to worship the local god (2 Kings 17:24–8).

15

GREECE, ETRURIA, ROME, AND
CONVEYING TRADITIONS

Religion was among [Napoleon's] favorite topics. It was his vague religiosity, perhaps a lingering attachment to childhood beliefs, which made him recoil from the cold materialism of Berthollet and attracted him to the more open-minded Monge. Also, religion had such obvious political usefulness!
— J. Christopher Herold, *Bonaparte in Egypt*, 1962, 53

They spoke in a pidgin language, so nuances were not ascertainable, but the guys kneeling on the Italian shore were captivated by what the foreigners were doing. They had bought, among other things, a sheep, and they were clearly intending to cook it, eat it, and share it with their trading partners in celebration of this so far successful voyage. The foreigners' wooden ship was skillfully anchored to a big rock onshore, and the wine they had bought they also shared generously.

They slaughtered the sheep near the fire, but then one of them cut a gash in the sheep's belly and thrust his hand in, drawing out the liver, which he then closely studied. The Italians asked him what he was doing, and he seemed to say that he was seeking there the will of the gods. The Italians looked at each other as if he were daft, but they were silent and tried to be respectful.

The foreigner turned to his fellows and said something the Italians understood to mean there would be fair winds tomorrow and it would be propitious to sail. Later during the meal, one of them asked the liver-man how he learned things from the liver, and the man produced from his pack a tiny clay model of a sheep's liver, with things written on it, and tried to explain the variety of answers you might get to questions. The Italian was impressed and wanted to learn more, but the language barrier impeded that.

Next morning did dawn fair, and as the foreigners took their leave, the liver-man thrust the liver model into the hand of the previous night's inquisitive Italian. The Italian tried to make him understand such was too great a gift. The foreigner refused to take it back, indicating he had more, and also saying something the Italian understood to mean that all people should be able to ask questions of the gods and get answers.

* * *

This may have been how the Etruscans began examining livers for omens and making teaching models of them in the style of the Ancient Near East (Falchetti and Romualdi 2001: 34).

The Ancient Near Eastern religions and the people who cared about them lived in a wider world, which they had an impact on through trade, arms, and the force of ideas. The latter is the hardest to document and to understand, for although a physical contact may be established with foreign cultures, the degree and nature of interaction cannot necessarily be established.

The premier example of such interaction which had profound and long-lasting influence on the Ancient Near East was the impact of Hellenism. By Hellenism we mean the culture of the Greeks as conveyed by the Macedonians before and after the conquests of Alexander the Great in the 330s BCE. There were interactions earlier, as one can see in the case of the Philistines, who appeared as the key opponents of the Israelites in their early history, but who archaeologically had affinities with peoples from the Aegean. The port of Dor on the Israelite coast was a site of interaction of Greeks and Western Asians. The movement of ideas from the Ancient Near East is clear at least with writing techniques and perhaps with the increasing complexity of a multi-money economy that the Phoenicians may have introduced (Brown 1981). Others have credited the Greeks themselves with elaborating both monetary and intellectual complexity as a result of coined money (Seaford 2004). In religion, however, the later Greeks could not see clearly how the impact might have come about, although they were quick to suggest equations between their traditional gods and those of the Ancient Near East. The underlying assumption, as perhaps of all polytheisms, may have been that the nature of the gods was similar everywhere, but cultures had different names for the gods and might divide up the divine attributes differently, not affecting the basic structure of how people interacted with the gods.

In the centuries after Alexander's death in 323 BCE most of the Ancient Near East was ruled by Greek-speaking rulers, and if not directly by such people, then by local despots who aspired to some of the finer things in Greek culture. These might include gymnasia, where elites could exercise together, and theaters, where almost everyone could come together to watch civic-sponsored spectacles that could include the plays that had become classics back on the Greek mainland. Hellenism might even include the structures, although never the substance, of Greek democratic assemblies. These latter sometimes tapped into local traditions of representative government, but their power was rarely more than local, and kings kept them well under control and allowed them little leeway.

Alexander and his successors sometimes founded new cities that were near older ones, and they were competitors for the commerce of the old cities. They tended to be laid out in rectangles and included spaces for markets, baths, and sometimes theaters, and they were frequently peopled by Greek-speaking veterans. These cities were not necessarily alien implantations, however, because the veterans married local girls, and the culture of the cities of the east may have continued to be bilingual.

In southern Iraq, we can trace this kind of Hellenization through cuneiform tablets, which continued to be produced both in Sumerian, a language already dead for millennia, and in Akkadian, which was certainly no longer spoken as anyone's first language but continued to be studied. We see in these records that people sometimes were given Greek names, perhaps to endear themselves to Greek-speaking rulers, but their children did not necessarily also have Greek names (Doty 1988). There was some waffling in the commitment to what was Greek, and the impact of Greek ideas may have been superficial (Momigliano 1975). Practically the assimilation of Greek ideas could affect even cuneiform astronomy, but it did not end any of the Ancient Near Eastern intellectual traditions (Scurlock and Al-Rawi 2006).

In the other direction, we can see the impact of the Ancient Near East in Greece. The whole idea of having a genealogy of gods, which was important as early as Hesiod, who wrote in central Greece in the 700s BCE, may have come from the east, as well as some of the ideas about water as the essence of the earliest beings. The high god, Zeus, a god of thunder corresponded to Baal on the Syrian coast. The idea of codifying laws may have owed something to the Ancient Near East, although the practices codified were rooted in local experience. An early law code was found at Gortyn in Crete inscribed around 450 BCE; its theological trappings were not so detailed as in the Ancient Near East, consisting only of the invocation of "Gods!" at the beginning (Willetts 1967: 39). More concretely, the study of the motions of the planets and stars permeated Greek thought, and the records from back to 747 BCE were available to the Greek-writing scholar Ptolemy, who was probably of Egyptian descent (Barker 1996).

There is a possibility that views of the netherworld were affected by Ancient Near Eastern ideas, but the mechanism for contact is not clear. It probably was not through traveling scholars (Röllig 2001: 314). The Greek heroes might owe something to the reverence for the benevolent ancestors that was cultivated early and late in the western part of the Near East (Merlo and Xella 2001: 287–8).

The use of Greek as a literary language across the Ancient Near East was a means of passing on the ideas of the various cultures in all directions. We have several compositions at least partly preserved in Greek that were the efforts of people from the Near East to convince the Greek readers that their Ancient Near Eastern cultures had value and ought to be studied for themselves.

The earliest of these efforts in Greek may be that of the Phoenician priest Sanchunyatan, imperfectly preserved in the writings of the church historian Eusebius. These show Phoenicians as interested in the rain god and revering his mountain home. Manetho wrote his history of Egypt in the third century BCE and gave a chronological framework for the whole (Waddell 1940).

Somewhat later was Berossus of Babylon, again purportedly a priest whose work Christian authors preserved. He wanted to emphasize the antiquity of his culture and its architectural monuments (Verbrugghe and Wickersham 1996).

Finally and most well known of this genre was Josephus, a first-century Jew writing for Romans but still in Greek, who was trying to show how philosophically deep his own tradition was and how much there was to learn from the Jewish tradition. He gave an account of many of the stories about Abraham and later Israelite leaders that we read in the Bible and had access to sources, since lost, about the period after the close of the canon around 200 BCE.

The Ancient Near Easterners had reason to try to explain themselves in Greek to the Greek-dominated world. The easterners could always boast of greater age and perhaps wisdom, but their wisdom was made to correspond to what Greeks thought ancient tradition should be.

Earlier there were interactions in religion, but the dates and nature of them are hard to pin down. The figure of Aphrodite, representing sexual joy as a woman, had something to do with the figure of Ishtar and Astarte, and it may have come to the Greeks through the Phoenicians. Aspects of her worship like her being depicted sometimes as a man but mostly as a woman and her quality as a warrior goddess may have derived from the older tradition (Burkert 1985: 152–6).

Athena, the goddess connected with Athens, has been suggested as coming somehow from Egypt and the name from Neith, a goddess of the night there (Bernal 1987), but the evidence is slight. More interesting is that her unexplained epithet of Pallas, always standing before the name, was Semitic *ba'alat*, "Lady of." Connection to shooting arrows may bind the "most Greek" god Apollo to Rashap, or Reshef, the West Semitic god of plague who also shot arrows (Burkert 1985: 139 n. 4, but see also 140, Pallas as a man's name; 143, 145).

The role of Demeter, the earth mother, representing grain, was very old in Greece, but her interaction with "the girl," Persephone, who was a symbol of fertility who died and had to be brought back, echoes Near Eastern stories about dying and rising gods, including the Hittite story of Telepinu and the story of Ishtar visiting the netherworld. Neither Telepinu nor Ishtar was actually retained in the netherworld, but "the girl" became an underworld goddess and remained married to her rapist, Hades, the underworld personified. The idea that gods could die and then rise again prepared the way for Christian views.

The Demeter story was also the focus of secret cults to which people had to be initiated, the mysteries, and this aspect seems not to have Near Eastern sources (Burkert 1985: 159–61). There is, nonetheless, the apparently unrelated mystery of the "mouth and tongue," known in a Middle Babylonian text; these parts of a god were supposed to become possessions of the initiate (Oppenheim 1966).

The origins of Dionysius, god of wine and ecstasy, were obscure. Although probably deriving some characteristics from Anatolia, particularly Phrygia, the southeastern region of Turkey, there may have been other influences as well. The alternate name, Bacchus, equally unexplained, may have something to do with the Semitic root for "weeping," *bky*, and the weeping for the missing Dionysius may derive from people like the women of Israel whom the prophet Ezekiel criticized for mourning for Tammuz (8: 14). The prophet must have observed this practice around 600 BCE; it recalled the death of the goddess Ishtar's husband, who had to replace her in the netherworld if there was to be any fertility during the year in southern Iraq. Alternatively, the prominence of Greek interest in the Egyptian god of the underworld, Osiris, may have brought Dionysius to his residence in the underworld (Burkert 1985: 161–7). Osiris was not connected to wine and intoxication, but drunken Syrian wakes for the dead may have influenced those characteristics (Lewis 1989: 93–4). The god of crafts and smithing, Hephaistos, was non-Greek, hailing from the island of Lemnos, off the Turkish coast, and the Greeks associated the people from there with Etruscans, the pre-Roman residents of the region of Italy just north of Rome. Smiths were important in the times when bronze was the most useful metal and remained so when iron, somewhat easier to work, came in (Burkert 1985: 167–8). The Ugaritic god Kothar-wa-Ḥasis, "ready and smart," may have been a model for some of his characteristics.

Other Greek gods, such as Hecate, a goddess of roads and crossroads, also had Near Eastern roots; she may have come from Asia Minor. Prometheus as a human-loving trickster god who tricked the others to steal fire may have owed something to Enki's concern for humans at the time of the flood. The idea that the sun rode in a chariot can be paralleled in Egypt but also in other Indo-European traditions. The mourning for Adonis reflected that for Tammuz, but the name of the god, from Semitic *Adon*, "lord," was not used in similar cultic acts (Burkert 1985: 171, 175, 177).

Greeks in antiquity were never politically united until Alexander's father Philip forced them to cohere, but they constituted a cultural unity even though their geography and organization in city-states led to their having various sets of gods in different cities. The great gods were revered everywhere, and some of them were influenced by developments further east. We cannot say that this means that Ancient Near Eastern religions lived on in Greece, but some peculiar facets of some gods and practices may have had their lives extended through translation into Greek (Ribichini, Rocchi, and Xella 2001).

ETRUSCANS TEACH AND HIDE

The Greeks thought that the people of Italy just north of Rome had come from remnants of the Trojans in the Trojan War. Although the Etruscan language was not related to any other, it is possible that examples of it were found in Anatolia, perhaps substantiating the idea of Trojan origins. The major factor in the takeoff of Etruscan art and letters was the influence of the Greeks, who had established colonies in Italy in the 700s, particularly the island colony of Pithekoussai, which was a major conduit for Greek ideas, probably including the alphabet. This borrowing means that we can read the letters that the Etruscans used, but apart from short formulaic inscriptions, we cannot translate Etruscan well. The Etruscans also had contact with the Phoenicians, and especially the Carthaginians across the Mediterranean (Bonfante 1986: 66–70, 76–84). The Etruscan-Phoenician bilingual on gold tablets from Pyrgi seems to be a burial inscription where the buried person was assumed to become a god, meaning a revered ancestor (Knoppers 1992: 106, 114–20).

The Etruscans were famous for their omens, and this aspect of their knowledge may have been connected with the Ancient Near East. They interpreted observed omens of birds, which was even called the "Etruscan teaching" by the Romans; they also observed the innards of sacrificed animals (Bonfante 1986: 233, 247–8). A liver model shows that they studied that flexible little organ, just as the Mesopotamians had. Like the Ancient Near Easterners, the Etruscans worried that everything could be a sign of the gods' wills, but they were not concerned as the Greeks were with an overarching fate that would make the omens absolutely unalterable (Pallottino 1955: 162, 166–7). The gods they honored could usually be equated with members of the Greek and then with the Roman pantheon (Falchetti and Romualdi 2001: 30–1, 33–4), and yet depictions in art showed that sometimes the characteristics of the gods were slightly different in Etruscan eyes.

The Etruscans taught the Romans something of the culture of the Ancient Near East in the form of the alphabet, and they probably conveyed some of the assumptions about the world being full of omens that wise persons could interpret. Because of the obscurity of their language and because of the chance of archaeology that we have found only Etruscan tombs and not houses, they have kept some of their influence to themselves. It may be that some of the differences in their depictions of gods derived from a desire not to explain everything that was known about the gods, making their religious approach something of a mystery religion, meaning one into which people had to be initiated to understand the full meaning. Their elaborate tombs and their sculptures show that the Etruscans were concerned to ensure their dead relatives a safe passage into the life beyond, conceived as a pleasant continuation of the best things in this life, somewhat like the Egyptians' view of the West.

ROME CAPTIVATED BY THE EAST

The poet Horace wrote that politically Rome may have conquered the east in the first two centuries BCE, but culturally it actually had found itself made captive by the East, and particularly the Greeks; "Captive Greece," he said, "captured her fierce captor and brought the arts into uncultured Latium" (Letter II, 1, 156). Although Roman armies were successful in incorporating Ancient Near Eastern kingdoms into their imperial system, Roman intellectuals looked to eastern models in many matters. Most leaders actually spoke Greek even in their homes because it was seen as a classier language than Latin.

The Greek influence conveyed eastern religious ideas to Rome. It makes sense that as the scope of Roman power increased even as early as the 400s BCE, there would have been more interest in things eastern. A key event was the bringing to Rome of the stone that represented the Great Mother in Phrygia in southern Turkey in 205 BCE. This was a piece of rock small enough to be carried by a single person; the leading general of the day was sent by the Roman authorities to usher it into Rome (Lewis and Reinhold 1966 i: 475–6, from Livy xxiv: 10–14). When the empire stretched even to Egypt, the interest in the goddess Isis and other Egyptian gods intensified, much to the disgust of the old-timers in Rome (Lewis and Reinhold 1966 ii: 574, with texts from the 200s CE).

However, it is frequently hard to judge whether Romans really borrowed aspects of religion from the Ancient Near East. This lack of clarity sometimes derived from the mediation of the Greeks. An example is the deification of kings; this was a spotty matter in most of the Ancient Near East, except Egypt. But in Egypt there seems to have been a decline in respect for actual kings in the first millennium, even though kings continued to have themselves depicted as divine. Alexander, who delighted in foreign ideas while pushing his own brand of Greek ones, had himself shown as a god, and many Hellenistic rulers followed suit. After the civil wars when the Romans came to concentrate power in the hands of a single person with the victory of Octavian around 27 BCE, the way was open to appropriate some trappings of divine kingship (Chaniotis 2003).

Christianity was just one of the eastern mystery religions that flooded the Roman religious marketplace in the first centuries of our era. Mithra, an Indo-Iranian god of war who appealed to soldiers, had a following, as did Isis, the Egyptian mother goddess. Roman traditionalists did not find these incursions appealing and persecuted not only Christians but others practicing what they saw as dangerous foreign cults. In this Rome accepted the change that had come to polytheism by asserting there were right and wrong gods and ways to worship them, an idea that had not been common in the Ancient Near East before the rise of monotheism. Perhaps there had not been any society so buffeted by outside influences as Rome after it had achieved its control of the Mediterranean. Conservatives saw the erosion of the old religion as undermining Roman values, the same argument monotheists had made since Ezra. The grip of the old ways was definitely felt to be loosening in the late Republic of the first century BCE (Lewis and Reinhold 1966 i: 477–8).

The influence of the East was, however, being forgotten, perhaps along with the decay of the living traditions of the Ancient Near East. Only in astronomy and astrology did Greeks and Romans remember that the Chaldeans, using the name of a prominent tribe to stand for the Babylonians, had amassed the data on the movements of stars and planets.

The ends of the Ancient Near Eastern literate traditions cannot be precisely dated, but the latest cuneiform tablet was an astronomical text dated from 74 CE. At that time, only a few families were still preserving the tradition in the old southern city of Uruk, where we first found cuneiform writing. The Egyptian evidence lasted longer and was more diffuse. Coptic writing, using Greek letters supplemented with others to stand for late Egyptian sounds, began to appear around 400 CE, although there might still have been some priests who could read hieroglyphics. The end of the writing traditions did not necessarily mean that other religious practices abruptly halted. The cities in which Mesopotamian traditions were based may have continued with little interruption through the Muslim conquest of the mid 600s CE and beyond, and yet Islam did make inroads in Iraq as it did in Egypt and Syria.

Later witnesses wrote, in the new languages, that in the 800s CE women of the Sabaeans were still roaming the Syrian hills near the city of Harran mourning for the dying and rising god Tammuz; Sabaeans were a cult sometimes tolerated by Muslim rulers but eventually suppressed (Carra de Vaux 1974). Tammuz still gives his name to the month of July in some of the languages of the modern Middle East, but such linguistic survivals do not represent any memory of earlier ways.

16

THE DEAD HAND OF THE PAST
AND THE LIVING GOD

To write the history of a religion, it is necessary firstly to have believed it (otherwise we should not be able to understand how it has charmed and satisfied the human conscience); in the second place, to believe it no longer in an absolute manner, for absolute faith is incompatible with sincere history.

– Ernest Renan, *Vie de Jesus*, 107

The intense young man with the beautiful eyelashes sat bent over the copies of the ancient Egyptian writing, playing with different combinations of signs along with the few that could already be recognized because of their appearance in royal names on the Rosetta Stone. The Rosetta Stone did not explain much, however, and he still had to work to understand the mass of signs and what was being said in every new inscription that reached him in his rural retreat.

He was in retreat because he was a person of whom the new government was suspicious, for he had supported the Revolution, and worse, Napoleon, hoping, he had told friends, for a new day without the horrible constraints of the old Catholic faith with its myriad rules. He had been one of those modern young men who thought people could be reinvented, made better, by casting off tradition and sharing the achievements of the modern age. Especially he hoped for the demise of the priesthood and its hold on education in France. The nation had been held back for so long by the mindless dictates of the priests that only radical Republicanism and then the Empire had seemed to offer a way out.

Now, against his hopes, the British and the Germans had thrown the emperor out definitively and brought back those idiot Bourbons. He had lost his job because he was politically unreliable. His brother still hung on and supported him, at least.

But wait, was this new inscription not to be read "The god Thoth has given birth" as the name Tutmosis seemed to mean? It was worth a try.

* * *

Jean-François Champollion in 1822 CE, in spite of himself, discovered a new world of gods hitherto known only indistinctly through the impressions of the Greeks, and he opened up the era of decipherment that made possible the work of hundreds of scholars in unearthing the ideas of the Ancient Near East (Adkins and Adkins 2000).

How we think about the religions of the Ancient Near East is affected by how we feel about our contemporary traditions. For some of us, these ways of thinking and doing seem to be the residue of superstition and lack of rational thought that people still detect among our own traditions. If the ancient traditions of the Near East still existed in a form other than mere echoes, perhaps we would find ourselves rebelling daily against them. Notions of lucky and unlucky days would seem silly to us, although we must admit that some of us do still look at horoscopes, more for amusement than religious guidance.

The Ancient Near Eastern traditions were concrete ways of looking at the universe and seeing it as actively engaged in our daily living and really concerned with our health and well-being. Our living traditions argue that this is the stance of the one God, and yet the problem of evil persists and has not ever been solved. The ancient traditions do live on as ways of thinking about powers higher than ourselves guiding us in our lives whether in Judaism, Christianity, Islam, or later formulations. Certainly the idea of monotheism itself comes from these ancient sources and has permeated the modern world.

Feelings about religion in modern society are more in flux than at any time in the past five hundred years, beginning from the time of the discovery of the New World and the Protestant Reformation. Ancient traditions from the Far East and elsewhere offer themselves in the marketplace of ideas, and many in the West look to them as ways of thinking about religion that seem less oppressive than home-grown traditions. Our ease of communication makes such ideas accessible, along with more recently founded alternative religions which may borrow from various cultures.

The religions of the Ancient Near East, at least late Egyptian religion in its Gnostic form, have been used as critical mirrors to the dominant Christian traditions (Pagels 1979). Although such exercises may be attractive guesses at what might have been, this sort of alternative history has in my view only a limited benefit in our current situation. I would not argue that any of the Ancient Near Eastern traditions is particularly helpful in current spiritual quests. They are rather signposts for important changes in human thought, which we will inevitably see from our own perspectives. They cannot be expected to appeal directly to us because our situations are very different from those of the ancients.

In this essay, we have been walking through a world of great strangeness, and we may be astonished at the differences, but the continuities in what humans feel and do may in the end be stronger despite technological advances. We still mourn people who die, and we still know that we shall all die one day too, even if our consumer culture refuses to take death into account.

The first fact to stress is that the Ancient Near Eastern cultures had no word for religion. This means that the things we have been examining did not represent an ancient category. We have chosen to look at matters that seemed to us to be analogous to what we find religious. The Latin term *religio* might come from a word for "binding," from Latin *religāre* and thus refer to traditions that people are bound to follow, or it might come from a word for "recounting," from *relegĕre* "to recover, read over, or recount" and thus mean "things people needed to recite." At any rate, the term came in as a general word for religious behavior only in the first millennium CE, and its modern sense of traditions we might choose among is even newer (Smith 1964: 23–6).

There are words that embody some important aspects of what we mean by religion in the Ancient Near Eastern languages. Sumerian ŠU-LU Ḫ-Ḫ-A means "hand washing" and was used to mean more than that, coming to represent the proper rites people might perform for the gods. The Akkadians borrowed the word but still kept it very specific (Oppenheim 1992 Š 2: 260–1). Although unrelated, the Hebrew word ʿavodah, meaning "work," came to mean in some contexts "worship," but it, too, does not seem so general as our term. In fact, the modern Hebrew word for religion, *dāt*, actually comes from Persian, where it might first mean "law," and then by extension "tradition" (Koehler and Baumgartner 1994–2000: I: 234).

We do not need words for a sphere of activity until it becomes necessary to question its correctness, and in late Hebrew the term for heresies was ʿavodah zarah "strange or foreign work," a phrase that was used as the name of a section of the Mishnah, the third-century book of Jewish teaching. Strange work was what others did; the rabbis were advising the work or worship of God.

Another issue that may be more important than the lack of a word for religion is the issue of belief. There were words in the Ancient Near Eastern languages for thinking that something was true and affirming that it was true. These words are frequently translated with words for belief and believing, and yet their force was not what it has become. The idea that proper religious behavior involved believing something was foreign to the Ancient Near East.

We can see how this worked by looking at the Akkadian word for "to believe," *qâpu*. It means "to give credence to," but it does not seem to have been applied in religious situations. Instead there were simple assertions such as "they do not believe that the king will come" in a Neo-Assyrian letter. The term also meant to entrust something to someone, and gods could do that to kings; it also meant to make a kind of loan and to guarantee loans (Oppenheim 1982 Q: 93–8).

In Hebrew the root *'mn* is translated as "to believe," but again in most instances, it seems to mean "to think someone or something is reliable," not necessarily to assert something about God. For example in Genesis 15:6, having received Yahweh's promise of a child, Abram "believed the Lord . . . ," presumably that the prediction would come to pass. In Exodus 14:31, the people of Israel, having witnessed the saving acts of Yahweh in extracting them from Egypt "believed in the Lord and in his servant Moses," meaning they found them trustworthy. Even in the late text Jonah 3:5, "the people of Nineveh believed God," that is, they thought what had been predicted would happen, and their city would be destroyed.

Closer to the later sense is 2 Chronicles 20:20, dated perhaps around 300 BCE, when the norms of monotheism had definitely taken hold in Israel. In connection with the reforms of Jehoshaphat, the narrator said that the Levites, the priestly tribe, were exhorted by the king, "Believe in the Lord your God, and you will be established; believe his prophets, and you will succeed." Isaiah 7:9b, from the eighth-century prophet, argued, after an oracle about the coming defeat of an enemy, "If you will not believe, surely you shall not be established." This does tend to sound like the later use of "belief." God wanted the king simply to think what had been predicted would happen, and then it would, but this may edge toward asserting the existence of God. At any rate, the term is sparsely used in the Hebrew Bible, and although logically we can see that it might have become more important in later texts, belief was certainly not an emphasis (Gladigow 1995: 22; Wildberger 1971: 192–3).

The idea that merely by believing, people did something that God wanted was not a usual one, but it came in toward the end of the period, perhaps along with the assertions of a book like Daniel, parts of which can be dated to the Maccabean rebellion around 164 BCE. The author pushed the idea that all would be well among those who merely bided their time and maintained their traditions. This was the response of politically disenfranchised people who did not feel that they could affect how even their own culture went, but they could remain faithful and affirm that "those who are wise shall understand" (Daniel 12:10b). The people in fact might not have to do anything because

God would bring about salvation: "But go your way till the end; and you shall rest, and shall stand in your allotted place at the end of days" (12:13). This feeling that witnessing was all a person could do was a theme in the slightly later books of Maccabees and was linked with valuing martyrdom. Allowing oneself to be killed for right belief only came about as the Jewish tradition embraced the idea that there would be reward and punishment after death (Shepkaru 2006).

This new idea about death became dominant between 250 BCE, when Ecclesiastes decisively rejected it, saying that the same fate would come to the wise person and to the fool, and 100 BCE when the Wisdom of Solomon asserted it as a general principle. This was an idea championed by the Jewish group called the Pharisees, and rejected by the Sadducees, who, however, were eliminated as an intellectual force with the destruction of the Second Temple by the Romans in 70 CE. Political powerlessness was the order of the day for Jews, and religious people saw that they might not be able even to practice their own private religious customs if the state intervened. They could believe the right things, however, and they came to see statements of Yahweh's power in the Hebrew Bible as statements of beliefs, indeed creeds, to use the Christian term. One was Deuteronomy 6:4: "Hear, O Israel: The Lord our God is one Lord; and you shall love the Lord your God with all your heart and with all your soul, and with all your might."

This development in thinking about religion arose partly because monotheism posed the question of getting religion wrong, although polytheisms, too, could become more rigid if they felt themselves threatened with change (Gladigow 1995: 25). The possibility of getting religion wrong by the late first millennium was a well established alternative to the freewheeling open-ended polytheism that had dominated earlier human thought. Jews were saying that most people had it wrong and therefore trusted in the wrong gods, who in fact did not even exist. The Jews trusted in the true God and could argue that He was worthy of trust. With monotheism came the possibility of persecuting people who were wrong, for their own good. When Jews were a persecuted minority, such an option was only theoretical, except for the forced conversions of Idumaeans from southeast of Israel in the first century BCE by the Maccabean leaders (Josephus, *Antiquities* 13.9.1). When Christianity became first a tolerated and then a state religion of Rome, however, persecution became not only a possibility but even a theological necessity because the persistence of wrong belief might be seen to threaten the salvation even of right believers. All of this was an offshoot of Ancient Near Eastern religions.

Now we will try to see how our information about the Near East might relate to ideas about religion in general. From within the field, the still dominant way of thinking about the history of religions is Thorkild Jacobsen's view, formulated as early as 1946, that objects of religious veneration derived from commodities that were important in early economic life (1946, 1976). He connected this view to Rudolf Otto's suggestion that religion came from numinous experience, the feeling of the uncanny or holy (1923). What organized religion was trying to do, in Otto's view, was to crystallize and recreate that sort of feeling. Otto's idea was rooted in the study of Roman religion, and particularly used the term *numen*, meaning "spirit" of any rank or sort, as a key inspirer of religious feeling. This approach has been questioned by students of Roman religion, who doubt whether Otto was right to speak of "the holy" as really equivalent to Roman *sacer*, and particularly to stress the idea of the contrast between sacred and profane. This might not be a universal and might not even stretch back to Roman times, but it might be something more recent and thus irrelevant to ancient thinking (Sabbatucci 1994).

In modern experience, too, it is not obvious that religious acts are really trying to induce feelings of the uncanny in worshipers. The so-called mountaintop experiences may happen in religious contexts and be endowed with religious meaning, or they may not. Furthermore, can we really say that all, most, or most significant religious acts are designed to induce or reproduce such feelings? In premodern societies, they must have been part of the daily texture of experience, and no particular feeling or fireworks were to be expected; sacrifice or omen taking were ways of communicating with the gods, and that could be helpful for the individual. It does not follow, however, that the individual wanted to feel anything besides a general assurance that a person was acting in accord with the gods' wishes. The great gods, at least in historic periods, were not limited to a single phenomenon as their areas of power (Ringgren 1973: 5).

In the western part of the Ancient Near East, there were ecstatics and prophets who were felt to be more in touch with the god or gods than ordinary people, but there was no desire on the part of anyone to emulate them or to practice a discipline that might lead to similar experience. There may have been mystics, people more in touch with the divine, in all societies, but it does not follow that their experiences were viewed as able to be imitated or that they dictated a cultural style. The exception may be in Ancient Israel, not that we know much about the discipline of becoming a prophet, but the argument has frequently been made that the prophets revolutionized Israel's religion. Their words, uncomfortable to those in power, were cherished and copied by those not in power, and when their reading of the precarious political situation of the kingdoms of Israel proved correct, the authority imputed to their words grew. By the time Deuteronomy was composed, before 622 BCE, the pious thinkers saw prophets as much more important for doing what God wanted than any other authority, including the priesthood. Again, however, it is unlikely that even the Deuteronomists wanted people to become prophets in imitation of the earlier ones. The word of the Lord had been proclaimed in the past, and for the Deuteronomists, the problem was to do it. And so we see an apparent legalism in their extensive stipulations.

The basis for Jacobsen's idea of what religion was may thus be open to question, but this might not invalidate his reading of the ancient texts. Jacobsen argued that there was a progression among the best thinkers and writers in Mesopotamia from an interest in the fourth millennium BCE in the gods as embodiments of economically important products. He thought that Tammuz represented the date and the date palm itself, and Inanna, Akkadian Ishtar, was the storehouse that made possible the preservation of the date. Jacobsen was certainly correct that in the swamplands of southern Iraq both the date and the storehouse were crucial for sustaining life, but this was also true after the fourth millennium.

Jacobsen's next stage emphasized the image of gods as royalty. He thought the rise of city-states led by kings created the context in which thinkers saw their gods not as elemental natural and economic forces but as great kings with courts who ruled the universe. He thought this sort of organization must have arisen in the third millennium BCE, when city-states became important.

The next stage was to see the gods as careful and attentive shepherds, who would take care of their human flock. Jacobsen considered this a hallmark of the second millennium BCE and looked to Hammurabi's code as a sign of this view of what the gods wanted. Human kings imitated the gods in expressing those concerns.

Jacobsen's interest waned in the first millennium BCE, and he thought that the major images of the gods continued but were not significantly elaborated by the Mesopotamians. He was not interested in the Axial Age developments because the Mesopotamians were not significant participants in those movements.

Jacobsen's formulations were based on his theory of development and were founded on texts copied in the Old Babylonian Period. Even his texts about Tammuz and Inanna, the personifications of the date and the storehouse, came from that period, but he argued they reflected earlier realities. He also recognized that all of his images persisted through time.

Although influential, Jacobsen's views do not seem particularly informative. They also partake of a belief in progress and development that needs to be proven rather than assumed. Everyone who looks at the ancient material sees that there was change over time, but it is not evident that it was moving along the lines Jacobsen suggested or even that it was moving in any one direction. It was an old assumption that animism, the idea that every thing had a spirit that might be placated or offended, was the basis of polytheism, with some things becoming more prominent than others for arbitrary, sometimes environmental, reasons. Yet we cannot be sure that this was necessarily a stage through which every culture passed, or that we have access in the cuneiform texts from the early second millennium BCE to such developments.

For example, I am not sure that this idea helps explain the prominence of the god Assur in northern Iraq. Here we have, as we have noted, an instance of a large rock being thought of as a god, and then, maybe for political reasons, it became the god of the city, gave the god's name to the city, and assumed the human characteristics of a reigning king (Lambert 1983). We could argue that in northern Iraq, rain was always more important for the success of agriculture than any particular rock, and yet the Akkadian god Adad and the Hurrian weather-god Teshub, although prominent, were never dominant in the region of Assur. The success of Assur in the long term was not predictable, and political factors were important.

Beyond Otto's and Jacobsen's views are others that have been influential in thinking about religions, but they all come from the early part of the twentieth century. One of the early views is that of the French sociologist Emile Durkheim, who wished to see in societies manifestations of human needs for particular functions. Religions for him were ways to build solidarity and give motives for organizing resources. The Polish ethnologist Bronislaw Malinowski in this vein proposed that myths, stories about gods, were designed as charters to authorize persons in authority to extract surpluses from their dependents and otherwise to set a course for societies (1948: 52–3). These thinkers did not necessarily see such efforts as malicious.

Marx and Engels had, however; for them religion was depicted famously as the "opium of the people," meaning religion was thought to be a set of false stories meant to induce obedience (Niebuhr 1964: 42). The context is not, perhaps, so negative as might first appear: "Religion is the sigh of the oppressed creature, the heart of a heartless world, just at it is the spirit of a spiritless situation. It is the *opium* of the people" (emphasis in original). The basic insight of Marx, that "Man makes religion; religion does not make man" seems widely accepted now, and not so radical as it may have been in 1844 (Niebuhr 1964: 40).

The Ancient Near Eastern evidence on the argument for religion as functional seems moot. There was an early emphasis, seen already in the southern Mesopotamian site of Eridu, on supplying fish sacrifices to the god and thereby giving occasions on which the god's priests and worshipers could feast. Settlements built storehouses to keep surpluses and to redistribute them as needed, and these were followed by large communal buildings serving as temples that demonstrated the devotion and power of the communities to their gods. Doubtless there was some coercion in this kind of organization (Liverani 1986: 141–50), but in southern Iraq, because of the lack of boundaries between communities and the primacy of water for irrigation, people could leave if oppression became unbearable. This probably limited the oppression. In Egypt, the boundaries between the Nile Valley and the surrounding desert were harsher, and perhaps movement along the river was more restricted.

Religion had a significant function in gathering resources, blessing them, and redistributing them to others who stood in need of them. Some of the recipients were just the sort of organizers, "mind workers," that Marx despised because he saw them as parasites on the people who did the actual producing of the food, but others were the destitute and widows and orphans. The communities had a common interest in maintaining potential dropouts from society and using their labor for the common good. This contributed to a social function, the preservation of the most desperate people in the communities. Not all stories that appear to be religious endow particular gods or their representatives with concern for the downtrodden, however. Mother goddesses seem to have had that inclination but warrior gods or goddesses not so clearly.

Max Weber, the German sociologist, emphasized not the origins or purpose of religion but rather its tendency to create institutions. He saw a repeated pattern of charismatic leaders arising within societies and inspiring followers to move in new directions; within a generation or two, the groups that the leaders had founded had become structured and even ossified with a logic of their own driven by goals of self-preservation and elaboration of their powers. In Ancient Near Eastern history, it is sometimes hard to catch glimpses of charismatic personalities, but we can trace the elaboration and preservation of institutions in some detail. Weber was probably thinking of the prophets of Israel as charismatic individuals, and there the institutions among their followers were not very clear (Weber 1968). Among the kings of the Davidic line the effort to build institutions is obvious, as is the long-term effect in the creation of the feeling that Jewish leaders ought to be descended from that family.

Part of our limitations in applying Weber's insights to the origins of institutions derives from the lack of personal writing in the Ancient Near East. In the continuum from staid clichés to personal creativity, the Ancient Near East usually preferred to emphasize the clichés, except perhaps in art. This reticence may have derived from the feelings among cultural leaders in all these regions that the institutions they were elaborating were in fact fragile and liable to fall apart with the least slip on their parts. In this they were usually correct, and disunity was much more common in Ancient Near Eastern history than unity, although it was the periods of unity that were celebrated in the cultures themselves and in our own (Brinkman 1984).

The study of the Ancient Near East does not thus appear to illustrate with clarity any of the great classical explanations of religious behavior, although descriptions of institutions and their elaboration do seem to ring true. In the area of brain research, it is now known that some forms of religious action reduce the activity in the brain areas that stress individualization and instead reinforce a feeling of well-being rooted in the group and the universe as a whole (Begley 2001). These findings may give another dimension to the arguments for the functionality of religion; people feel better after having done some of those practices – for example, prayer – and this aspect of pleasure may have appealed to the ancients as it does to moderns. It does not explain why these prayers and not others, why in languages we can no longer understand and not in others, why a large communal exercise and not a small personal petition.

The late Italian historian of religions Angelo Brelich, following up on ideas of Raffaele Pettazzoni, presented an argument that appears to clarify some aspects of Ancient Near Eastern religions. He considered the category of polytheism. It was coined modernly by Jean Bodin in 1580 (Sabbatucci 1998: 9), although the term had been used by Philo of Alexandria as a pejorative description of non-Jewish religious practice (Marcus 1961: 240). Brelich argued that polytheisms were not a universal development from simpler forms of religiosity but rather rarely attested ideologies that accorded usually with complex social formations. He asserted that there is no such thing as a perfect polytheism, and so individual instances inevitably carry forward aspects of earlier religious thinking. Previous students, he felt, had concentrated on simpler stages because they were influenced by evolutionary thinking and wanted to study origins, but this tactic left the study of particular religious traditions with antiquated methods and ideas (Brelich 2007: 24). Not every religious tradition that is not monotheism is polytheism, but that is a specialized development only in some societies, and it is relatively new in contrast to earlier forms (Brelich 1960: 132–3).

In particular, Brelich contrasts polytheisms with the veneration of ancestors and other spirits (1960: 126). Such veneration is widespread, and the sometimes deified heroes of polytheisms may result from such ancestors.

However, polytheisms arise only in cultures with writing, an advanced and productive agriculture, and differentiation of labor, so that not everyone has to be a farmer. Exceptions to this rule are only the religions of the Guinea coast, the Yoruba and Dahomey, and Polynesians. Elsewhere more complex cultures have polytheisms, but China does not, and so agricultural complexity is quite possible without polytheism (Brelich 1960: 133; Shaughnessy 2007: 511–16). Polytheisms can exist without mythology, as the case of Rome shows; all the good stories were borrowed from the Greeks (2007: 79).

Brelich is adamant that trying to trace particular gods back to agricultural or other phenomena is a vain effort in polytheisms, because the gods of complex polytheisms always have personalities and characteristics. He studied at length gods who were clearly associated with particular phenomena, including the Indian god of fire, Agni, whose name means fire, and showed that the association with fire was culturally determined and could not be used to predict what Agni was actually felt to have done (Brelich 2007: 29, 43–4). He also generalizes that gods whose names are transparent tend to be rather poor in personal characteristics and stories about them, mentioning Egyptian *Ma'at* in particular as a rather wan figure (2007: 72). These gods may be relics of earlier times, and the existence of lots of minor gods may show that complex polytheisms are not necessarily thorough in endowing gods with personalities. The gods of rivers and springs too may show that there is a persistence of animism, or "predeistic" ideas, even in polytheisms (2007: 102–3, 109).

The conclusion to be drawn from these studies is that the Ancient Near Eastern religions are more likely to have more in common with other polytheisms than with perhaps neighboring traditions that seem less developed in the characteristics of their gods. One objection I would make to Brelich's formulations has to do with his description of the gods. He writes that a god must be a being who intervenes in human affairs, has a permanent existence, is worshiped, and is not of human origin (2007: 29). By permanent existence, he means immortality, but, as I suggested earlier, Ancient Near Eastern gods die, and although they may last forever in that they were worshiped over long periods and felt to be important in human affairs, gods like Osiris really did die, and he was not alone in doing so. Gods were certainly of a higher power of magnitude than any human, but not all lived forever. We are influenced doubtless by the Greek epithet of the gods as immortal, *athanatoi*, but this is not a universal characteristic of polytheisms. If it were, some of the struggling of the gods would seem much less heroic and important to human experience, as we see even in Christianity still.

Burkhard Gladigow suggests that we still do not have a truly applicable categorization of polytheisms, but he ventures a definition as "a form of religion ... in which are conceived the actings of a large group of personally depicted gods [eine Religionsform ... in der ein Handeln einer Mehrzahl persönlich vorgestellter Götter]." Gladigow refrains from trying to relate polytheisms to the makeup of their societies (Gladigow 1983: 294, 297, 303; Sabbatucci 1998: 16, 121).

Golzio attempts to compare Mesopotamian and Indian temples with some success, finding that there were similarities in the cosmic ideas about the houses of the gods in each culture. Both saw temples as "the stages for the great temple celebrations" (Golzio 1983: 175). Yet Golzio does not attempt to look at the living traditions of India but only the classically literate ones. Comparison in that sphere might be more enlightening, as is suggested by casual perusal of Babb (1975).

We may ask whether, aside from the wisdom ideas and monotheism that are our legacy, we can see in the Ancient Near East any encounter with what is divine that may still speak to us. In a wonderful book, the late Welsh Assyriologist H. W. F. Saggs argued that the ancient Mesopotamian material showed many of the assumptions and aspects that became important in the later Hebrew traditions. Saggs argued that since the Protestant Reformation, the emphasis on religion as belief instead of religion as ritual has increased, but it was ahistorical. He explicitly refused to try to understand origins because origins were too difficult and lost in the past, especially trying to distinguish Sumerian from Semitic religious thought (Saggs 1978: 26–8).

Saggs examined Israelite and Mesopotamian ideas of creator gods and found them both in the Bible and Mesopotamia, but in early stages the Israelites' God was not a creator god. He noted that Yahweh in the Moses stories was not omniscient because he could not tell the difference between Israelite and Egyptian houses. It may have been under the influence from the image of Marduk that Israel's God was seen as a creator. The Canaanite god El had been a creator, but Saggs saw his association with Yahweh as late (Saggs 1978: 36, 42, 45, 49).

Saggs maintained that the idea of God and gods intervening in history was common to the whole Ancient Near East. People could choose to join the association that was Israel and people could leave that community, but the criteria had nothing to do with belief. When Mesopotamians tried to explain why the demon Lamashtu killed babies, they had two answers; one was that she was rebelling against the benign plan of the great gods, and one was that her role was part of the plan to control overpopulation. In both Israel and Mesopotamia, the problem of undeserved evil remained unresolved (Saggs 1978: 67–8, 98, 104, 124).

The mechanisms for communication with the divine included divination and prophecy in parts of Mesopotamia and in Israel. The prophets of Old Babylonian Mari were addressing rather narrow problems for the benefit of people in authority. The prophets from whom we have writings in Israel were not; they seemed to address the whole people, and although they may have advocated particular policies, they placed those policies on a wide canvas. They were moving beyond traditional Ancient Near Eastern religion, including earlier Yahwism, especially in rejecting the efficacy of the cult, the things people did to placate the god (Saggs 1978: 125, 150–2).

On the question of universalism, Saggs began with a discussion of popular versus elite religion, concluding that the popular is difficult to get at. He said that "the idea sometimes expressed that ancient man's life was dominated by religion is quite without basis." In Second Isaiah, there was an explicit universalism, indicating Israel's God cared for all people, and this did not occur explicitly in Mesopotamia. In fact Assyrian royal inscriptions showed Assyrians thought even their enemies were cared for by the sun-god, and the Mesopotamian hymn to the sun-god showed he was concerned for everyone (Saggs 1978: 159, 178–80).

Having established that Israelite religion was in most ways an Ancient Near Eastern religion and that Israel shared the main ideas seen in Mesopotamian texts, Saggs tried to say what the differences really were. He concluded that the lateness of the Israelite tradition made it more critical of institutions. Israel simply had less reverence for its tradition because it was not so very old, and its religious thinkers were less tolerant of deviation from their ideas than polytheistic Mesopotamians. This is especially obvious after the return from Babylonian exile, where Israelite leaders had been exposed to Mesopotamian practices and thought (Saggs 1978: 183, 185–6).

In a couple of places Saggs expressed his own belief that the Mesopotamians, like the Israelites, were struggling toward encounters with the real divinity. This was a statement of faith, of course, and we may or may not wish to echo it, but it does underline the basic fact that the religions of the Ancient Near

East are still with us, whether or not we choose to acknowledge them in all their variety, in their light and darkness.

Some traditions practiced in the Ancient Near East seem strange and alien to us now, such as the Egyptian treatment of the dead and the Mesopotamian omen. There is one aspect of these traditions that still seems particularly vibrant and accessible, however, and that is what in Hebrew Bible study we call the wisdom tradition. As noted before, there is no such clear term in Mesopotamia, and in Egypt the instruction form may include what we mean by wisdom. These were practical texts that attempted to inform and educate privileged young men in the skills necessary to advance in their societies.

To a large extent, these texts are still accessible to us, and the values they convey, although rooted in their own particular traditions, translate to us. The Egyptians advised their young men to practice *ma'at*, the fairness and balance that maintained order but also gave underlings the feeling that they were being listened to, even if they were not going to be satisfied with actual results. The Egyptians also stressed silence, and simply being quiet in a difficult situation was better than running off at the mouth in ways that might get you into trouble. This studied reticence was also a feature of what Mesopotamians valued, although they did not call it silence. In Hebrew wisdom material, there was an emphasis on learning and keeping your proper place, on not exceeding your status, at least without invitation from the master of the house. The values conveyed in general seem to be ones that worked in many later societies, and of course some of the attitudes advised persisted in the Bible, which was studied by the later monotheistic traditions.

The wisdom texts seem to convey the basic assumptions of the elites of these societies, and they influence our own. They also show the depth of our own traditions, even of behavior. Modern movements like Alcoholics Anonymous echo and endorse the view that "Man proposes, but God disposes" (= approximately Proverbs 16:9: "The heart of a man thinks about his way, but Yahweh makes firm his step"). The idea is that a higher power must sensibly be acknowledged, or people will be frustrated with how things work and how they do not work.

17

EXPERIENCING ANCIENT NEAR EASTERN RELIGION

Thus would a sort of polytheism return upon us – a polytheism which I do not on this occasion defend, for my only aim at present is to keep the testimony of religious experience clearly within its proper bounds. Upholders of the monistic view will say to such a polytheism (which, by the way, has always been the real religion of common people, and is so still today) that unless there be one all-inclusive God, our guarantee of security is left imperfect.
>   – William James, *Varieties of Religious Experience*, 1912, 525–6

First, the sound. The great bombilating blasting of a drum magnified beyond normal hearing by the narrowness of streets and the height of buildings, a distant crashing accompanied by the much less dominating sounds of distant harp music and cymbals. Then the crowd stirred and pressed forward to see the beginning, still blocks away. The hawkers and the gossipers were quieter as the trumpets peeled out in the distance and the sounds grew louder as the procession came closer. People shouted that they could see the beginning, although they could not. The army marshals came first pushing people back on either side of the narrow alleys, and then came the lines and lines of priests, wearing old-fashioned robes of white, singing in their high-pitched voices in archaic language that people could not understand, the language, perhaps, of the gods themselves.

More priests came, and their servants, and their squires, and then the king himself, in a cart crowded with his officers and followed by others on horses, or perhaps they were guards, all armed with polished ceremonial swords. They did not sing, but then people could not hear them not singing because the huge drums followed the king and went immediately before the towering statue of the god's wife, carried by naked priests on a palanquin decked in flowers, and under the flowers the precious metals of it glinted. She was very tall and made of gold and silver, but the striking thing was her jet-black eyes of semiprecious stone that seemed to look deeply into the distant future, up the street and out into the countryside, where they were all headed.

She sparkled in the hot sun, for that was her name, was it not? "Sparkly," Ṣarpanitum, the aid and helpmate of the great god and first of his court. Other statues of lesser gods followed, the great god's courtiers and messengers, servants and slaves, all similarly arrayed in multicolored garments over their gold and silver bodies, and with the penetrating eyes.

The drums were far in advance now, and people could hear that the crowd was hushed in the expectation of the advent of the chief god. When he appeared, he was markedly more magnificent than any of the others, taller, with many heads, and many black, penetrating eyes, looking in all directions, sparkling in the sun as the priests who bore him bobbed along the street, singing softly the ancient story of his triumphs in the impossibly distant past. Only when they said his name, slowly, and with great emphasis, did the people in the crowd begin to cheer, as they had all the way back to his temple, which he had just left. "Lord," they cried. "Son of the Sun-god," they yelled. For it seemed to everyone that all would be well in the year to come since obviously this year, unlike in earlier unfortunate times, the ruler of the world would in fact take the hand of the lord and lead him into the house of the New Year, and would perform the necessary rites, speak his pieces just as he was supposed to do. The lord, indeed all the gods, would be happy with their people and grant them good harvests and all the successes they could imagine. People turned after the lord had passed and became part of the procession, sweeping the vendors and foreigners along, out on the narrow streets and into the countryside, with a feeling of happiness and hope, expecting the blessings to be immediate and continual.

* * *

So it must have been for those watching the New Year's procession many springs ago at the equinox in Babylon. We can follow at a very great distance in understanding what was going on because a text has been preserved that prescribed the ritual at least for the beginning of the New Year's festival, but it is broken, and we cannot follow it to its end.

We have here stressed the affective impression these rites must have had on witnesses, but the evidence is slight. In a sense, we join those witnesses, trying to feel what they might have felt at these great spectacles, which seem, however, very different from those we actually have witnessed in our own traditions. Still, we can see in the acts how the world was viewed by at least some of the participants.

The text itself is from a late period in Mesopotamian history, from Seleucid times, meaning from 330 to 100 BCE, and it is a prescriptive ritual, not a description of what really happened but rather a set of orders for what was supposed to happen. This means it was an ideal vision of how the ceremony was supposed to go, not necessarily how it actually did go. Because it was so late in a very long history, we may question whether it really reflected things that were happening earlier. Yet the "New Year" and the "New Year's House" are known from much earlier, and some of the aspects of the texts may show things that had great continuity with the distant past. Religious texts are notoriously conservative, although it is clear, too, that they change slowly under new conditions.

The text begins on the second of the month Nisannu, April, with a priest arising at night to praise the lord Marduk, son of the sun-god, "lord of the countries." He stressed those eyes with their mighty glance, and yet also the mercy that could proceed from him. The priest begged him to "grant mercy to your city, Babylon! . . . Establish the 'liberty' of the people of Babylon, your subordinates." By liberty was meant the series of exemptions from taxes in kind, money, and labor, which the ancient cities had wrestled from kings. It was important to everyone in Babylon, and yet it was frequently threatened, especially by kings insensitive to ancient tradition, as those Greek-speaking Seleucid kings may have sometimes been (Bottéro 2001: 58–64; Sachs 1969; Thureau-Dangin 1921: 127–54). The ideal of exemption from services and taxes was legendary, however.

The colophon, or editorial notation at the end of the text, says that these were actually "secrets of the temple . . . [whoever rev]eres the god Bel [lord] shall show them to nobody except the . . . priest. . . . " So we as later readers are trespassing on forbidden ground.

After the nighttime recitation, the priest was to open the gate, and many other priests came in to perform "their rites, in the traditional manner" before the lord and his wife. The text has now grown fragmentary, but the rites included exorcism and curses on enemies and bandits. A crown of the old heaven-god also was mentioned, and so maybe the lord was taking on some of his characteristics.

On the next day, the priest entered three hours after sunrise, got together some craftsmen, gave them materials, and asked them to make rather small figures, about 6 inches or 15 centimeters tall, of wood with stones and metal on them. The craftsmen were to be paid with pieces of meat from a sheep slaughtered and offered to the lord. The figures made were to be kept and offered food until the sixth day, when the slaughterer was to strike off their heads, and they then were burned in a fire. Somehow they must have embodied evil forces that had to be overcome.

On the fourth day, the priest was to arise early, still in the night, and address the lord with another prayer. The priest praised the lord especially for giving the scepter to "the king who reveres" him. The priest also recited a prayer to the lord's consort. She was called one "who brings complaints, who defends, who impoverishes the rich, who causes the poor to become wealthy, who fells the enemy who does not fear her divinity, who releases the prison, grasps the hand of the fallen."

Then the priest was to go out into the courtyard and let in the various officiants, who conducted their traditional rites, which were not further described. After the late afternoon meal, the priest was to recite the composition called "When on high." This is what we know as the "Creation Epic," the story of the exaltation of the authority of the lord Marduk leading to his destruction of the forces of chaos and the organization of the world as we know it. The text notes, "While he recites 'When on high' to the god Bel [the lord], the front of the tiara of the god Anu [the sky-god] shall be covered," perhaps because the sky-god would be offended by the story of Marduk's successes.

This is an important passage because it shows the use of a literary text that we know from other places. Of course we do not know whether "When on high" was composed to be used in this festival, or it may have been an older text for another purpose that has been adapted for use here. I noted earlier the likelihood that it was composed on the occasion of Nebuchadnezzar I's successful retrieval of the statue of Marduk from Elamite captivity around 1200 BCE (Lambert 1964). Was it the entire seven-tablet text, which must have taken hours to recite, or some shorter version (Foster 2005: 439–86)?

The next day, the priest arose and bathed and again addressed a prayer to the lord. The gist of it was asking that the lord and all the astral deities in particular should be calm. He spoke similar sentiments to the lord's consort, stressing female deities. Later that day the temple was to be purified and exorcized, and a ram was to be slaughtered, then thrown into the river. The two men involved in that act then left town and did not return until the twelfth day of the month, when the ceremonies were presumably over. This may have been an effort to concentrate the evil that might be in a place onto a scapegoat and then to banish that evil by getting rid of the animal and incidentally those involved in the ritual, at least temporarily. The rite raises the problem of whether evil and impurities were thought of as physical things that might be disposed of. It shows that evil might magically be transferred to something else and then eliminated.

The main priest who had led the ceremony was not even to see the purification rituals; perhaps he might himself have become impure if he saw how impurity was eliminated. He came now and prayed again to the lord. He spoke of the purification of the temple and made offerings of food and wine.

Later the reigning king entered the temple. When he nearly reached the presence of the lord, in an antechamber before where the statue of the lord stood, the priest took away his "scepter, the circle, and the sword." The scepter, a simple staff, was an old symbol of rulership, and presumably the sword stood for the king's military prowess. The circle (*kippatu* in Akkadian) is more obscure but perhaps connected to a sense of totality associated with the rule of all lands. The priest brought the objects before the lord and put them on a chair within the sanctuary.

The priest then returned to the king and struck his cheek. Then he brought him into the lord's presence, dragging him by the ears and making him bow to the lord. The king then gave a speech in which he denied having done bad things: "I did not sin, lord of the lands. I was not neglectful of your godship. I did not destroy Babylon; I did not commend its overthrow, . . . I did not rain blows on the cheek of a subordinate [as had just happened to him!]."

The priest then admonished the king not to fear, for the lord would hear his prayer and would exalt his kingship. The king then had his symbols of office restored. Perhaps the priest again struck the king on the cheek, and the text notes that it would be a good omen if the king cried then, but if he did not cry, people could deduce that the lord was angry. Other rites followed in which the king participated, but the rest of the tablet is broken.

This extraordinary scene shows the king reigning at the pleasure of the lord, and it briefly put the religious authority above the king. This implies that there were recognized standards of royal behavior, extending beyond an ability to cry at will, that could be crossed by powerful kings, but such transgressions would certainly result in criticisms from religious figures. It is known from other texts that the priests and theologians distrusted kings and particularly criticized the king's absences from this set of ceremonies because they saw his participation as helping to ensure the fertility of the land and the orderly action of the universe for the new year. The phrase they used was "the king took the lord's hand," and we think, although this did not occur in the text we have, that it involved leading the statue of the lord as he left the city to live briefly in the New Year's House outside the city.

The difference between the scene we depicted at the beginning of this chapter and the one we have been following from the ritual text is who was present, who could see, who could hear. The ritual was practically secret, and maybe all of it really was supposed to be kept secret. But procession would have been public. This difference parallels the problem of official and popular religion. We know much more about the former than the latter because of the limited access to writing in the society. The king and his priests could write down what at least in tradition they were supposed to do. The roles and thoughts of the people in the crowd remained their own.

* * *

Religion divides us in ways that seemed impossible a few years ago, and yet divisions over religion are mostly old, stemming from long before the Modern Period since 1500 CE. The origins of these divisions will remain a matter for study and engagement for a long time to come.

With the study of religion we are faced with the profound temptation to try to explain ourselves and how we got to be as great as we are. Any study of the past begins from ourselves, and there is a tendency to ignore those strains of a tradition that may not lead obviously to later developments. Yet to do so is to close off in advance other possible futures that might have developed but did not.

We cannot really experience Ancient Near Eastern religion. We can at most imagine. But we should.

REFERENCES

Adams, Robert McC. 1966. *The Evolution of Urban Society*. Chicago: Aldine.
──────. 1981. *Heartland of Cities*. Chicago and London: University of Chicago Press.
Adkins, Lesley, and Roy Adkins. 2000. *The Keys of Egypt*. New York: HarperCollins.
Allen, James P. 2006. "Monotheism in Ancient Egypt." In G. Beckman and T. Lewis, eds. *Text, Artifact, and Image. Revealing Ancient Israelite Religion*. Providence: Brown Judaic Studies, 319–25.
Ariès, Philippe. 1982. *The Hour of Our Death*. New York: Vintage. French edition: 1977.
Armstrong, Karen. 2006. *The Great Transformation*. New York: Knopf.
Asmussen, J. P. 1969. "Manichaeism." In C. J. Bleeker and G. Widengren, eds. *Religions of the Past*. Leiden: Brill, 580–610.
Assmann, Jan. 1990. *Ma'at. Gerechtigkeit und Unsterblichkeit im Alten Ägypten*. Munich: Beck.
──────. 1997. *Moses the Egyptian*. Cambridge: Harvard University Press.
──────. 2002. *The Mind of Egypt*. New York: Henry Holt.
Augé, Marc. 1982. *La génie du paganisme*. Paris: Gallimard.
Babb, Lawrence A. 1975. *The Divine Hierarchy: Popular Hinduism in Central India*. New York: Columbia University Press.
Barker, Andrew. 1996. "Ptolemy." In S. Hornblower and A. Spawforth, eds. *The Oxford Classical Dictionary*. Oxford: Oxford University Press, 1273–5.
Beaulieu, Paul-Alain. 1989. *The Reign of Nabonidus, King of Babylon, 556–539 B.C.* New Haven and London: Yale University Press.
──────. 1998. "The Turbaned Standard of Ištar." In Jan Braun et al., eds. *Written on Clay and Stone. Ancient Near Eastern Studies Presented to Krystyna Szarzyńska*. Warsaw: Agade, 25–6.
Beckman, Gary. 1983. *Hittite Birth Rituals*. Wiesbaden: Harrassowitz.
──────. 1999. *Hittite Diplomatic Texts*. Atlanta: Scholars.
Begley, Sharon. 2001. "Searching for the God Within." *Newsweek* 29 January: 59.
Benz, Frank. 1972. *Personal Names in the Phoenician and Punic Inscriptions*. Rome: Pontifical Biblical Institute Press.
Bernal, Martin. 1987. *Black Athena. The Afroasiatic Roots of Classical Civilization. Volume 1: The Fabrication of Ancient Greece, 1785-1985*. New Brunswick, NJ: Rutgers University Press.
Bianchi, Ugo, and Yuri Stoyanov. 2005. "Dualism." In Lindsay Jones, ed. *Encyclopedia of Religion*. Detroit: Thomson, Gale, 2504–17.
Boemer, R. M. 1957-71. "Götterdarstellungen in der Bildkunst." *Reallexikon der Assyriologie* 3: 466–9.
Bonfante, Larissa, ed. 1986. *Etruscan Life and Afterlife*. Detroit: Wayne State University Press.
Bonogofsky, Michelle. 2004. "Including Women and Children: Neolithic Modeled Skulls from Jordan, Israel, Syria and Turkey." *Near Eastern Archaeology* 67: 118–19.
Bottéro, Jean. 1972. "Habiru." *Reallexikon der Assyriologie* 4: 14–27.

_____. 2001. *Religion in Ancient Mesopotamia.* Chicago and London: University of Chicago Press. French edition: 1998.

Boyce, Mary. 1975. *A History of Zoroastrianism.* Volume I. Leiden: Brill.

_____. 1979. *Zoroastrians.* London: Routledge and Kegan Paul.

_____. 1992. "Zoroaster, Zoroastrianism." In D. N. Freedman, ed. *The Anchor Bible Dictionary.* New York: Doubleday, Volume VI 1168–1174.

Brandon, S. G. F. 1967. *The Judgment of the Dead.* New York: Scribner's.

_____. 1969. "The Weighing of the Soul." In J. Kitagawa and C. Long, eds. *Myths & Symbols. Studies in Honor of Mircea Eliade.* Chicago and London: University of Chicago Press, 91–112.

Breasted, James. 1934. *The Dawn of Conscience.* London: Scribner's.

Brelich, Angelo. 1960. "Der Polytheismus." *Numen* 7: 123–36.

_____. 2007. *Il politeismo.* Rome: Riuniti.

Brewer, Douglas. 2005. *Ancient Egypt. Foundations of a Civilization.* Harlow and London: Pearson, Longman.

Brinkman, J. A. 1984. "Settlement Surveys and Documentary Evidence: Regional Variation and Secular Trend in Mesopotamian Demography." *Journal of Near Eastern Studies* 43: 169–80.

Brown, John P. 1981. "Proverb–Book, Gold–Economy, Alphabet." *Journal of Biblical Literature* 100: 169–91.

Bulliet, Richard W. 1979. *Conversion to Islam in the Medieval Period.* Cambridge: Harvard University Press.

Burkert, Walter. 1985. *Greek Religion.* Cambridge: Harvard University Press. German edition: 1977.

Caplice, Richard. 1974. "An Apotropaion against Fungus." *Journal of Near Eastern Studies* 33: 345–9.

Carra de Vaux, B. 1974. "Al-Sabi'a. The Sabaeans." In H. A. R. Gibb and J. H. Kramers, eds. *Shorter Encyclopedia of Islam.* Leiden: Brill, 477–8.

Chaniotis, Angelos. 2003. "The Divinity of Hellenistic Rulers." In A. Erskine, ed. *A Companion to the Hellenistic World.* Malden, MA: Blackwell, 431–45.

Claburn, W. E. 1973. "The Fiscal Basis of Josiah's Reform." *Journal of Biblical Literature* 92: 11–22.

Clay, A. T. 1912. *Personal Names of the Cassite Period.* New Haven and London: Yale University Press.

Cogan, Mordechai. 1974. *Imperialism and Religion: Assyria, Judah, and Israel in the Eighth and Seventh Centuries B.C.E.* Missoula, MT: Society of Biblical Literature.

Cooper, Jerrold. 1983a. *Reconstructing History from Ancient Inscriptions: The Lagash-Umma Border Conflict.* Malibu, CA: Undena.

_____. 1983b. *The Curse of Agade.* Baltimore and London: Johns Hopkins University Press.

Cunningham, G. 1999. *Religion and Magic.* Edinburgh: Edinburgh University Press.

Daniels, Peter. 1990. "Fundamentals of Grammatology." *Journal of the American Oriental Society* 110: 727–31.

David, Rosalie. 2002. *Religion and Magic in Ancient Egypt.* London: Penguin.

Dearman, John. 1988. *Property Rights in the Eighth-Century Prophets.* Atlanta: Scholars.

Dhorme, Edouard. 1949. *Les Religions de Babylonie et d'Assyrie.* Paris: Presses universitaires de France.

Di Vito, Robert. 1993. *Studies in Third Millennium Sumerian and Akkadian Personal Names. The Designation and Conception of the Personal God.* Rome: Pontifical Biblical Institute Press.

Dodd, E. R. 1951. *The Greeks and the Irrational.* Berkeley and Los Angeles: University of California Press.

Doty, L. Timothy. 1988. "Nikarchos and Kephalon." In E. Leichty and M. Ellis, eds. *A Scientific Humanist: Studies in Memory of Abraham Sachs*. Philadelphia: Babylonian Fund, 95–118.

Edzard, Dietz Otto. 1997a. *Gudea and His Dynasty*. Toronto: University of Toronto Press.

———. 1997b. "Incantations." In Hallo and Younger, 1997: 426.

Falchetti, Franco, and Antonella Romualdi. 2001. *Die Etrusker*. Darmstadt: Wissenschaftliche Buchgesellschaft. Italian edition: 2000.

Falkenstein, Adam, and Wolfram von Soden. 1953. *Sumerische und Akkadische Hymnen und Gebete*. Zurich and Stuttgart: Artemis.

Feeney, John. 2003. "The Last Nile Flood." *Aramco World* 57(3): 24–33.

Fine, Hillel. 1952–3, 1954. "Studies in Middle-Assyrian Chronology and Religion." *Hebrew Union College Annual* 24: 187–273, 25: 107–68.

Finkelstein, Jacob J. 1962. "Mesopotamia." *Journal of Near Eastern Studies* 21: 73–92.

Foster, Benjamin R. 2005. *Before the Muses*. Bethesda: CDL.

———. 2007. "Mesopotamia." In J. Hinnells, ed. *A Handbook of Ancient Religions*. Cambridge: Cambridge University Press, 161–213.

Frankfort, Henri. 1948. *Kingship and the Gods*. Chicago and London: University of Chicago Press.

Frayne, Douglas. 1990. *Old Babylonian Period (2003–1595 BC)*. Toronto: University of Toronto Press.

———. 1997. *Ur III Period (2112–2004 BC)*. Toronto: University of Toronto Press.

———. 2008. *Presargonic Period (2700–2350 BC)*. Toronto: University of Toronto Press.

Freud, Sigmund. 1938. *The Basic Writings of Sigmund Freud*. New York: Modern Library.

Frye, Richard. 2000. "Parthian and Sasanian History of Iran." In John Curtis, ed. *Mesopotamia and Iran in the Parthian and Sasanian Periods*. London: The British Museum, 17–22.

Fulco, William. 1976. *The Canaanite God Rešep*. New Haven: American Oriental Society.

Gelb, I. J. 1972. "The Arua Institution." *Revue d'Assyriologie* 66: 1–32.

George, Andrew. 1999. *The Epic of Gilgamesh*. London: Penguin.

Gladigow, Burkhard. 1983. "Strukturprobleme polytheistischer Religionen." *Saeculum* 34: 292–304.

———. 1995. "Struktur der Öffentlichkeit und Bekenntnis in polytheistischen Religionen." In H. Kippenberg and G. Strousma, eds. *Secrecy and Concealment: Studies in the History of Mediterranean and Near Eastern Religions*. Leiden: Brill, 15–35.

Glassner, Jean-Jacques. 1986. *La Chute d'Akkadé*. Berlin: Reimer.

Goetze, Albrecht. 1947. *Old Babylonian Omen Texts*. Yale Oriental Series 10. New Haven and London: Yale University Press.

Golzio, Karl-Heinz. 1983. *Der Tempel im alten Mesopotamien und seine Parallelen in Indien*. Leiden: Brill.

Grayson, A. Kirk. 1987. *Assyrian Rulers of the Third and Second Millennium BC (to 1115 BC)*. Royal Inscriptions of Mesopotamia. Assyrian Periods 1. Toronto: University of Toronto Press.

Grignaschi, Mario. 1966. "Quelques spécimens de la littérature sassanide conservés dans les bibliothèques d'Istanbul." *Journal Asiatique* 254: 1–142.

Groenewegen-Frankfort, H. A. 1987 (1951). *Arrest and Movement. Space and Time in the Art of the Ancient Near East*. Cambridge: Harvard University Press.

Gröndahl, Frauke. 1967. *Die Personnennamen der Texte aus Ugarit*. Rome: Pontificial Biblical Institute Press.

Guinan, Ann K. 1997. "Divination." In Hallo and Younger, 1997 1: 421–6.

———, et al., eds. 2006. *If a Man Builds a Joyful House: Assyriological Studies in Honor of Erle Verdun Leichty*. Leiden: Brill.

Gurevich, Aaron. 1992. *Historical Anthropology of the Middle Ages*. Chicago: University of Chicago Press.

Gurney, O. R. 1977. *Some Aspects of Hittite Religion*. Oxford: Oxford University Press.

Hallo, W. W. 1963. "Royal Hymns and Mesopotamian Unity." *Journal of Cuneiform Studies* 17: 112–18.

_____. 1996. "Enki and the Theology of Eridu." *Journal of the American Oriental Society* 116: 231–4.

_____, and J. J. A. Van Dijk. 1968. *The Exaltation of Inanna*. New Haven and London: Yale University Press.

_____, and K. Lawson Younger, Jr., eds. 1997. *The Context of Scripture. Volume One. Canonical Compositions*. Leiden: Brill.

_____, and K. Lawson Younger, Jr., eds. 2000. *The Context of Scripture. Volume Two. Monumental Inscriptions*. Leiden: Brill.

Harden, Donald. 1962. *The Phoenicians*. New York: Praeger.

Harris, Rivkah. 1975. *Ancient Sippar*. Istanbul: Nederlands Historisch-Archaeologisch Instituut.

Helck, Wolfgang. 1977. "Götter, fremde in Ägypten." *Reallexikon der Ägyptologie* II: 643.

Hodder, Ian. 2006. *The Leopard's Tale*. London: Thames and Hudson.

Hornung, Erik. 1999. *Akhenaten and the Religion of Light*. Ithaca and London: Cornell University Press.

Jacobs, Bruno. 2006. "Die Religion der Achämeniden." In A. Koch, ed. *Pracht und Prunk der Großkönige. Das persische Weltreich*. Stuttgart: Historisches Museum der Pfalz Speyer and Theiss, 213–21.

Jacobsen, Thorkild. 1939. *The Sumerian King List*. Chicago: University of Chicago Press.

_____. 1946. "Mesopotamia: The Cosmos as a State." In H. Frankfort et al., eds. *The Intellectual Adventure of Ancient Man*. Chicago: University of Chicago Press, 125–219.

_____. 1957. "Early Political Development in Mesopotamia." *Zeitschrift für Assyriologie* 52: 91–140 (Moran 1970: 132–56).

_____. 1976. *The Treasures of Darkness. A History of Mesopotamian Religion*. New Haven and London: Yale University Press.

_____. 1987. *The Harps That Once . . . Sumerian Poetry in Translation*. New Haven and London: Yale University Press.

James, T. G. H. 1984. *Pharaoh's People*. London and New York: Tauris.

Janssen, J. J. 1975. *Commodity Prices from the Ramessid Period*. Leiden: Brill.

Jaspers, Karl. 1953. *The Origin and Goal of History*. New Haven and London: Yale University Press. German edition: 1949.

Josephus. *Antiquities of the Jews. The Life and Works of Flavius Josephus*. New York: Holt, Rinehart and Winston, 1977.

Kaufmann, Yehezkel. 1960. *The Religion of Israel*, abridged by Moshe Greenberg. New York: Schocken, 1972. Hebrew edition: 1937–56.

Kent, Roland G. 1953. *Old Persian. Grammar. Texts. Lexicon*. New Haven: American Oriental Society.

Klengel, Horst. 1991. *König Hammurapi und der Alltag Babylons*. Zurich: Artemis.

Knoppers, Gary. 1992. " 'The God in His Temple': The Phoenician Text from Pyrgi as a Funerary Inscription." *Journal of Near Eastern Studies* 51: 105–20.

Koehler, Ludwig, and Walter Baumgartner. 1994–2000. *The Hebrew and Aramaic Lexicon of the Old Testament*. Leiden: Brill.

Kunin, Seth D. 2003. *Religion. The Modern Theories*. Baltimore and London: Johns Hopkins University Press.

Lambert, W. G. 1957–71. "Götterlisten." *Reallexikon der Assyriologie* 3: 473–9.

————. 1964. "The Reign of Nebuchadnezzar I: A Turning Point in the History of Ancient Mesopotamian Religion." In W. S. McCullough, ed. *The Seed of Wisdom. Essays in Honor of T. J. Meek.* Toronto: University of Toronto Press, 3–13.

————. 1983. "The God Aššur." *Iraq* 45: 82–6.

Lewis, Bernard. 1994. *The Shaping of the Modern Middle East.* New York and Oxford: Oxford University Press.

Lewis, Naphtali, and Meyer Reinhold. 1966. *Roman Civilization: Sourcebook.* 2 volumes. New York: Harper.

Lewis, Theodore. 1989. *Cults of the Dead in Ancient Israel and Ugarit.* Atlanta: Scholars.

Lichtheim, Miriam. 1976. *Ancient Egyptian Literature. Volume II: The New Kingdom.* Berkeley: University of California Press.

Limet, Henri. 1971. *Les légendes des sceaux cassites.* Brussels: Palais des Académies.

Liverani, Mario. 1971. "ΣΥΔΥΚ e ΜΙΣΩΡ." *Studi in onore di Edoardo Volterra* 6: 55–74.

————. 1986. *L'origine delle città.* Rome: Riuniti.

Livy (Titus Livius), *The War with Hannibal.* In Radice, Betty, ed. London: Penguin, 1965.

Mahan, Alfred T. 1902. "The Persian Gulf and International Relations." *National Review* September: 26–45.

————. *Retrospect and Prospect.* Boston: Little, Brown, 1902, 209–54.

Malinowski, Bronislaw. 1948. *Magic, Science and Religion.* New York: Doubleday.

Marcus, Ralph, ed. 1961. *Philo. Supplement II.* London and Cambridge: Heinemann and Harvard University Press.

Marx, Karl, *Capital.*

Maul, Stefan. 1994. *Zukunftsbewältigung. Eine Untersuchung altorientalischen Denkens anhand der babylonisch-assyrische Löserituale (Namburbi).* Mainz: Zabern.

Merlo, Paolo, and Paolo Xella. 2001. "Da Erwin Rohde ai Rapiuma ugaritici: antecedenti vicino-orientali degle eroi greci?" In Ribichini, Rocchi, and Xella, 2001: 281–97.

Meskell, Lynn. 2002. *Private Life in New Kingdom Egypt.* Princeton: Princeton University Press.

Momigliano, Arnauldo. 1975. *Alien Wisdom.* Cambridge: Cambridge University Press.

Moran, William L., ed. 1970. Thorkild Jacobsen, *Toward the Image of Tammuz and Other Essays.* Cambridge: Harvard University Press.

————. 1992. *The Amarna Letters.* Baltimore and London: The Johns Hopkins University Press.

Murnane, William. 2000. "Imperial Egypt and the Limits of Power." In R. Cohen and R. Westbrook, eds. *Amarna Diplomacy.* Baltimore and London: The Johns Hopkins University Press, 101–111.

Niebuhr, Reinhold, ed. 1964. *Marx and Engels on Religion.* New York: Schocken.

Nissinen, Marti, et al. 2003. *Prophets and Prophecy in the Ancient Near East.* Atlanta: Scholars.

Oggiano, Ida. 2006. "'Categorie interpretative dell'architectura': gli edifici di culto del Levante del 1 millennio a.c." In M. Rocchi and P. Xella, eds. *Archeologia e religione.* Verona: Essedue, 141–68.

Oppenheim, A. Leo. 1936. "Die akkadischen Personennamen der 'Kassitenzeit.'" *Anthropos* 31: 470–88.

————. 1966. "Analysis of an Assyrian Ritual (KAR 139)." *History of Religions* 5: 250–65.

————. 1967. *Letters from Mesopotamia.* Chicago and London: University of Chicago Press.

————, et al., eds. 1960. *The Assyrian Dictionary.* Chicago and Glückstadt: Oriental Institute and J. J. Augustin.

————. 1960. Volume I and J.

————. 1982. Volume Q.

————. 1992. Volume Š II.

Otto, Rudolf. 1923. *The Idea of the Holy*. New York: Oxford University Press. German edition: 1917.

Pagels, Elaine. 1979. *The Gnostic Gospels*. New York: Random House.

Pallottino, Massimo. 1955. *The Etruscans*. Harmondsworth: Penguin.

Pardee, Dennis. 1997. "The 'Aqhatu Legend." In Hallo and Younger, 1997, volume 1: 343–56.

———. 2002. *Ritual and Cult at Ugarit*. Atlanta: Society of Biblical Literature.

Peters, F. E. 1970. *The Harvest of Hellenism*. New York: Simon and Schuster.

Pfiffig, Ambros Josef. 1972. *Einführung in die Etruskologie*. Darmstadt: Wissenschaftliche Buchgesellschaft.

Pisi, Paola. 2001. "Dumuzi-Tammuz. Alla ricerca di un dio." In Xella, 2001a: 31–62.

Pomponio, Francesco, and Paolo Xella. 1997. *Les dieux d'Ebla*. Munster: Ugarit.

Pope, Marvin, and Wolfgang Röllig. 1965. "Syrien." In H. Haussig, ed. *Götter und Mythen im vorderen Orient*. Stuttgart: Klett, 219–312.

Redford, Donald B. 1984. *Akhenaten. The Heretic King*. Princeton: Princeton University Press.

———. 1992. *Egypt, Canaan, and Israel in Ancient Times*. Princeton: Princeton University Press.

Renan, Ernest. 1974 (1863). *Vie de Jesus*. Paris: Gallimard.

Renger, Johannes. 1972–5. "Heilige Hochzeit. A. Philologisch." *Reallexikon der Assyriologie* 4: 251–9.

Ribichini, Sergio, Maria Rocchi, and Paolo Xella, eds. 2001. *La Questione delle influence vicino-orientali sulla religione greca*. Rome: Consiglia nazionale delle ricerche.

Ringgren, Helmer. 1973. *Religions of the Ancient Near East*. Philadelphia: Fortress. Swedish edition: 1967.

Rochberg, Francesca. 2004. *The Heavenly Writing. Divination, Horoscopy, and Astronomy in Mesopotamian Culture*. Cambridge: Cambridge University Press.

Rochberg-Halton, Francesca. 1982. "Fate and Divination in Mesopotamia." In H. Hirsch and H. Hunger, eds. *28ᵉ Rencontre assyriologique internationale. Archiv für Orientforschung Beiheft* 19: 363–71.

Röllig, Wolfgang. 2001. "Myths about the Netherworld in the Ancient Near East and their Counterparts in the Greek Religion." In Ribichini, Rocchi, and Xella, eds., 2001: 307–14.

Roth, Martha. 1997. *Law Collections from Mesopotamia and Asia Minor*. Atlanta: Scholars.

Rutten, Maggie. 1938. "Trente-deux modèles de foies en argile inscrits provenant de Tell-Hariri (Mari)." *Revue d'Assyriologie* 35: 36–52.

Sabbatucci, Dario. 1994. "Terminologia sacrale in Roma." In U. Bianchi, ed. *The Notion of "Religion" in Comparative Research*. Rome: "L'Erma" di Bretschneider, 141–4.

———. 1998. *Politeismo*, 3 volumes. Rome: Bulzone.

Sachs, Abraham. 1969. "Temple Program for the New Year's Festival at Babylon." In J. Pritchard, ed. *Ancient Near Eastern Texts*. Princeton: Princeton University Press, 331–4.

Safar, F. et al. 1981. *Eridu*. Baghdad: Ministry of Culture and Information.

Saggs, H. W. F. 1978. *Encounter with the Divine in Mesopotamia and Israel*. London: Althone.

Sallaberger, W. 2004. "Pantheon. A. I. In Mesopotamien." *Reallexikon der Assyriologie* 10: 294–308.

Scandone Matthiae, Gabriella. 2001. "Osiride, l'Africano, ovvero la morte reale." In Xella, ed., 2001a: 15–30.

Schippmann, Klaus. 1990. *Grundzüge der Geschichte des sasanidischen Reiches*. Darmstadt: Wissenschaftliche Buchgesellschaft.

Scurlock, JoAnn. 2005. "Ancient Mesopotamian Medicine." In Snell, 2005a: 302–15.

Scurlock, JoAnn, and Farouk Al-Rawi. 2006. "A Weakness for Hellenism." In Guinan et al., eds., 2006: 357–81.

Seaford, Richard. 2004. *Money and the Early Greek Mind*. Cambridge: Cambridge University Press.

Shaughnessy, Edward. 2007. "The Religion of Ancient China." In J. Hinnells, ed., *A Handbook of Ancient Religions*. Cambridge: Cambridge University Press, 490–536.

Shaw, Ian, and Paul Nicholson. 1995. *The Dictionary of Ancient Egypt*. London and New York: The British Museum and Abrams.

Shepkaru, Shmuel. 2006. *Jewish Martyrs in the Pagan and Christian Worlds*. Cambridge: Cambridge University Press.

Sherwin-White, Susan, and Amélie Kuhrt. 1993. *From Samarkhand to Sardis. A New Approach to the Seleucid Empire*. Berkeley: University of California Press.

Sigrist, Marcel. 1992. *Drehem*. Bethesda, MD: CDL.

Silverman, David P. 1991. "Divinity and Deities in Ancient Egypt." In B. Shafer, ed. *Religion in Ancient Egypt*. Ithaca and London: Cornell University Press, 7–87.

Simpson, William Kelly, ed. 2003. *The Literature of Ancient Egypt*. New Haven and London: Yale University Press.

Sjöberg, Å. 1957–71. "Götterreisen." *Reallexikon der Assyriologie* 3: 480–3.

———. 1994. *The Sumerian Dictionary*. A. Part II. Philadelphia: University Museum.

———, and E. Bergmann. 1969. *The Collection of the Sumerian Temple Hymns*. Locust Valley, NY: Augustin.

Skjaervo, Prods Oktor. 2005. "Introduction to Zoroastrianism." Cambridge: Harvard University, Near Eastern Languages.

Slanski, Kathryn E. 2003. *The Babylonian Entitlement narûs (kudurrus)*. Boston: American Schools of Oriental Research.

Smith, Mark. 2009. "Democratization of the Afterlife." *UCLA Encyclopedia of Egyptology*. www.uee.ucla.edu.

Smith, Wilfred Cantwell. 1964. *The Meaning and End of Religion*. New York: Mentor.

Snell, Daniel. 1974. "The Mari Livers and the Omen Tradition." *Journal of the Ancient Near Eastern Society of Columbia University* 6: 117–23.

———. 2000. "The Structure of Politics in the Age of David." In S. Graziani, ed. *Studi sul vicino oriente antico dedicati alla memoria di Luigi Cagni*. Naples: Istituto universitario orientale, 2131–42.

———, ed. 2005a. *A Companion to the Ancient Near East*. Malden, MA: Blackwell.

———. 2005b. "The Invention of the Individual." In Snell, 2005a: 357–69.

Stadelmann, Rainer. 1977. "Ägyptische Götter im Ausland." *Reallexikon der Ägyptologie* 2: 630–2.

———. 1984. "Seevölker." *Reallexikon der Ägyptologie* 5: 814–22.

Steinkeller, Piotr. 1998. "Inanna's Archaic Symbol." In Jan Braun et al., eds. *Written on Clay and Stone. Ancient Near Eastern Studies Presented to Krystyna Szarzyńska*. Warsaw: Agade, 87–101.

———. 2002. "Archaic City Seals and the Question of Early Babylonian Unity." In Tzvi Abusch, ed. *Riches Hidden in Secret Places. Ancient Near Eastern Studies in Memory of Thorkild Jacobsen*. Winona Lake, IN: Eisenbrauns, 249–57.

Stone, Elizabeth. 2005. "Mesopotamian Cities and Countryside." In Snell, 2005a: 141–54.

Sweeney, D. 2001. "Walking Alone Forever, Following You: Gender and Mourners' Laments from Ancient Egypt." *NIN: Journal of Gender Studies in Antiquity* 2: 27–48.

Szpakowska, Kasia. 2008. *Daily Life in Ancient Egypt*. Malden, MA: Blackwell.

Taracha, Piotr. 2009. *Religions of Second Millennium Anatolia*. Wiesbaden: Harrassowitz.

Thureau-Dangin, F. 1921. *Rituels accadiens*. Paris: Leroux.

Trigger, B. G., B. J. Kemp, D. O'Connor, and A. B. Lloyd. 1983. *Ancient Egypt. A Social History.* Cambridge: Cambridge University Press.

Tsevat, Matitiahu. 1966. "The Meaning of the Book of Job." *Hebrew Union College Annual* 37: 73–106.

Tubb, Jonathan. 1998. *Canaanites.* Norman: University of Oklahoma Press.

Vanstiphout, Herman. 2003. *Epics of Sumerian Kings.* Atlanta: Society of Biblical Literature.

Veldhuis, Niek. 2006. "Divination: Theory and Use." In Guinan, et al., eds., 2006: 487–97.

Verbrugghe, Gerald, and John M. Wickersham. 1996. *Berossos and Manetho.* Ann Arbor: University of Michigan Press.

Vermes, Geza. 1987. *The Dead Sea Scrolls in English.* London: Penguin.

Waddell, W. G. 1940. *Manetho.* Cambridge and London: Harvard University Press.

Wagner, Andreas, ed. 2006. *Primäre und sekundäre Religion als Kategorie der Religionsgeschichte des Alten Testaments.* Berlin: De Gruyter.

Watrin, Luc. 2003. "Lower-Upper Egyptian Interaction during the Pre-Naqada Period: From Initial Trade Contacts to Ascendancy of Southern Chiefdoms." In Zahi Hawass, ed. *Egyptology at the Dawn of the Twenty-First Century.* Volume 2. Cairo and New York: American University of Cairo Press, 566–91.

Weber, Max. 1968. *On Charisma and Institution Building.* S. N. Eisenstadt, ed. Chicago and London: University of Chicago Press.

Wente, Edward. 1990. *Letters from Ancient Egypt.* Atlanta: Scholars.

Westenholz, Joan Goodnick. 1997. *Legends of the Kings of Akkade.* Winona Lake, IN: Eisenbrauns.

Wilcke, Claus. 1976–80. "Inanna/Ištar." *Reallexikon der Assyriologie* 5: 74–87.

Wildberger, H. 1971. "'mn fest, sicher." In E. Jenni and C. Westermann, eds. *Theologisches Handwörterbuch zum Alten Testament.* Volume 1. Gütersloh: Kaiser and Gütersloher, 177–209.

Wilkinson, Richard H. 2003. *The Complete Gods and Goddesses of Ancient Egypt.* London: Thames and Hudson.

Willetts, R. F. 1967. *The Law Code of Gortyn.* Berlin: de Gruyter.

Wyatt, Nicholas. 1999. "Astarte." In K. Van der Toorn, B. Becking, and P. W. Van der Horst, eds. *Dictionary of Deities and Demons in the Bible.* Leiden and Grand Rapids: Brill and Eerdmans, 109–114.

———. 2007. "The Religious Role of the King in Ugarit." In K. Lawson Younger, Jr., ed. *Ugarit at Seventy-Five.* Winona Lake, IN: Eisenbrauns, 41–74.

Xella, Paolo. 1988. "Tradition und Innovation. Bemerkungen zum Pantheon von Ebla." In H. Waetzoldt and H. Hauptmann, eds. *Wirtschaft und Gesellschaft von Ebla.* Heidelberg: Heidelberger Orientverlag, 349–58.

———, ed. 2001a. *Quando un dio muore. Morti e assenze divine nella antiche tradizioni mediterranee.* Verona: Essedue.

———. 2001b. "Da Baal di Ugarit agli dei fenici. Una questione di vita o di morte." In Xella, 2001a: 73–93.

Yamauchi, Edwin M. 1990. *Persia and the Bible.* Grand Rapids, MI: Baker.

Younger, K. Lawson, Jr. 2009. "The Deity Kur(r)a in the First Millennium Sources." *Journal of Ancient Near Eastern Religions* 9: 1–23.

Zabkar, Louis V. 1968. *A Study of the BA Concept in Ancient Egyptian Texts.* Chicago: Oriental Institute.

INDEX

Lightning Source UK Ltd.
Milton Keynes UK
UKOW05f1600080617

302958UK00001B/142/P